FINDING PEACE AND PURPOSE

LIFE LESSONS FROM SRI RAMAKRISHNA & VIVEKANANDA

SWAMI KRITARTHANANDA

Vitasta

TO THOSE SPIRITUAL ASPIRANTS
IN SEARCH OF THE ELUSIVE IDEAL
IN A WORLD FULL OF ADVERSITIES
MOVING ADRIFT LIKE BOATS
WITHOUT ANCHORS

Published by
Renu Kaul Verma
Vitasta Publishing Pvt Ltd
4348/4C, Ansari Road, Daryaganj
New Delhi - 110 002
info@vitastapublishing.com

ISBN: 978-81-19670-40-6

First Edition 2025
MRP ₹595

Editor: Oswald Pereira
Typeset and Cover Design by Somesh Kumar Mishra
Printed by Chaman Enterprises, New Delhi

Contents

Preface

Spiritually elevated persons are born in different times, countries, climes and creeds. They live their unique, enlightened lives and leave behind a legacy of teachings or guidelines for people of their own time, as well as future generations to follow. For those who believe in the legacy, the teachings seem like an incessant stream of holy water flowing close to them. As these spiritual aspirants go deeper and imbibe the teachings, they may even find the path to freedom from bondages of this world. And if they seek material prosperity, they might also get that by following the guidelines of those holy men or women. This can be seen as the practical part of spirituality, which is an important aspect in day-to-day life.

People often mistakenly think that spirituality and householder life are two incompatible paths. They wrongly believe that a householder is less spiritual than a renunciate and that spiritual life is meant only for old age. But the fact is that spirituality is not exclusive to any particular lifestyle or any individual. Everyone can lead a spiritual life, including a householder, by following the right path.

The Hindu religion believes in one distinct idea: this world is not merely an object of illusion. When someone sees a rope in dim light, he mistakes it for a snake and reacts to it with fear. He first sees 'something,' and then imagines it as a snake. That 'something' is the reality, and not the snake which the seer conjures up in the mind. So, Hinduism says that behind even the illusion there is reality. This reality has to be discovered in this world full of *māyā* or illusion.

Hindu legends like *Mahābhārata* and others exemplify this fact by citing the story of a hermit and a householder woman. The hermit lives in the forest, observes austerities, and becomes endowed with some mystic power, which he boasts about, feeling elated.

Once, the hermit comes with a begging bowl at the door of a chaste woman, who is busy with household chores. She asks him to wait for a while. The hermit gets angry, thinking that the 'ignorant' woman does not know about his inner power. But the moment such a thought crosses his mind, pat comes the voice of the woman from the inner apartment, 'My son, I am serving my ailing husband, and shall not be long; don't be impatient with me. I am not the crane in the jungle whom you just a while ago reduced to ashes by your yogic power.' The hermit gets dumbfounded, and when the woman finally appears to give alms, he humbly seeks her advice.

Swami Vivekananda's chief aim was to bring Vedanta from the seclusion of the forest to daily life. That, indeed, is Hindu teaching coming down the ages. The ways Vivekananda showed us to achieve this are very practicable, and can transform even worldly people into spiritual persons. Sri Ramakrishna, his master asked, 'Is meditation possible only with closed eyes, and not with open eyes?' This question sets us all thinking. Following in his footsteps, Swami Vivekananda discovered a revolutionary idea, naming it as 'Practical Vedanta.' God can also be seen in all walks of life. As a matter of fact, there is nothing but God, and no world at all.

Such sublime ideas have been given expression in the articles collected in this book. First comes the lives of some spiritual stalwarts who lived and practised lofty ideals in their own lives, and then the practical applications have been demonstrated in and through various articles that follow.

If this book pleases the readers, I would consider my endeavour successful.

Swami Kritarthananda

PART 1

SRI RAMAKRISHNA THE IDEAL

Sri Ramakrishna:
Scriptures Embodied

SWAMI VIVEKANANDA had said on several occasions that everything a true Hindu does—right from birth till his last breath—is in accordance with a scriptural injunction. Indeed, a true Hindu's life is moulded after the pattern laid down by the scriptures, he often said, while speaking to a Western audience.

Great souls descend on Indian soil from time to time to prove the veracity of such statements in their lives. Their exemplary lives inspire humanity to live in conformity with the scriptures, making God-realization their ultimate goal of life.

These great souls are called *avataras*. Buddha, Rama, Krishna, Sankara, Ramanuja, Chaitanya, among others, were such *avataras*, who were born with super-human qualities of head and heart. They all learnt the wisdom inherent in the scriptures from their very childhood. They had many dazzling glories shining in through their personalities, making them unique in many respects.

Education in Nature's school

Sri Ramakrishna, Vivekananda's guru, was one exemplary, dazzling light. He was born in a devout, learned, yet humble and steadfast Brahmin family. He was endowed with a few prominent traits, which acted as strong shields in protecting his life from many odds, leading him smoothly towards the goals of human life and spirituality.

Driven with a passion for truth, he set out to experience truth from various revelations of the 'open book of nature'. So, he embarked on an adventurous journey towards truth by going to school with many other chums of his village. He was always in a playful mood with them, yet with a little distinction. Unlike others, he had a unique penetrative gaze that could judge things in depth with an unbiased mind by diving through the obstructive covering. It is the first weapon necessary to storm the gate of the spiritual mansion. So even amidst his play, he discovered that the great scholars had their minds fixed on mere bread-earning education, instead of acquiring that knowledge of the Immutable one.[1] As the boy Gadadhar (Sri Ramakrishna's childhood name) started learning his Mathematics lessons on addition (yoga), he found it acceptable. But the problem arose in subtraction. His question was: how could anything be taken away from another? Isn't everything pervaded by God? So, if you reduce something from another, where can the remainder be kept? The scholarly teachers found such questions too much to answer. Hence, Gadadhar's learning ended up in merely enjoying the company of friends. For him, all those complicated problems of accounts were merely meant for material prosperity that he disliked. As a result, his education could not cross the threshold of the village school.

One day, he saw two brothers, who were quarrelling over land, dividing it into two with a rope, claiming one side for each. The next day, both of them died for reasons unknown. Little Gadadhar could see the hand of unseen Providence. Then he saw a doctor falsely assuring relatives of a dying man that he would survive, knowing well that the patient's life-span was over. When the man died, Gadadhar realized the limitations of human capacity.[2]

These are a few incidents from the *open book of nature* that made little Gadadhar wise even without continuing with traditional school. He possessed another rare quality called *Medhā*: to hold firmly the wisdom perceived long ago. When a student absorbs something into his system with all love and confidence (called *Śraddhā*), it makes an indelible impression in the mind and comes out spontaneously at the time of crisis. Gadadhar's observations were so keen and carried in their trail such a will to do good to all, that even those very events which aroused adverse reactions in common minds would reveal to him something special about God.

In later years, once a devotee asked Sri Ramakrishna how to fix the mind in God. He saw at once down memory lane a market place at Kamarpukur. Two lady vendors were in a roadside shanty husking rice from paddy by means of a country-made pounding contraption, simultaneously conversing with the buyer, while attending to various tasks at the same time, including one of them breast-feeding her child. All the while her careful gaze was on the pounding stone, which fell periodically on the husking rice.

Sri Ramakrishna spoke of *abhyāsa*-yoga or the yoga of constant practice to the questioner by narrating this incident. When he was taken to see the Calcutta Circus, he saw a young girl standing on one leg on a running horse. That reminded him of intense spiritual practice, which leads to perfection. And even when his horse carriage was clopping past the grog shop where a few tipsy people were revelling in a spell of intoxication, Sri Ramakrishna pushed his neck out of the carriage window and cheered them up in a loud voice. The sight had actually reminded him of the joy of God-intoxication! This is another unique power of *Medhā*—to convert even commonplace, profane experiences into divine happenings.

The illiterate scholar

Neither did Sri Ramakrishna continue his school studies nor did he possess bookish scriptural knowledge. Then how could he mould his life according to scriptural injunctions? He didn't follow scriptures, but on the contrary scriptures followed him. It all started even as he was a little boy. Dhani, a woman of blacksmith caste, became the midwife at the time of his birth. She was also like his second mother. Once when left alone with him, she extracted from the little one a promise that he would beg his first alms from her at the time of his investiture with the sacred thread. And poor that she was, she started saving money bit by bit from that day, trusting that little boy's promise.

It was the first time in Indian history that a Brahmin boy begged his first alms from a so-called low-caste blacksmith lady. Was it a mere childish prank of a simple boy to violate age-old customs? The answer would be, to hold on to truth. But that is not the only answer. The renowned law-maker Manu gave an injunction in his *Smriti* that, 'A Brahmin boy may beg his first alms after investiture ceremony from his mother, sister, aunt, or one who gives full dignity to him.'[3] But how did the child know all this at that tender age?

One has no answer to this question except that scriptures follow him who is the real Pundit. Now, what is the true meaning of this word Pundit? The greatest commentator of the eighth century, Acharya Sankara clearly comments in his *Gītā-bhāṣya* (2:11) that one who has *paṇḍā*, that is, a clear knowledge of the *ātman*, is fit for that name.[4] He further explained this term in the *Bṛhadāraṇyaka Upaniṣad:* '*Pāṇḍitya* means knowing the *ātman* in a special way.'[5] Hence, judging by this standard laid down by our commentators, can we not call Sri Ramakrishna a Pundit in the real sense of the term? Of course, though he himself never liked to hear such titles about himself in his lifetime.

Almost all children below the age of ten are seen to be playful pranksters. Sri Ramakrishna as a boy, Gadai, was no exception to that. His mischievous behaviour in the company of his chums, his playful mimicry of the Pundits in an assembly threw even elders into side-splitting laughter. Yet he had a distinction that made him stand head and shoulders above all his mates. He was not merely a keen observer but a keen listener too. Whereas his chums got themselves lost in the amusement of various pranks, he would have a part of his receptive mind fixed on the discussions and disputes raised by the assembled scholars.

In one such assembly of scholars during a debate on a certain issue nobody could come to any decisive conclusion. But Gadai whispered to one of the participant scholars a possible solution to the dispute. The scholar was amazed and announced Gadai's solution to the rest of the members to their astonishment and applause.

In Sanskrit there is a word *bālya-bhāva,* interpreted as childish attitude or prank. The *Bṛhadāraṇyaka Upaniṣad*, however, has used the word *bālya* to mean strength of spiritual knowledge. It says, 'The knower of Brahman, having known all about scholarship, should try to live upon that strength which comes from knowledge.'[6] It is this strength of knowledge that compelled child, Gadai to give his solution to settle the dispute among the scholars; it is, again, the same strength which opened the gates of knowledge even to his guru Totapuri by freeing him of his age-old superstition.

Sankara has elaborated the meaning of the word *bala* as, 'Strength is the total elimination of the vision of the objective world by Self-knowledge.'[7] Then what does Self-knowledge do? It merges the objective world into the divine. Sri Ramakrishna meant exactly this when he said, 'I see the world is soaked in God.' He never looked upon the phenomenal world as anything other than God. In his eyes even fallen women became veritable representations of the Divine Mother; the drunkards' noisy revelry seemed to him as born of the bliss of God. He could not see anything apart from that. Even the lower states of enjoyment were nothing but a speck of that bliss of God in his eyes. This has also been spoken of in the *Upanishad*.[8] But Sri Ramakrishna knew and saw this truth from direct (*aparokṣa)* realization, and not from scriptural study. This is why he was a real Pundit even without studying scriptures; moreover, he became verily the embodiment of scriptures.

Sri Ramakrishna evinced another childlike trait which has been explained by Sankara in his commentary on the *Brahma-Sūtra* 3:4:50. Here the acharya refutes the opposition's doubt by saying that in the case of a monk of realization the word *bālya* does not mean a freaky or wayward nature of a child. It actually means that a monk who is a knower of Brahman often behaves like a child who, owing to its immature sense organs, never tries to display his knowledge, wisdom, or spirituality to others; he keeps himself free from all vanity, ostentatiousness and the like.[9] Those who are acquainted with the life of Sri Ramakrishna know only too well how his behaviour fitted into such scriptural definition of *bālya-bhāva*.

Rani Rasmani, the founder of Dakshineswar temple, had made such provisions for charity that no beggar, saint, or scholar would go away empty-handed from the temple precincts. The temple became a haven for all pilgrims irrespective of caste, creed, or sect. Scholars of various denominations would spend a few days at Rasmani's temple precincts on their way to pilgrimage discussing various scriptural topics. Sri Ramakrishna with his keen and receptive mind would participate in the discussions. Occasionally there would be discussions on higher states of realization of saints, when he would compare notes with his own realizations and ecstasies.

In the trail of the scriptures

Sri Ramakrishna, in his youth, with his photographic memory and strong power of *medhā* or wit and intelligence absorbed a vast knowledge of scriptures and their commentaries by listening to the discussions of scholars. In later years, like an affectionate mother, he would guide spiritual aspirants coming to him for advice with that unceasing flow of knowledge. Even renowned scholars would wonder about the source of Sri Ramakrishna's knowledge.

Once Sri Ramakrishna went to see the scholar Iswar Chandra Vidyasagar, hearing of his great scholarship and compassionate nature. And there he spoke such a truth which even for a scholar like Vidyasagar seemed unique. Speaking on Brahman, he said, 'All things in the world…have been defiled…for they have been read or uttered by the tongue. Only one thing has not been defiled in this way, and that is Brahman. No one has ever been able to say what Brahman is.'[10] But even though Vidyasagar had never heard such an apt illustration before, it truly existed in the *Jñāna-saṅkalinī Tantra.*[11]

Sri Ramakrishna often cited the examples of some devotees adopting a tricky way to extract a number of boons from God in the name of one boon. He said, 'Once the Divine Mother was pleased with a man's austerities and said to him, "You may ask a favour of Me." "O Mother," said he, "if you are so pleased with me, then grant that I may eat from a gold plate with my grandchildren".' In one boon the man got everything: grandchildren, wealth, and gold plate.[12] This is a very oft-quoted illustration used in many scriptural contexts by renowned commentators, and is known as *vṛddha-kumārī-vara-nyāya.* So is the story of four blind men visiting an elephant.[13] Śaṅkara illustrated the same story in his commentary on the *Chandogya Upanishad.*[14]

Śaṅkara and other commentators on scriptures often cited picturesque examples from everyday life to simplify or illustrate an intricate subject. Sri Ramakrishna also did the same to drive home certain difficult points in question. For example, demonstrating how people foolishly depend on hearsay leaving aside direct vision, Sri Ramakrishna made a sardonic statement one day: 'A man said to his friend,

"Yesterday...I saw a house fall with a crash." "Wait," said the friend, "let me look it up in the newspaper." But this incident was not mentioned in the paper. Then the friend said, "But the paper doesn't mention it." The man replied, "I saw it with my own eyes." "Be that as it may," said the friend, "I can't believe it as long as it isn't in the paper".'[15]

The *Bṛhadaranyaka Upanishad* makes a similar statement: 'If even today two persons come disputing, one saying, 'I saw it,' and another, 'I heard of it,' we believe him only who says, 'I saw it.'[16] Commenting on this statement, Śaṅkara says, 'What a man hears of may sometimes be false, but not what he sees with his own eyes. So we do not believe the man who says, "I heard of it".'[17] That is why, people jokingly say that the difference between truth and falsehood is 'four inches,' meaning the distance between the eye and the ear.

To know the real worth of a valuable thing like a diamond, one must go to the right person who can evaluate its worth. Sri Ramakrishna used to tell his devotees the story of a rich man with a diamond.[18] Śaṅkara, in his commentary on the *Chandogya Upanishad*, said the same thing: 'It is seen in the world that a professional trader of jewels can recognize the worth of a jewel much better than a hunter who finds it perchance.'[19] In speaking about the secret of creation, Sri Ramakrishna would say, 'After the destruction of the universe, at the end of a great cycle, the Divine Mother garners the seeds for the next creation....After the creation, the Primal Power dwells in the universe itself.'[20]

Strikingly enough, Śaṅkara, the exponent of the Advaita system, also spoke of a similar phenomenon. He said in his commentary on *Brahma Sūtra* 1:3:30: 'When this universe gets dissolved, it dissolves by keeping its latent power intact, and the next creation emerges from that latent power.'[21] Another illustration given by Sri Ramakrishna is cited here. 'A man once said, 'There are many horses in my uncle's cow-shed.' From that one could know that the man had no horses at all. No one keeps a horse in a cow-shed.'[22]

This is also an echo of Śaṅkara's comment on *Brahma Sūtra*, 'Unless one is a fool, one will not conclude by seeing a cow in a stable that it must be a horse.'[23] Still in another context Sri Ramakrishna said, 'By touching any part of a cow you undoubtedly touch the cow herself. Even by touching her horns you touch the cow. But the milk comes through the cow's udder.'[24] And Śaṅkara comments on *Brahma Sūtra* as, 'If the whole abides in its totality in each part, then since the whole has competence to perform all its own functions, and since it is the same, it should perform the duties of the teats even through the horn.'[25]

If there is an entity called God, why don't we see him? This is an age-old question asked by sceptics. Sri Ramakrishna's apt answers were different under different situations and to different types of aspirants. One of those answers was, 'The stars are not seen in the sky in the daytime. Does it mean they do not exist at all? As soon as the sun goes below the horizon and darkness prevails, they reveal themselves in the vault.' In the opposition's view on *Brahma Sūtra*, we find a similar statement—'It is a well-known fact that the luminaries moon, stars, etc. do not shine in the daytime when the bright sun keeps shining.'[26]

Like other men of realization, Sri Ramakrishna too compared God sometimes to a wealthy person or a king and he used to say that in order to meet the king one has to please his gate-keeper with repeated requests or bribes or by any other means.[27] Śaṅkara also holds the same view in his commentary on *Chandogya Upanishad*: 'In the world the gate-keepers are to be propitiated by prayer and then they will usher in the visitor to the king's presence.'[28] Śaṅkara again cites the king's illustration in his commentary on *Br. Upanishad*: 'When a king goes to inspect some place in his kingdom, his deputed servants keep ready beforehand all the necessary provisions like victuals, carpets, etc. in order to provide every comfort to the king.'[29]

Sri Ramakrishna used that very parable in this way: 'When a rich master decides to visit the house of his servant, he sends various things to the house, such as a carpet, a hubble-bubble for smoking, and the like.'[30] Speaking on one-pointedness in concentration, Sri Ramakrishna used to tell the story of a hunter.

'A hunter was aiming at a bird. A bridal procession passed along beside him, with the groom's relatives and friends, music, carriages and horses. It took a long time for the procession to pass the hunter, but he was not at all conscious of it. He did not know that the bride-groom had gone by.'[31] And what did the great Śaṅkara say? In refuting the opponent's proposition in *Brahma Sūtra* 3:2:10, he said, 'The arrow-maker, whose attention had been fully engaged, says afterwards, "I was perceiving simply the arrow so long".'[32]

In another context of spiritual practice, Sri Ramakrishna said, 'He who has learnt to dance correctly never makes a false step.'[33] Śaṅkara also commented on the *Brahma Sūtra* 3:3:54 thus, 'A trained actor does not ride on his own shoulder.'[34] We have another similar reference in the *Bhagavatam* where it is said that one submitted to God never comes under delusion; even when such a person runs with closed eyes, one never falls down.[35]

Sri Ramakrishna quite frequently used to mention one very important but simple statement for all spiritual aspirants. 'The goal of life is the attainment of God.'[36] Similarly, Śaṅkara says: 'The knowledge of Brahman is the highest goal of man,'[37] which corroborates the universality of the fact. In his commentary on the *Brahma-Sūtra* also, Śaṅkara pinpoints the same truth with more accentuation.[38]

Sri Ramakrishna's favourite catchphrase was: 'Go forward and stop not.' To illustrate this he gave the parable of the wood-cutter. The translation of the word 'go forward' in the Vedas is *caraiveti*. In a couple of telling verses, the *Ṛg-Veda* emphazises this idea.[39] Swami Vivekananda took this cue from the Vedas and declared boldly that ever since the advent of Sri Ramakrishna, Satya Yuga has started; for Sri Ramakrishna always taught people to aspire for higher things and not get stuck up in one or two achievements.

Sri Ramakrishna never tired of instructing his devotees. Often, he would repeat the same story several times, a fact corroborated in the *Gospel of Sri Ramakrishna*. He himself was well aware of this. Said he: 'Hriday used to say to me: "Uncle, please don't give out your stock of instructions all at once. Why should you repeat the same things over and over again?" I would reply: "You fool, what's that to you? These are my words and if I like I shall repeat them a hundred thousand times. You keep quiet!"'[40] Śaṅkara defended repetition in the scriptures. Commenting on the *Īśopaniṣad,* he said that the verses are untiring in their emphasis. He again fortified his statement in another Upaniṣad thus: 'Many illustrations are meant for understanding the multiform differences in the things illustrated, as also *for firm conviction*.'[41]

Another beautiful example of Sri Ramakrishna was: 'An

insignificant tenant was once engaged in a lawsuit with a big landlord. People realized that there was a powerful man behind the tenant. Perhaps another big landlord was directing the case from behind. Man is an insignificant creature. He cannot fulfil the difficult task of a teacher without receiving power direct from God.'[42] Even this illustration gets its support from Śaṅkara. He said: 'As in life a householder contending even with the king, who is the most powerful of all, so also a weak man hopes to defeat a man stronger than himself through the strength of righteousness.'[43]

Significantly, even after Sri Ramakrishna had reached the height of spirituality, his behavioural patterns continued to follow scriptural injunctions. Sri Ramakrishna could not eat anything offered by physicians, lawyers, and people of questionable character. His explanation was that they extract money even from people under afflictions. Manu, the law-maker, enjoins in his code of law that a true Brahmin should not eat the food given by a backbiter, nor by a habitual liar, or one who accepts money for sacrifice, an actor, or an ungrateful person.[44]

Sri Ramakrishna was quite reserved in his discussions on God-realization. When a person of Narendranath's (Vivekananda) stature enquired about God-vision, he would reply, 'Certainly; and even I can show you.' Again, in the case of 'M' (Mahendranath Gupta) he replied to the same question as, 'God can be seen; one has to seek Him ardently and humbly.' But when a haughty man foolishly challenged him saying, 'Sir, we hear that you see God. If you do, show Him to us,' Sri Ramakrishna just passed over without answering. The reason is clearly given in the *Bhagavad Gita*[45] and *Manu-Smṛti*.[46] Of these two the *Manu-Smṛti* is uncompromising, and enjoins—'One must not speak of spiritual things to another unasked, or improperly asked, and should behave like an idiot before such persons.'

There are at least three examples when Sri Ramakrishna cited from scriptures in terms of day-to-day examples. The *Yoga-Vāsiṣṭha-Sāra* speaks of 'getting back' one's real nature by giving the example of one who looks for a supposedly lost necklace everywhere except around his neck out of absent-mindedness.[47] Sri Ramakrishna's version is: 'Another man looked everywhere for his towel. Finally, he discovered that it had been on his shoulder all the time.'[48]

The second example is also from the same scripture which says that a man embraces his wife and daughter with different attitudes of mind.[49] Sri Ramakrishna gave the exact reference in the *Gospel:* 'The mind is everything. A man has his wife on one side and his daughter on the other. He shows his affection to them in different ways. But his mind is one and the same.'[50]

The third example was his last advice to Adhar Sen, a deputy magistrate. He was a householder devotee whom Sri Ramakrishna loved. The devotee hankered for a higher position. But Sri Ramakrishna could foresee his imminent, untimely death. So he warned the disciple, 'Look here. All these are unreal—meetings, school, office, and everything else. God alone is the substance, and all else is illusory. One should worship God with one's whole mind.'[51] The *Mahābhārata* conveys the same thing: 'One should observe piety even from youth, because life is so transient. Who knows when death stalks one?'[52]

Going beyond scriptures

As Sri Ramakrishna followed the scriptures so meticulously, sometimes it seemed that the scriptures were following him. The state of a man of wisdom as depicted in the philosophical treatise *Vivekacūḍāmaṇi* fitted so exactly with him, that sometimes it seemed that the verses were written after seeing Sri Ramakrishna. It is said about him: 'Sometimes with and sometimes without any clothes on, sometimes like a mad man, a ghoul, or a five-year-old, he wanders about in the world empowered by wisdom.' Again, 'As a child plays with its toys forgetting hunger and bodily pains, the man of realization too moves about happily without the sense of 'I' or 'mine.'[53]

Another remarkable trait in him was that he could not tie the cloth he wore to his waist with a knot. As a result, more often than not, especially during his frequent ecstasies, his cloth would fall down of itself. This should not be seen as mere carelessness, as it had its complete sanction in the *Bhagavatam*. There it has been said, 'Just as a drunkard fails to keep his cloth tied to his waist, so a realized soul cannot take care if his mortal body remains or is destroyed.'[54] But it is important to note that the scriptures say that such a man never enjoys unrestrained licence by doing as he likes, for then there will be no distinction between a dog and a knower of truth.[55]

That is why even though Sri Ramakrishna looked upon fallen women as veritable representations of Divine Mother, he was extremely cautious in dealing with them. When wine was brought to him as a necessary ingredient to be consumed when he was practising tantric disciplines, he didn't drink it but put a drop on his forehead as a sign of respect, and would be merged spontaneously in the name of the real Cause of the universe.[56] It is true that he was taken to the place where male-female couples were engaged in the most secret tantric discipline called ānanda-āsana or *bhairavī-cakra*. But the very sight transported him into the blissful aspect of Divine Mother instead of giving rise to any mental aberration. A living free soul that he was, such precautions were not meant for himself, but were lessons for the world. Sometimes when he found a wayfarer monk behaving contrary to the scriptures, he would warn him to behave in the right way.

It is given to great souls like Sri Ramakrishna to go sometimes beyond the scriptures. It is said in scriptures that a man of true realization stands on the head of the Vedas like a crest-jewel. Once Sri Ramakrishna asked his guru Totapuri about the need to practise meditation every day. His guru pointed to the brass pot of drinking water around and said that to keep it glossy like gold it has to be scrubbed every day. But Sri Ramakrishna meant something still deeper than the general way of thinking. He forthwith said, 'But if the water pot itself be of gold, then?' The master had to admit that no scrubbing is needed in such a case.

What Sri Ramakrishna really had in mind was the spontaneous state of samadhi under all circumstances. That, is indeed, a state beyond ordinary scriptures. On another evening, as Totapuri was seated before a blazing fire, of which he was an ardent worshipper, an illiterate person came in search of a fire for his hookah, and took a piece of glowing charcoal from the fire. Totapuri got terribly annoyed at the sacrilegious act of the person. But Sri Ramakrishna laughed. Surprised at the reaction of his disciple, the master asked him the reason. Sri Ramakrishna asked, was it not ridiculous for a person who looks upon the whole universe as identified with Brahman to be affected by such petty things as anger? One must be true to what one preaches. This silenced the guru and he promised not to allow himself to be swept away by emotions.

We will now narrate an incident to demonstrate how a knower of Brahman stands, as it were, on the head of the Vedas. One day at Dakshineswar, the senior priest of Vishnu temple was carrying the image of the deity to the adjacent room when he slipped on the floor and broke the leg of the deity. The Rani was in a fix and sought the verdict of scholars in scriptures about the repair or replacement of the image. The verdict went in favour of replacement.

But the Rani's heart did not consent since she had been offering her heart's love so long to the old deity; and it is not so easy to shift the focus of love to another newly built image. Torn between the verdict of scholars and her own feelings, the Rani, maybe led by the inscrutable will of Providence, sought the opinion of Sri Ramakrishna, the younger priest of the Kali temple. He assessed the whole situation from the Vedantic point of view. The Vedanta has made its invulnerable basis with three strong weapons of *śruti* (scriptural injunction), *yukti* (reason), and *anubhūti* (feeling). Among these, the second is an analytic function, that is, intellectual power; and the third is that of the heart.

Our scriptures say that the heart is the repository of the intellect. Now, according to Śaṅkara, 'When a thing is the support of another, the former is more powerful than the latter.'[57] The main point here is that the three items named are three steps from lower to higher. In other words, *yukti* is higher than *śruti*, and *anubhūti* is higher than *yukti*. Sri Ramakrishna saw that all the scholars unanimously sided with the first two only, but did not care for the last or the highest one. On the other side stood the Rani with her whole-hearted devotion, but devoid of the power to oppose the scholars. Under such circumstance, Sri Ramakrishna came forward to fulfil the devotee's desire.

He stood, as it were, on the head of the scriptures and gave his verdict, 'If any son-in-law of the Rani breaks his leg due to an accident, will she discard him and look for another? Or will she get the latter medically treated and cured? So let the old image be mended and the daily service of worship etc. go on as before.'

Later, Sri Ramakrishna himself mended the broken leg with a sculptor's adept hand and re-established the deity in its old throne. And lo behold! The whole rank of scholars accepted the verdict without any opposition. How? Behind that verdict was an inexorable force which no mortals can counter. The *Brihadaranyaka Upanishad* clearly states, 'In this state the scriptures become nullified, the world becomes zero, and the gods lose their resplendence.'[58] This is the significance of going beyond scriptures.

Significance of symbol worship

There is an age-old dispute between image or symbol worshippers and the followers of God without attributes or form. A careful study of our primary scriptures can settle this dispute quite easily. In refuting the opponent's misleading view, the *Vedanta Sutra* brings in a discussion on symbols. An aphorism says, 'The aspirant should not identify himself with a symbol, for he cannot understand himself to be so.'[59] We in India are quite familiar with the worship of symbols. But many do not know the inherent truth behind that.

The fact is that some particular stone or wood reminds one of God with certain attributes. This is called superimposition of a superior entity on an inferior one. Śaṅkara clarifies this point in his commentary on the next aphorism, namely, 'The sun etc. are to be looked upon as Brahman because of the consequent exaltation.'[60] He further says, 'It is seen that the king's charioteer is honoured as the king himself. This is a case of superimposition of the higher on the inferior. But the king is never looked upon as the charioteer.'[61]

Sri Ramakrishna served this very truth to 'M' with a master stroke of an expert artist when he objected to image worship arguing, 'Certainly God is not the clay image!' To this Sri Ramakrishna promptly replied, 'But why clay? It is an image of Spirit.'[62] By this he meant that though an image is made of clay, it has no importance in worship. The image or the symbol is built on the thought of Brahman with various attributes. And the worshipper invokes life into that clay image before offering worship to the deity. After worship the vital force is withdrawn by the worshipper from the clay image to his own heart, and the image is consigned to water to be dissolved in it, but the living spirit will endure forever in the heart of the devotee.

Sri Ramakrishna further explained this point to 'M': 'You were talking of worshipping the clay image. Even if the image is made of clay, there is need for that sort of worship. God Himself has provided different forms of worship. He who is the Lord of the Universe has arranged all these forms to suit different men in different stages of knowledge. The mother cooks different dishes to suit the stomachs of her different children.'[63]

Sri Ramakrishna applied this very truth in pacifying the

stubbornness of 'M.' When 'M' in an ecstatic mood, refused to immerse the image of the Divine Mother Durga in water, Sri Ramakrishna said to him, 'So long the Mother accepted your worship by living in the image. From now She will live in your heart.' And this solved the impending problem.

Ultimately this act of superimposition of the superior on the inferior leads to the worship of God in living beings. People in India are seen to feed animals, birds, and famished people as a part of worship. This type of service based on worship helps the aspirant overcome his human limitations and formulate his own life on higher thoughts, not seeing the gross form of the object of worship or its limitations. The inherent divinity of all beings will reign supreme in his heart. By transforming the scriptural theory of immanence of God into the great maxim *shiva jñāne jīva sevā*, Sri Ramakrishna gave the world a new message of living happily.

Going beyond samadhi

There is a very common faulty belief among the people that samadhi is the endpoint or consummation of spiritual life. Those who have walked the path of spiritual life, however, say just the opposite, that is, real spiritual life begins with samadhi. This raises another doubt: If samadhi means realization of God, then what remains to be further realized? Sri Ramakrishna has given a fitting answer to this question in his characteristic candid way. 'If one is able somehow to reach Calcutta, one can see the Maidan[64] and the museum and other places too. The thing is how to reach Calcutta.'[65]

Here 'coming to Calcutta' signifies entering samadhi. It is only after one reaches there that one can be guided to various places in that realm. To know that God is, implies a distant knowledge about Him; this is called *jñāna* in Indian term; whereas, to meet Him and know from Him about His territory, possessions, is known as *vijñāna* in India. In Sri Ramakrishna's language, 'There is a stage beyond even *Brahma-jñāna*. After *jñāna* comes *vijñāna*.'[66] Śaṅkara also gave similar definitions of the two terms in his commentary on the *Gita*. In his opinion, '*jñāna* implies forming an overall concept about *ātman*, having known about it from the preceptor and the scripture; whereas *vijñāna* is to realize that in particular.'[67] He also said in his commentary, '*jñāna* is the overall knowledge of the objects mentioned in the scriptures; but *vijñāna* is the name of relating to oneself the knowledge as it is gained from scriptures.'[68] This very phenomenon of relating to oneself has been represented by Sri Ramakrishna as 'getting nourished by milk.'

The long and short of it is that only a real knower of Brahman (*Brahma-vijñānī*) knows clearly about every nook and cranny of that difficult path; and so, he alone can tell with confidence the subtle difference between the four statuses, namely, *brahmavid*, *brahmavid-vara*, *brahmavid-varīyān*, and *brahmavid-variṣṭha* or the four types of *jnanis* or liberated sages. Madhusūdana Sarasvatī, the great exponent of Advaita Vedanta from Bengal, has discussed all these states in his gloss on the Gita (3:18) by quoting from the scripture *Laghu-Yoga-Vāsiṣṭha*. There the sage Vasiṣṭha has described a knower of Brahman in terms of seven different stages, namely, the plane of knowledge called good resolve, deliberation, fineness of the mind, experience of reality, non-relationship, absence of objects, reaching the *turīya*.[69]

The glossator then goes to explain, 'Among these the first is the desire for liberation, which starts from discrimination between the eternal and the non-eternal and culminates in its fruit. Then, after approaching the guru, *vicāra* in the form of *śravaṇa* and *manana* on the Upanishadic texts is the second. Then the third is the ability of the mind to grasp subtle things with concentration accomplished through the practice of *nididhyāsana* or thinking. These three stages are called the waking state by the yogin. That yogin who has reached the fourth stage is called *brahmavit*. To him the world appears as a dream. However, the fifth, sixth, and seventh stages are the secondary divisions of *jīvanmukti* itself. The state of *nirvikalpa*-samādhi, which comes when the mind becomes withdrawn through the practice of *savikalpa*-samādhi, is called *asaṁsakti* (non-relationship) and *suṣupti* (sleep).

From this state he emerges by himself. One attaining this state is called *brahmavid-vara*. The sixth state called *padārthābhāvanī* and deeper sleep is a state from which the yogin cannot come out of his own effort. He has to be awakened by others. Such a yogin is called *brahmavid-varīyān*. The seventh stage called *turīyagā* is one of total absence of perception of duality. From this state, the yogin cannot emerge either by his efforts or through that of others, but remains in every way self-absorbed, as a mass of supreme bliss alone, with his bodily functions managed by others, and his vital forces controlled by the Supreme Lord. One attaining this stage is called *brahmavid-variṣṭha*.[70]

The various states of ecstasies and absorption experienced by Sri Ramakrishna tally in every respect with these descriptions. When he went into a deep thought of Shiva while enacting as the god, or when he listened to the glories of the Divine Mother on his way to the temple of Vishalakshi, he was in the fourth stage of ecstasy. At that time, according to his narrative, the whole world appeared as a dream.

Next, during his madness for a vision of the Divine Mother at the Kali temple in Dakshineswar, when he was endowed with a vision of Her, he had attained the fifth state, for he came back to normal consciousness with his own effort. When, under the guidance of Totapuri, he attained nirvikalpa samadhi in three days' effort, he was brought back to consciousness by his guru only. So that state of absorption tallies fully with the sixth state. But when even after that he developed a desire to enjoy the state of nirvikalpa samadhi unceasingly, he remained in that state continuously for six months, and his body function was maintained by Providence, while an unknown monk who stayed by him for that whole period pushed in food through his mouth by force, just to keep his body alive.

Judging by such scriptural standards, one wonders who Sri Ramakrishna was. All his states of samadhi had clear sanction of the scriptures. Hence, one is left with no doubt that he was a knower of Brahman par excellence. It is he and he alone who had the right to say that there are stages even beyond samadhi. Such men only deserve the worship of all as *Avatāra-variṣṭha* (the greatest among the avatars of Bhagavan).

In the course of time, so many other facts about his life and teachings will be uncovered, enabling the people to have more in-depth understanding of his life in the light of scriptures. The devout heart cannot but sing paeans of joy in his name and say, 'O God! O indweller of all beings, Sri Ramakrishna! Who is ever capable of singing the true glory of you who are beyond all concepts and repeller of all misery? Hence, I offer you my homage.'[71]

Endnotes

1 *Muṇḍakopaniṣad,* 1:1:5.

2 Cf. 'M', *The Gospel of Sri Ramakrishna,* (Tr. Nikhilananda), [Henceforth *Gospel*] Chennai Sri Ramakrishna Math, Feb.2000, pp.323-24 (conversations with Keshab Sen in his house on 28-11-1883).

3 *Mātaraṁ vā svasāraṁ vā māturvā bhaginīṁ nijām/bhikṣeta bhikṣāṁ prathamaṁ yā cainaṁ nāvamānayet//* Manu, 2:50.

4 *Paṇḍā ātmaviṣayā buddhir-yeṣāṁ te paṇḍitāḥ.*

5 *Etad ātma-vijñānaṁ pāṇḍityam.*

6 *Tasmād brāhmaṇaḥ pāṇḍityaṁ nirvidya bālyena tiṣṭhāset*— Br. Up.3:5:1.

7 *Balaṁ nāma ātmavidyayā aśeṣa-viṣaya-dṛṣṭi-tiraskaraṇam*— Sankara's commentary on ibid.

8 *Etasyaivānandasyānyāni bhūtāni mātrām upajīvanti*— Br. Up. 4:3:32.

9 *Āntaro bhāvaviśeṣo bālasya aprarūḍhendriyatvādiḥ iha bālyam āśrīyate. Yathā bālaḥ aprarūḍhendriyatayā na pareṣām ātmānam āviṣkartum īhate, tadvad jñānādhyayana-dhārmikatvādibhiḥ ātmānam avikhyāpayan dambha-darpādi-rahito bhavet*—Br.Sū. 3:4:50 Sankara's commentary.

10 *Gospel*, Chennai Sri Ramakrishna Math, Feb.2000, p.102.

11 *Ucchiṣṭaṁ sarva-śāstrāṇi sarva-vidyā mukhe mukhe/ Nocchiṣṭaṁ brahmaṇo* jñānam avyaktaṁ cetanāmayam//—verse 52.

12 *Gospel*, Chennai, 2000, p.647 (conversations on 29-09-1884).

13 Ibid, p.191 (conversations on 11-03-1883).

14 See Sankara's commentary on Ch. Up.5:18:1.

15 *Gospel*, Chennai, 2000, p.789 (conversations on 13-06-1885).

16 *Yad idānīṁ dvau vivadamānau eyātām, aham adarśam, aham aśrauṣam iti, ya evaṁ brūyād aham adarśam iti, tasmā eva śraddadhyāma*—Br. Up.5:14:4.

17 *Śrotur mṛṣā śravaṇam api sambhavati, na tu cakṣuṣo mṛṣā darśanam. Tasmāt na aśrauṣam iti uktavate śraddadhyāma*—Sankara's commentary on ibid.

18 *Gospel*, Chennai, 2000, pp.759-60 (conversations on 12-04-1885).

19 *Dṛṣṭaṁ hi loke vaṇik-chabarayoḥ padmarāgādi-maṇivikraye vaṇijo vijñānādhikyāt phalādhikyam*—Sankara's commentary on Ch. Up.1:1:10.

20 *Gospel*, Chennai, 2000, p.135 (conversations on 27-10-1882).

21 *Pralīyamānam api idaṁ jagat śaktyavaśeṣam eva pralīyate, śaktimūlam eva ca prabhavati.*

22 *Gospel*, Chennai, 2000, p.316 (conversations on 26-11-1883).

23 *Na hi aśvasthāne gāṁ paśyan aśvo'yam iti amūḍhaḥ adhyavasyati*—B.S. 1:4:1.

24 *Gospel*, Chennai, 2000, p.883 (conversations on 25-10-1885).

25 *Yadi gotvādivat pratyekaṁ parisamāptaḥ avayavī syāt, yathā*

gotvaṁ prativyakti pratyakṣaṁ gṛhyate, evam avayavī api pratyavayavaṁ pratyakṣaṁ gṛhyeta| na ca evaṁ niyataṁ gṛhyate| pratyekaparisamāptau ca avayavinaḥ kāryeṇa adhikārāt, tasya ca ekatvāt, śṛṅgenāpi stanakāryaṁ kuryāt|—B.S. 2:1:18.

26 *Tejasvabhāvakaṁ hi candra-tārakādi tejaḥsvabhāvake eva sūrye bhāsamāne ahani na bhāsate iti prasiddham.*—B.S. 1:3:22 Although it comes in the opponent's proposition, we quote it since it is a common experience to all.

27 Cf. *Gospel*, Chennai, 2000, p.482 (conversations on 30-06-1884).

28 *Loke dvārapālāḥ rājñaḥ upāsanena vaśīkṛtāḥ rājaprāptyarthā bhavanti*—Sankara's commentary on Ch.Up.3:13:1.

29 See Sankara's commentary on Bṛ Up.4:3:37.

30 *Gospel*, Chennai 2000, p.203 (conversations on 7-04-1883).

31 Ibid., p.744 (conversations on 12-04-1885).

32 *Iṣukāro jāgradapi iṣvāsaktamanastayā na anyān viṣayān īkṣate; iṣukāro hi vyāpṛtamanā bravīti, 'iṣumeva aham etāvantaṁ kālam upalabhamāna abhuvam*—Sankara's commentary on B.S.3:2:10.

33 *Gospel*, Chennai 2000, p.220, (conversations on 2-05-1883).

34 *Na hi naṭaḥ śikṣitaḥ san svaskandham adhirohati*—Sankara's commentary on B.S.3:3:54.

35 *Śrīmad Bhāgavatam*, 11:2:35.

36 *Gospel*, Chennai 2000, Part I, p.460, (conversations on 15-06-1884).

37 *Brahmavidyā puruṣārtha-sādhanam*—Br. Up.2:4:1 (introductory).

38 *Brahmāvagatiḥ hi puruṣārthaḥ*—B.S. 1:1:1.

39 Aitareya Brāhmaṇa, 7:15:4, 5. [*Kaliḥ śayāno bhavati, sanjihānastu dvāparaḥ/uttiṣṭhaṁstretā bhavati, kṛtaṁ sampadyate caran—caraiveti caraiveti. Caran vai madhu vindati, caran svādum udumbaram/paśya sūryasya śremāṇaṁ yon a tandrayate caran—caraiveti caraiveti.*]

40 *Gospel,* Chennai, Part 2, Appx.B, p.528.

41 न मन्त्राणां जामिता अस्ति।—I.Up.5; अनेकदृष्टान्तोपादानं दार्ष्टान्तिक-अनेकभेद-अनुगमार्थं दृढप्रतीत्यर्थं च ।—Ch. Up. 6:1:6.

42 *Gospel*, Chennai, Part 1, Ch.7, conversations on 14 December 1882.

43 यथा लोके राज्ञा सर्वबलवत्तमेन अपि कुटुम्बिक: (तथा दुर्बलतर: आत्मनो बलवत्तरम् अपि धर्मेण बलेन जेतुं कामयते)—Br. Up. 1:4:14.

44 *Piśunānṛtinoścānnaṁkratu-vikrayiṇastathā/śailūṣa-tantuvāyānnaṁ kṛtaghnasyānnameva ca//*—Manu-smṛti, 4:214.

45 *Idaṁ te nātapaskāya nābhaktāya kadācana/na cāśuśrūṣave vācyaṁ na ca māṁ yo'bhyasūyati//*—18:67

46 *Nāpṛṣṭaḥ kasyacid brūyān-na cānyāyena pṛcchataḥ/jānan-napi hi medhāvī jaḍavalloka ācaret//*—Manu-smṛti 2:110.

47 *Svakaṇṭhe'pi sthitaṁ vastu yathā na prāpyate bhramāt / bhramānte prāpyate tadvadātmāpi guruvākyataḥ //* 1:14.

48 *Gospel,* Chennai 2000, Part 1, Ch.27, p.525 (conversations on 27 September 1884).

49 *Yenaivāliṅgitā kāntā tenaivāliṅgitā sutā*—Yoga-vāsiṣṭha-sāra, 4:8.

50 *Gospel,* Chennai 2000, Part 1, Ch.5, p.137 (conversations on 27 October 1882).

51 *Gospel,* Chennai 2000, Part 1, Ch.20, p.419 (conversations on 9 March 1884).

52 *Yuvaiva dharmaśīlaḥ syād animittaṁ hi* jīvitam / ko hi jānāti kasyādya mṛtyukālo bhaviṣyati //—Mb.Cr. Edn., 12:169:14, 15.

53 Vivekacūḍāmaṇi, 540, 537.

54 *Śrīmad Bhāgavatam,* 11:13:36.

55 *Buddhādvaita-satattvasya yatheṣṭācaraṇaṁ yadi/śunāṁ tattvavidāṁ caiva ko bhedo'śucibhakṣaṇe//*—Sureśvarācārya, *Naiṣkarmya-siddhiḥ*, Ch.4, verse 62.

56 Wine is generally called in Indian language *kāraṇa-vāri*. The word *kāraṇa* also means cause in Sanskrit.

57 *Yasmin hi yadāśritaṁ bhavati, tasmād āśritād āśrayasya balavattaraṁ prasiddham*—Sankara's commentary on Bṛ Up. 5:14:4.

58 *Atra lokā alokāḥ, deva adevāḥ, vedā avedā bhavanti*—Bṛ. Up. 4:3:22.

59 *Na pratīke na hi saḥ*—B.S. 4:1:4.

60 *Brahmadṛṣṭir-utkarṣāt*—B.S. 4:1:5.

61 *Utkṛṣṭadṛṣṭir-hi nikṛṣṭe adhyāsitavya iti laukiko nyāyaḥ, yathā rājadṛṣṭiḥ kṣattari. Na hi kṣatradṛṣṭi-parigṛhīto rājā nikarṣaṁ nīyamānaḥ śreyase syāt.*—Sankara's commentary on B.S. 4:1:5.

62 *Gospel,* Chennai 2000, p.80 (conversations on March 1882).

63 Ibid, p.81.

64 Meaning Eden Gardens.

65 *Gospel*, p.468 (conversations on 25-06-1884).

66 Ibid. p.287 (conversations on 09-09-1883).

67 *Jñānaṁ śāstrataḥ ācāryataśca ātmādīnām avabodhaḥ; vijñānaṁ viśeṣataḥ anubhavaḥ*—Sankara's commentary to the *Bhagavad Gītā,* 3:41.

68 *Jñānaṁ śastrokta-padārthānāṁ parijñānam; vijñānaṁ tu śāstrato jñātānāṁ tathā eva svānubhavakaraṇam*—Ibid, 6:8.

69 *.Jñānabhūmiḥ śubhecchākhyā prathamā parikīrtitā/Vicāraṇā dvitīyā syāt tṛtīyā tanumānasā//Sattvāpattiś-caturthī syāt tato'saṁsaktināmikā/padārthabhāvanī ṣaṣṭhī saptamī turyagā smṛtā//*—Laghu-Yoga-Vāsiṣṭha, Lavaṇa-Upākhyāna, 3:9:13, 14

70 Cf. Madhusūdana Sarasvatī's gloss to B.G.3:18 for the detailed discussion.

71 *Tvāṁ stotuṁ ko'tra śaktaḥ syād bhāvātītam anāmayam/ Bhagavan sarvabhūtātman rāmakṛṣṇa namo'stu te//*—A hymn by Swami Abhedananda.

Sri Ramakrishna and the Bodhisattva Ideal

Be ye like a banyan tree

SRI RAMAKRISHNA once made an epochal remark in his advice to Narendranath. When Narendranath badgered him persistently for a state of complete absorption in God for days together, he reproached him, 'Fie upon you! I thought you would be like a huge banyan tree under the cool shade of which many a tired traveller of life will find rest and peace. No, my boy, there are higher stages than what you crave for (samādhi). Don't you sing, 'Thou art whatever exists'? This was not the only occasion. A keen reader of the life and gospel of the great master will find such pregnant ideas gushing forth in streams from Sri Ramakrishna whenever occasion demanded.

A few days before his final departure, he implored Sri Sarada Devi (Sri Ramakrishna's wife), 'Would you not do anything, dear?' She dithered, 'What can I, a helpless woman, do?' To that Sri Ramakrishna retorted, 'Oh no! You will have to do much more than what this body has done. The people of Calcutta are wallowing like insects in the mire of the world. You must look after their welfare.'

Long before the devotees started flocking around him, Sri Ramakrishna, after achieving the consummation of all spiritual paths, felt an indomitable desire within, and would go to the terrace of the office building in Dakshineswar to call aloud at the top of his voice, 'Come, all ye! I have been waiting for you.' It seemed he could delay no more to distribute at large whatever he had earned in the course of his spiritual struggle. What force impelled him to do good to the world voluntarily? What prodded him to train a band of people to sacrifice their lives for the noble cause of doing good to others as a way of achieving freedom for oneself as well as for others?

Indeed, it was a radically new ideal of modern religious thought that Sri Ramakrishna promoted. This ideal contained the best elements of all the then extant philosophies of the world. Such a beautifully proportionate blend was done only once before in the religious annals of India—during the regime of Śrī Kṛṣṇa.

Today we all remember Sri Ramakrishna as the harmonizer of religions. But very few among us have a clear idea of how he effected this feat. To know this, we have to discuss some of the less-known views of Advaita philosophy as also some remarkable features of some other contemporary religious philosophies of India. An avatāra like Sri Ramakrishna comes not to destroy or throw away anything already established by the earlier prophets but to build a unique philosophy befitting the present age by blending in his own life all the best aspects of different religions, some of which were on the verge of being lost due to neglect or misunderstanding. Here we will study mainly two lesser-known aspects to suit the present context. One is the Bodhisattva ideal and the other is the Sarvamukti ideal (meaning 'liberation of all'). These two have come to bear upon the spirit of 'serving God in all' with an attitude of worship in great measure.

The Bodhisattva ideal

The Bodhisattva forms such a core doctrine in Mahāyāna Buddhism that it is also known as the Bodhisattva-yāna. The word Bodhisattva literally means the essence (sattva) of wisdom or supreme intelligence (bodhi). It is a state, compared to the threshold of a house, from which both the inside and the outside can be seen. Here inside means the phenomenal universe while the outside is the superconscious existence.

The Bodhisattva state is one of perfect balance between the faculties of the head and the heart. The essential nature of Bodhisattva is a great loving heart, and all sentient beings constitute the object of his love. Kenneth Saunders describes the characteristics of a Bodhisattva in the following way in his *Epochs in Buddhist History*:

'Charming, gentle, and compassionate, full of tender and affectionate thought, unbiased, serene, he is ever zealous, and ever girded for the duties of his high calling, and has no thought that is not pure and wise. He rouses others to good deeds.'[1]

One of the outstanding characteristics of a Bodhisattva is his eagerness for vicarious salvation. He is ready to give up his own salvation to help others find salvation. He is ready to exchange others' sins for his own merits. This fact points to the superhuman courage a Bodhisattva possesses.

The Bodhisattva ideal originated in India and got developed and popularised in China (in Judo school) and Japan (Honen and Shiuran Shonin school). There are ten steps leading to the Bodhisattva stage. Of them, the initial three, known as *dānapāramitā, śīlapāramitā*, and *kṣāntipāramitā*, are meant for moral and ethical practices that form the basis of all spiritual aspirations. The word *pāramitā* in Buddhism has the same meaning as the Sanskrit word *parākāṣṭhā*, meaning the extreme limit. In the fourth plane, known as *vīryapāramitā*, the aspirant continues in his practice with enthusiasm. The fifth level, known as *dhyānapāramitā*, is meant for the practice of meditation.

In the next stage, the aspirant is directed for *prajñāpāramitā* when the aspirant gains the knowledge of the real nature of the objective world and its cause-effect network in the right perspective. This is an intermediary level between the temporal and liberated stages. The seventh plane opens the gate to non-dual realization. The aspirant acquires enormous qualities of an enlightened person (Buddha). This is the consummation of all spiritual practices. Then the aspirant (Bodhisattva) may merge himself in nirvā*ṇ*a (cessation of all mundane bondages, that is, liberation). But his desire to do good to all prevents him from entering the citadel of nirvāṇa for himself alone.

So he continues in his journey, and reaches the eighth stage to attain the power of forbearance. The Bodhisattva at this level goes beyond all taints of karma. Moreover, all the previously enlightened ones appear before him and open their store of inexhaustible wisdom for him. It is by virtue of this wisdom that the Bodhisattva earns the capacity to do good to others.

One point may be noted from this in passing: without acquiring the right knowledge, one cannot do good to others effectively. Here, again, one gains the capacity to control others. Next, he ascends the ninth stage where the powers due to knowledge and work and many kinds of samādhi come to his possession. In the tenth or final stage, the Bodhisattva becomes endowed with a resplendent body, emitting divine rays in all directions. These divine rays bring cessation to all miseries of living beings.

Thus, the Bodhisattva is a person who does not seek to escape from the cycle of transmigration into nirvāṇa, but, realizing the essential unity of the cycle and nirvāṇa, he continues to live in the cycle for the enlightenment of all other beings. The Bodhisattva feels that he cannot enjoy eternal bliss while other beings suffer, because he knows that there is no essential difference between them and him.

For him personal nirvāṇa is a vanity and selfishness as long as a single creature remains unenlightened. This profound principle points to the fact that the finite and the infinite, the secular and the spiritual, the mundane and the cosmic, are not incompatible. To put it philosophically, the immanent and the transcendent are just two perspectives of the same truth. The *Lankāvatāra Sūtra* has gone a step further in boldly proclaiming that 'There is no Nirvana except where there is Samsara; there is no Samsara except where there is Nirvana; for the condition of existence is not of a mutually exclusive character.' When Swami Vivekananda advised his disciples to have equal enthusiasm in meditation and work, he had this point in view.

The long and short of it is that the infinite can be worshipped only through the finite, and not to the complete exclusion of it. Swami Prabhavananda in his 1947 book, *The Upanishads* writes that the *Īśāvāsyopaniṣad* vouches for this truth clearly in the following mantras:

> To darkness are they doomed who worship only the body, and to greater darkness they who worship only the spirit. Worship of the body (the finite) alone leads to one result, worship of the spirit (the infinite) leads to another. We have heard from the wise. They who worship both the body and the spirit, by the body overcome death, and by the spirit achieve immortality.[2]

What Sri Ramakrishna used to call states of *bhāvamukha, Īśvarakoti,* and *Avatāra* bear a striking semblance to this Bodhisattva state. The following passage from M's *The Gospel of Sri Ramakrishna* clarifies the point in question:

> Take the case of a man who stands by a wall on both sides of which there are meadows stretching to infinity. If there is a hole in the wall, through it he can see everything on the other side. If the hole is a big one, he can even pass through it. The ego of the Incarnations and other Īśvarakotis is like the wall with a hole. Though they remain on this side of the wall, still they can see the endless meadow on the other side. That is to say, though they have a human body, they are always united with God. Again, if they will, they can pass through the hole to the other side and remain in samādhi. And if the hole is big enough, they can go through it and come back again. That is to say, though established in samādhi, they can again descend to the worldly plane.[3]

Sarvamukti ideal

According to Appaya Dīkṣita, practitioner of Advaita Vedanta School of Hindu philosophy, there were a number of schools of Advaita philosophy. Of these, only the Vivaraṇa school advocated the view of Sarvamukti. The word does not imply that all the souls will be liberated together on a fine morning. As a matter of fact, every individual soul, after getting enlightenment, attains oneness with *Saguṇa* Brahman, meaning, personal God. He then goes on leading his own exemplary divine life while maintaining an attitude of benevolence towards others. Such a soul is said to have attained the state of Īśvara.

Even after the dissolution of the body, he does not get complete liberation but continues to live in a particular region of transcendental existence. From there he may at times come back to temporal existence with a view to helping others get liberation. But this descent is not comparable with the usual transmigratory existence of the common run of individuals who take birth according to the inexorable law of Karma.

Professor M Hiriyanna has pointed out that this Sarvamukti theory does not admit of a complete individual perfection so long as the other bodies in the system continue to be imperfect. Here we have to bring in the name of Bhartṛprapañca, a lesser known pre-Śankarite Advaita philosopher who was one of the supporters of the Sarvamukti ideal. He lived a couple of centuries before Śankara, and is known as an interpreter of the Upaniṣads like *Bṛhadāraṇyaka, Kaṭha, Īśa*, and possibly of the Vedanta-Sūtras. Even Śankara in his commentary on the *Bṛhadāraṇyaka Upaniṣad* has referred to his views (though he refuted them). Both of them held the view that non-dualism was the ultimate teaching of the Upaniṣads. But while Śankara differentiated between the two states of Brahman, namely, the absolute (*parā)* and the relative (*aparā*), calling the latter as appearance, Bhartṛprapañca held them both as equally real.

This theory is known as *bhedābhedavāda*. Again, whereas Śankara restricted the scope of the Upaniṣads within the concept of unity alone, Bhartṛprapañca promoted the concept of unity in diversity (*dvaitādvaita*) in the Upaniṣads. He also felt it necessary to co-ordinate *jñāna* (knowledge) with *karma* (ritual work) on the way to attain *mokṣa* (liberation). Some other views of this great savant need mention. Those unique views will help us to link Sri Ramakrishna's significant views directly to the Advaita foundation.

For one thing, Bhartṛprapañca holds that genuine indifference to worldly objects comes as a matter of course through some kind of actual experience. This 'some kind' is prescribed in the Upaniṣads as a conscious participation in universal life. This is called *apavarga* (liberation from mundane existence) through *bhoga* (actual experience).

For another thing, Bhartṛprapañca recognized the variety of the universe in eight modes or *avasthās* of Brahman. They are, 1) *antaryāmin,* 2) *sākṣin,* 3) *avyākṛta,* 4) *sūtra,* 5) *virāj,* 6) *devatā,* 7) *jāti,* 8) *piṇḍa.* These eight can be broadly subdivided into two distinct aspects, namely, the spiritual (1 and 2), and the secular (3 to 8).

From the discussion on the two concepts, namely, the Bodhisattva and the Sarvamukti, two points get clarified. In the first place, the Bodhisattva ideal shares some common features with at least some schools of pre-Śankarite Advaita philosophy. Secondly, the Sarvamukti ideal as expressed in Buddhism is not altogether alien to Hindu philosophy.

These two points are important; for, Sri Ramakrishna in the modern era utilized these two features in propounding a wonderful and unprecedented work philosophy that is as deep as a stream in its Advaitic depth, as it is broad in its humanness and love for humanity.

Sri Ramakrishna's synthesis

One of the main contributions of Sri Ramakrishna to the world is the concept of the harmony of all religions. This harmony is based on several facts. In the first place, the goal of all religions is the same, namely, to realize God or truth or perfection. Secondly, the essential elements of all the paths lead to the wellbeing of humanity. That religion which does not cater to the welfare of people will perish in no time. In the third place, all religious paths are equally true and valid. Hence no question arises as to the survival of one to the exclusion of others. This idea was tersely clarified later by Swami Vivekananda in his concluding address at the Parliament of Religions, Chicago:

> The Christian is not to become a Hindu or a Buddhist, nor a Hindu or a Buddhist to become a Christian. But each must assimilate the spirit of the others and yet preserve his individuality and grow according to his own law of growth.[4]

This statement points to the peaceful coexistence of all religions in a multi-religious world. The fourth implication is that there are, in all religions, elevated personalities of divine stature. So, however defective a religion may look in the eyes of the common man, its need should not be undermined. As a fifth implication, harmony of religions leads to mutual enrichment through sympathy and right understanding. Interfaith dialogues enable us to dive deep into the essence of religions.

Interestingly, Sri Ramakrishna never had any intention of harmonising religions. After he attained perfection in one path, he felt an irrepressible desire within to taste the same bliss from different perspectives. To him it was all a divine play of the Mother. Through his punctilious adherence to every minute detail of some of the chief religious paths he reached perfection in each of them, realizing the truth that God has made various provisions for people of different temperaments. Hence, all dissension over religions is meaningless.

There is no evidence of Sri Ramakrishna following the disciplines of Buddhism; but from his own statements in the Gospel we come to know that he had a deep reverence for Gautama Buddha. He spoke highly of Buddha, refuting others' allegation that he was an agnostic. Moreover, he was highly impressed by the Bodhisattva ideal. By dint of his irresistible spiritual potential, he attained the non-dual unity of the Vedanta and remained in that state continuously for six months—an unprecedented episode in religious annals. But an inscrutable power brought him down to the normal plane of existence. Thereafter, he received a command from the High to remain in *Bhavamukha*. This was the starting point of his divine mission.

Noble souls like Sri Ramakrishna come not to destroy but to build. Even those paths of Tantric discipline that were berated by others for the immoral practices associated with them were held in good esteem by Sri Ramakrishna with the remark, 'At least some people have attained to perfection through that path also. It may be like a postern gate meant only for the menial servants of the house, but it's also a way nevertheless.'

Śankara had to release pure Advaita philosophy from the clutches of Buddhism. Hence, he had to defeat his Buddhist opponents in scriptural debate. As per the local custom prevalent in his era, the defeated had to embrace the winner's philosophy or perish. Thus, Śankara succeeded in converting a good number of Buddhist savants into his way of thought. But that could not strip Buddhism of its essential and humanitarian elements.

The Bodhisattva ideal, chiefly propagated by Mahāyāna Buddhism and the Sarvamukti ideal, held by some pre-Śankarite Advaita philosophers of the Vivaraṇa school have striking similarities in them. This implies that the Bodhisattva ideal was not alien to Hindu thought. Sri Ramakrishna, either through his spiritual intuition or through a divine dispensation, felt an intense desire to apply this important element to the welfare of people at large.

To bring about an all-round development of the human race, he did not stop merely by creating a group of monastic disciples to carry his humanitarian message to the people; he also set his mind to give the ideal of householder a new dimension. Ideal monks will be born only when the common people start living the lives of ideal householders, he believed. Besides, he left a number of dedicated women disciples including his own wife to ameliorate the condition of the other sex. He realized that to improve a race both the sexes must strive together for upliftment.

His followers remember reverentially his refusal to leave a group of poor, ill-nourished and famished villagers of Vaidyanath Dham before each of them were well-fed, and properly clad. This he did with sternness in the face of a strong opposition from the leader of the pilgrimage, Mathuranath. It was not his soft emotion that came into play at the sight of misery; it was a feeling of identity born of Advaitic realization and the heart of a Bodhisattva who is ready to sacrifice his all for the common weal, who is ready to return love for hate, virtue for vice, happiness and peace for misery.

Unmitigated the Advaita ideal may render one devoid of any feeling for others. On the other hand, excess of emotional outburst as found in the dualistic philosophies runs the risk of degrading and even corrupting man. A balance between the two was badly needed for the present age. That is precisely what Sri Ramakrishna did in his process of synthesis.

Another point needs special mention. Sri Ramakrishna had said that after realization when the aspirant comes down to the normal plane of consciousness by a reverse process called *viloma*, he finds that this world is made up of the same element as that of Brahman. He exemplified it by citing the terrace and the staircase, both made of the same elements of cement, lime and brick, among other ingredients. He named this realization as *vijñāna*.

This view is not accepted by the orthodox schools of Advaita Vedanta. Though Buddhism has a theory called *vijñānavāda*, it has no similarity with what Sri Ramakrishna believed. Some people trace this concept of vijñāna to the Viśiṣṭādvaita school of Rāmānuja. This is also not fully correct. Whatever name may be ascribed to it, the state of a *vijñānī* as placed by Sri Ramakrishna is purely an Advaitic view in a modified form. And as an outcome of this view, one is propelled by the desire to do good to the world.

In the present age, work has become an indispensable part of human life. Man has to earn his living through work, which connects each individual to the world. In other words, the relationship between man and the world can be established only through work. And there is a beautiful element in Advaita philosophy which says that the relative and the absolute, secular and spiritual are one and the same from the non-dualistic perspective. This wonderful idea gives rise to a new hope that by spiritualising our work, by changing our attitude to work, we can also have spiritual realization.

Another story narrated by Sri Ramakrishna that M writes about in the *Gospel of Sri Ramakrishna* illustrates the Bodhisattva ideal well.

> There was an infinite field beyond a high wall. Four friends tried to find out what was beyond the wall. Three of them, one after the other, climbed the wall, saw the field, burst into loud laughter, and dropped to the other side. These three could not give any information about the field. Only the fourth man came back and told people about it. He is like those who retain their bodies, even after attaining Brahmajñāna, in order to teach others.[5]

Implementation by Swami Vivekananda

It is not that Sri Ramakrishna followed the Bodhisattva ideal in toto. He blended the Bodhisattva of Buddism and the Sarvamukti of the Advaita schools, to make it suitable for the present age, and to enhance the collective liberation of all. Swami Vivekananda took off from Sri Ramakrishna and broadcasted it all over the world. Whereas Buddha preached the motto of *bahujana-hitāya, bahujana-sukhāya ca* (for the happiness of the many, for the welfare of the many), Swami Vivekananda placed a unique motto for the monks of the Ramakrishna Order. He put it as *ātmano mokṣārtham jagad hitāya ca*—for one's own liberation as also for the welfare of the world simultaneously. When he founded the Ramakrishna Mission on 1 May 1897, immediately after his triumphant return from the West, Vivekananda put this motto as the ideal before the monks. Before leaving for the West a second time in June 1899, he said in an address to the monks:

> To go ahead of others in salvation is wrong. One must learn sooner or later that one cannot get salvation if one does not try to seek the salvation of his brothers. You must try to combine in your life immense idealism with immense practicality. You must be prepared to go into deep meditation now, and the next moment you must be ready to go and cultivate these fields. You must be prepared to explain the difficult intricacies of the Shāstras now, and the next moment to go and sell the produce of the fields in the market. You must be prepared for all menial services, not only here, but elsewhere also.[6]

Sri Ramakrishna sometimes compared avatāras to a ship or a huge vessel that can carry many people across an ocean. The Sanskrit word for a vessel is *yāna*, and the words *mahāyāna* and *hīnayāna* in Buddhism point to the same meaning of two types of vessel that carries many souls across the ocean of life to salvation. Swami Vivekananda also mentioned this idea in three of his lectures in India. The appeal was so strong that it cannot but move the hearts of people even after a long gap of a century. Said he in his touching style:

> This national ship, my countrymen, my friends, my children—this national ship has been ferrying millions and millions of souls across the waters of life. For scores of shining centuries it has been plying across this water, and through its agency, millions of souls have been taken to the other shore, to blessedness. But today, perhaps through your own fault, this boat has become a little damaged, has sprung a leak; and would you therefore curse it? Is it fit that you stand up and pronounce malediction upon it, one that has done more work than any other thing in the world? If there are holes in this national ship, this society of ours, we are its children. Let us go and stop the holes. Let us gladly do it with our hearts' blood; and if we cannot, then let us die. We will make a plug of our brains and put them into the ship, but condemn it never…I have come to you, my children, to tell you all my plans. If you hear them I am ready to work with you. But if you will not listen to them, and even kick me out of India, I will come back and tell you that we are all sinking! I am come now to sit in your midst, and if we are to sink, let us all sink together, but never let curses rise to our lips.[7]

When Swami Vivekananda returned to India from his Western mission in 1897 and founded the Ramakrishna organization of monks with its missionary schedule of activity, many brows were raised in suspicion. Even his brother-disciples protested against the proposal, alleging that Vivekananda was influenced by the missionary zeal of the West. But he replied to that with full confidence that what all he had done till then were forcibly done through him by 'a ghost named Sri Ramakrishna.' This statement endorsed the fact that whatever he propagated was actually prompted by Sri Ramakrishna and was not his own brainchild. Another statement by Vivekananda reflects the Bodhisattva ideal better. He said:

> It may be that I shall find it good to get outside of my body—to cast it off like a disused garment. But I shall not cease to work! I shall inspire men everywhere until the world shall know that it is one with God.[8]

This is an ideal meant for each and every member of the Ramakrishna Order—not to care for his own liberation until the whole world rediscovers its unity with God. For a monk of the Ramakrishna Order, however spiritually advanced, there is no question of personal liberation. He will have to come back again and again to work for the enlightenment of his fellow brothers and sisters with renewed enthusiasm.

Endnotes

1 Kenneth Saunders, *Epochs in Buddhist History,* p.90.

2 Prabhavananda Swami, & Manchester, F.(Trs.), *The Upanishads,* (Hollywood, 1947) *Īśāvāsyopaniṣad,* verses 9,10.

3 M, *The Gospel of Sri Ramakrishna,* (Henceforth Gospel) Sri Ramakrishna Math, Chennai, Feb.2000, p.760.

4 *The Complete Works of Swami Vivekananda,* (Henceforth CW) Mayavati Memorial Editionm, Vol.1, p.24.

5 M, *Gospel,* Sri Ramakrishna Math, Chennai, 2000, p.354.

6 *CW,* Vol.3, P.447.

7 *CW,* Vol.3, p.227.

8 *CW,* Vol.5, p.414.

Practicality in Spiritual Life

'IN A village there lived a grumpy venomous snake in the meadows in its own hole, who would not allow people to pass by his hole,' Sri Ramakrishna drew an anecdote from a bucolic scene with his natural sweetness. 'The villagers were scared of him and signalled that zone as dreadful. One day a holy man happened upon that place. The shepherd lads came running to forewarn him. Having listened to their warning, the holy man smilingly continued his journey in the same direction to the utter horror of the villagers. The snake came as usual, saw the holy man, and was conquered by the power of certain mystic words. The upshot was, he became his disciple and gave up his harmfulness forever.'

'The holy man wended his way after promising to come back again to enquire of the disciple's spiritual development. After a year he was back on the spot and called out the snake who came out dragging himself with difficulty after a long time. The holy man was astonished to find a haggard-looking disciple prostrating before him. On critical enquiry the truth came out. The snake said he lived on a vegan diet and gave up anger; taking advantage of his meek nature the village urchins trounced him till the poor fellow vomited blood and became senseless. Taking him for dead, the boys left him proudly. At this the holy man said reprimanding, "My child, I had forbidden you to bite; why didn't you hiss at the evil-doers?'"

The story is an eye-opener for all spiritual aspirants. Our old culture depicts a spiritual aspirant as a morose, eccentric, out-of-the world fellow who has little room for others in his heart, who lacks all concern about the world. In our present day society monks and spiritual aspirants are generally looked down upon as beggars or parasites with no concrete contribution to society. Sri Ramakrishna's teachings, enlivened by his exemplary life, lash upon such age-old misconceptions and establish the truth that spirituality and practicality are not only compatible but also complementary. To put it in Einsteinian style, spirituality without practicality is lame; practicality without spirituality is blind.

However, practicality and a down-to-earth attitude are not one and the same thing. Materialism often appears in the cloak of practicality to delude the unwary. Instead of helping spiritual aspirants move forward in their journey, materialism stunts their growth. In contrast, practicality implies the application of common sense in day-to-day life. Great souls are born in every age to re-establish the hoary truth that spirituality can be attained even by living in the world and, wherever we live—in a busy metropolis or in the stillness of the deep forest—common sense must be applied in every step of our journey to the goal. Spirituality is not miracle mongering. It is the courage to face the realities of life and find a solution.

Synthesis of the Duo

Sri Ramakrishna emphasized that spirituality is the goal of human life. The soul has to wend its way through innumerable sharp curves and crossroads. Practicality is one of the chief factors that make this cumbersome journey pleasurable. Both are abstract concepts and so, their synthesis can best be effected in human life. Sri Ramakrishna himself did this blending so well in his life.

Even as an adolescent boy, he had a probing mind which would dive headlong into the bedrock of matters to find a viable answer to certain critical questions. He was a keen observer of day-to-day happenings, from which he would draw his own conclusions. For example, he saw scholars well versed in scriptures constantly reeling off quotations on spirituality, while their minds were engrossed in hoarding money. From this he concluded that formal education that had brought them to such a state couldn't take the aspirant Godward. So, he refused to undergo such education. Instead, he set his mind to learn that supreme knowledge (*parā-vidyā*) by which the Indestructible can be known.[1]

In his spiritual pursuits, Sri Ramakrishna insisted on creating the exact environment demanded for attaining perfection. Without any ego, he did not hesitate to clean the toilet of the scavenger's house, with his long-grown dishevelled hair, stealthily at dead of night in fear of not being allowed to do that. By this action, he proved that the concept of practicalising spirituality worked.

When devotees started pouring in from all walks of life, he took all precaution to see that he did not disappoint anybody. An ideal that is too high to attain is not a practicable one. He clearly saw that all are not equally fit to reach the ultimate goal. Following his own analogy, he would cook the same fish in different dishes to suit the stomach of each of his children. To souls like Narendranath he would give spiritual experience with a mere touch, to others he would ask them to wait or carry on with hearty prayer and devotion.

Training Holy Mother

His method of training the Holy Mother Sri Sarada Devi was one of its kind. As he moulded her life in a spiritual cast, he did not undermine her practical relationships with people around. In matters of divine pursuit he taught her, 'Just as the moon is everybody's uncle, so is God most closely related to all and appears before us whenever called upon with intense longing.' This teaching clearly shows that God-realization is not esoteric, and open to a selected few only. Anybody following the prescribed conditions is capable of His vision.

His advice to her on worldly matters was: 'When you take on a boat trip in a group, you should first get aboard and at the end of the journey come out last after making sure everything has been brought and nothing is left in the boat. In his teaching of behavioural science Sri Ramakrishna gave a rule of thumb to follow: "In all worldly dealings, act in accordance with time, place, and person."'[1]

'Give everyone his due.' This teaching has a wide practical bearing in our interpersonal dealings. When we live in society, we have to give importance to others' sentiments also, since they are part of society. Giving a patient hearing to others' opinion is an art of being both happy and human.

Dr W Beran Wolfe, an eminent Adlerian psychologist, has given some tips: If after mature thought and consideration you really believe in the truth of a certain proposition, and wish to convey it to another, it is always best to put it in such a form that your listener can accept your word without losing his self-esteem.... Develop a stoic disregard for trifles, and extend your horizons to such a degree that trifles can never affect the even tenor of the pursuit of your goals.[2]

Training Swami Vivekananda

Swami Vivekananda, then Narendranath, was the foremost of his monastic disciples. Naren, with his sound family background, was thorough in matters of practicality. One day, in a fit of heated argument with a person at the behest of Sri Ramakrishna, Naren's tongue slipped with the remark, 'That is due to your blind faith.' At once Sri Ramakrishna interrupted his disciple to correct him, 'What do you mean! Does faith have an eye that you say blind faith? Faith itself is blind.' This silenced Naren, who realized his own folly.

We live in an age in which work is indispensable for bare existence. Sri Ramakrishna introduced a unique work philosophy through Swami Vivekananda. One day, in an abstract mood, Sri Ramakrishna said, 'Compassion to others! Who are you to bestow compassion, petty creature that you are? No, not compassion but service to mankind in a spirit of worship to God.' This comment hit its mark in the heart of Swami Vivekananda who in later years engineered a powerful machine named the Ramakrishna Organization that would cater to the wellbeing of people in all fields irrespective of caste, creed, and religion in such a way as to bring about the liberation of both the worshipper and the worshipped. The motto of the Ramakrishna Order, which talks of individual liberation, coupled with welfare and wellbeing of the world, propounded by Swami Vivekananda, is the best example of the synthesis of meditation and work, spirituality and practicality.

Advice to Swami Brahmananda

Sri Ramakrishna taught his boy-disciple, Rakhal, later Swami Brahmananda, how to keep commonsense above false emotion. Once Sri Ramakrishna accompanied by Rakhal and others attended a Brahmo festival at Calcutta. At the end of the ceremony, the guests had a sumptuous feast. It was past 9 pm and the hosts were waiting for the distinguished guests, while Sri Ramakrishna and his retinue remained unnoticed. This angered Rakhal, who said in a huff, 'Let us get away from here this very moment.' But Sri Ramakrishna was wise enough and bore no malice to the householders for the lapse. On the contrary, he said with a smile, 'Don't be silly; who will pay the hackney fare? You wax irritated without a penny in your pocket. Besides, who is going to feed you at such a late hour at Dakshineswar?'

Teaching Swami Premananda

Sri Ramakrishna loved congregational dance to the accompaniment of devotional music. He would often get into a spiritual trance while dancing on such occasions, oblivious of the external world. On one such occasion, he was absorbed in dance along with many other devotees when his gaze fell on his boy-disciple Baburam (later Swami Premananda). Sri Ramakrishna noticed that the boy was spent with hunger. He at once retrieved some fruits and sweets brought for himself, ate a little himself to give it the status of an offered food, and made Baburam help himself with the rest. The incident showed, 'Religion is not for the empty stomach.'

Instructions to Swami Adbhutananda

Sri Ramakrishna was mindful even in mundane affairs. When he would stay at a devotee's house, he would take every care not to inconvenience him. Once Latu (later Swami Adbhutananda) was accompanying him on a visit. On the way the boy confessed to Sri Ramakrishna that he had forgotten to carry towels for the stay. Latu tried to cover up his slip saying the hosts were well-to-do and would not mind providing one for Sri Ramakrishna if asked. But Sri Ramakrishna was vexed and took the unmindful disciple to task for his forgetfulness and said, 'In an exuberance of ecstasy I often cannot keep to the norms of my own dress, yet I am so punctilious on worldly matters. And you are so forgetful at this tender age! Go back and fetch the towels, or the hosts might think some trouble-mongers have come to them.'

Lessons for Swami Yogananda

This disciple came at a very tender age to Sri Ramakrishna. Hailing from a high-caste Brahmin family, he had no experience in business matters. The master decided to strengthen his disciple in practical dealings. One day, he asked Yogen (later Swami Yogananda) to buy an iron wok from the market. The boy bought it, but the wok was found to have a crack. On asking the callow disciple, he regretted having trusted the devotional pretence of the shopkeeper.

Sri Ramakrishna said in a serious tone, 'Should you be a simpleton just because you are a devotee? The shopkeeper is a businessman by nature and not pious. Cheating is his business. You should rather be wary in dealing with such people. As a rule, you should call at three or four shops before you decide to buy, and bargain with them.'

Monks are supposed to stick to the principle of

harmlessness. Some people interpret this quality as non-killing also. Swami Yogananda in his earlier days held this view. So when one day Sri Ramakrishna took out a living cockroach from his hand box and asked Yogen to kill it outside the room, Yogen thought, being a monk Sri Ramakrishna must not have literally meant to kill it. Yogen was very soft-hearted by nature, so he just let go the cockroach out in the courtyard. But intent that Sri Ramakrishna was on training his disciple in the practical affairs of life, he caught the infraction and severely scolded him for holding on to his short-sighted judgement in preference to a prudent decision of the master.

Another incident bears mention in this context. Ever since Mathuranath was in charge of the temple, provision was made to send a share of the offerings of the Kali temple to Sri Ramakrishna's room. One day the temple authority inadvertently forgot to send the usual quota to Sri Ramakrishna's room. Yogen was present at the scene. To his consternation Sri Ramakrishna straightaway questioned the manager for his lapse, and after getting an apologetic reply, gently warned the manager not to repeat the mistake.

The whole affair evoked suspicion from the boy-disciple: 'Wasn't it the repetition of the hoarding nature of all priests?' And pat came the reply from Sri Ramakrishna who was also an expert thought-reader, 'The offered food is used here for the devotees; thereby the purpose of the arrangement devised by Rani Rasmani will be rightly served; whereas the quota fixed for the other priests of the temple are for the most part sent to ill-natured people. I have seen it for myself. Thereby the Rani will incur demerit with all her pious intents and purposes.'

The young disciple was now in awe of Sri Ramakrishna's deep sense of practicality.

Cue for Balaram Bose

Balaram Bose, a householder, was a staunch Vaishnavite. In the vow of harmlessness, Vaishnavites share the same belief as Jains. One day, as this disciple was meditating in his room, his concentration was distracted every now and then by mosquito-bites; still he was hesitant to kill the mosquitoes. As the problem was weighing heavily on his mind, he went to ask the master a solution. But, as he approached Sri Ramakrishna's room to his utter amazement he saw Sri Ramakrishna was killing bugs in his pillow! The disciple got his lesson: killing harmful creatures does not in any way impede spiritual growth.

Sri Ramakrishna and practical vedanta

Sri Ramakrishna's life shows how he practicalized the principles of Advaita Vedanta. These principles are: unity of all existence and truth of all religions. Sri Ramakrishna's life demonstrates his feeling of oneness with all. When a boatman slapped another person on a boat on the Ganga, Sri Ramakrishna not only cried aloud in pain, but welt marks appeared on his back. When someone walked past the verdant lawn in front of his home, he went out of breath as if someone had trampled on his chest.

People talk glibly about empathy without even realizing its significance, mistaking it for sympathy. Throwing a few coins at a beggar is not empathy. Empathy doesn't mean simply looking at poverty with compassion, but feeling it impact one's own life. For instance when the young prince of Śākya dynasty, on an outing, saw disease, old age and death, he placed himself mentally in the shoes of the suffering people. Feeling their pain, after some time, he gave up his royal attire and princely life, and went out to find out a solution to all the problems of human life, going deep into meditation. This was real empathy.

Sri Ramakrishna too was full of empathy. That is why he could give real solutions to seekers. Only practical spirituality can give us empathy, which can offer viable solutions to worldly problems. However, solving worldly problems permanently maybe utopian. According to *Śrīmad Bhāgavatam*, there is only a spiritual solution to the threefold misery of life described as *ādhidaivika, ādhibhautikia*, and *ādhyātmika*.[3] Only a person who remains undisturbed by the miseries given by one's own body or mind, or those given by others or by nature can have a steady mind. Such a person is free from attachment, fear and anger, and is almost like a sage.

When a bereaved Mani Mallick shared his agony with Sri Ramakrishna at the untimely demise of his only young son, he did not console the father but, instead, with spiritual fervour he beckoned humanity to be armed with the shield of spirituality, which even death cannot pierce. Both birth and death are the two extremities of a set of six different phases (birth, existence, growth, maturity, decay, and death) of a constantly changing system called life. When you accept one of them, you have to accept all the five others. There is no respite from them. If you want to go beyond the phenomenon called death, you must look beyond life.

Sri Ramakrishna's transparent attitude toward the truths of all religions is also purely scientific. Unless one treads each of the religious paths oneself and discovers the intricacies empathically, all attempts to harmonize religions will be brought to nought. What is important is the practical application of religion. What Sri Ramakrishna preached, he practised in his own spiritual life.

Practical Vedanta was preached long ago by Sri Krishna to Arjuna shortly before the Kurukshetra war. The very venue Sri Krishna selected for delivering his epochal message of the Upanishads attests to the fact that the Vedanta can be translated, not only in our day-to-day dealings but also in the busiest place of life—the battlefield. Sri Ramakrishna came one step forward and drew unparalleled examples from human life to guide the sincere aspirant in worldly ways. Here is another example cited by M in *The Gospel of Sri Ramakrishna*:

> One must be careful about these few things. First, an influential man who has much money and many men under his control. He can injure you if he wants; you must be careful while talking to him; perhaps you may have to approve what he says. Second, a dog. When it chases you or barks at you, you must stand still, talk to it gently, and pacify it. Third, a bull. If it runs after you with lowered horns, you must calm it with a gentle voice. Fourth, a drunkard. If you arouse his anger, he will abuse you, naming fourteen generations of your family. You should say to him: 'Hello uncle! How are you?' Then he will be mightily pleased and sit by you and smoke.
>
> In the presence of a wicked person, I become alert. If such a man asks me whether I have a pipe for smoking, I say, 'Yes, I have.' Some people have the nature of a snake; they will bite you without warning. You have to discriminate a great deal in order to avoid the bite; otherwise your passion will be stirred up to such an extent that you will feel like doing injury in return. The companionship of a holy man is greatly needed now and then. It enables one to discriminate between the Real and the unreal.[4]

What an amazing degree of practicality these lines bear! One wonders how a person totally absorbed in divinity can give such insights into worldly matters.

Endorsement of scriptures

The Vedanta philosophy, in explaining the phenomenal universe, poses three dimensions of reality or truth: *Pāramārthika* or absolute, *Prātibhāsika* or apparent, and *Vyāvahārika* or practical. To explain this further, we may look at the popular analogy of rope and snake. Suppose a man is walking in a dimly lit alley where a piece of rope is lying on his way. At a little distance from it, the man catches sight of it, mistakes it for a snake, and gets scared. How did the thought of snake come in his mind? It came from a previous experience of a snake. Once the man finds out the truth, that it is a rope, he never again sees a snake. But as long as he sees the snake, he does not see the rope either. Here the rope is the *pāramārthika* truth, while the snake is the *prātibhāsika* truth. One thing is to be noted here; even the appearance has a modicum of truth in it. Unless the snake is previously experienced, its memory will not come. In a Sanskrit hymn on this ultimate Reality called *parabrahman*, this idea bears out: 'I bow to that Reality in which the whole world, though insentient, appears sentient like a snake in a rope.'[5]

The phenomenal world also has truth in it. So long as one is within its purview, one cannot deny its existence. It is then that the need of practicality sets in. When one feels the tang of hot chilli and yet says it is not hot, he is lying. Likewise, when one's finger burns with fire and while feeling the pain of burn one says there is no fire, he is wrong. Only one who has gone beyond the feelings

> of pain or pleasure can say that. What should the rest of mankind do? The answer is very simple: they should accept the practical reality and pave their way through it. Sri Ramakrishna's story of the mahut-Nārāyaṇa brings to bear upon this fact of practical reality. It goes as follows: The guru had taught his disciple that everything was Nārāyaṇa. A mad elephant was coming toward the disciple, but he did not move away since he believed the guru's words. He thought that the elephant was Narayana. The mahut shouted to him: 'Get away! Get away!' But the disciple did not move. The elephant picked him up and threw him to the ground. The disciple was not quite dead; when his face was sprinkled with water, he regained consciousness. Being asked why he had not moved away, he said: 'Why should I? The guru said, 'Everything is Narayana.' 'But, my child,' said the guru, 'why didn't you listen to the words of the māhut Narayana?'[6]

In the *Mārkaṇḍeya Purāṇa*, queen Madālasā, born with the knowledge of the ultimate reality, taught her first three sons about the absolute so that as they grew up they left the world embarking on a search for that truth. But when the fourth and the last son was born, she, at the entreaty of the king, trained her child on the practical application of the eternal truth.

The *Hitopadeśa,* a treatise on moral and ethical values through stories, advises: 'A greedy person should be appeased with money, a haughty fellow with folded hands; an ignorant person should be brought under control with favourable views, while an erudite may be encountered with a speech of truth.' It also says, 'A real friend should be won over by intimacy, the relatives with ceremonious behaviour, the wife and servant with gift, and honour, and the others with generosity.'[7]

The secondary Hindu scriptures, namely, the *Smṛtis* of Manu, *Yājñvalkya, Pasrāśara,* and *Raghunandana*, enjoin humanity to practicalize the principles of the Vedanta in day-to-day life. In different periods of history these ethical and moral rules vary—sometimes even contradict the earlier ones—according to the existing pattern of life. So they are arbitrary truths and not eternal. In the *Gītā*, which harmonizes the eternal truth and its practical application in life, this idea of practicality finds fulfilment. The same reality scintillates through all existence, even activities—secular as well as spiritual. Vedanta will have meaning to people in all walks of life only when they can relate to its principles in their respective positions in life. The *Gītā* endorses this fact in the eighteenth chapter (verse 45, 46) in this way: 'Man attains to perfection by continuing with his enjoined duties. Now listen to how man attains it: By worshipping that Lord, who is the creator and pervader of all beings, through one's own work one attains perfection.'[8]

Again, in the case of Swami Adbhutananda, we have seen Sri Ramakrishna cautioning his disciple against forgetfulness. *Vivekacūḍāmaṇi*, a primer on Vedantic studies, warns the aspirant against carelessness by corroborating the view of the *Mahābhārata* ('I call inadvertence death itself'—vide *Sanatsujātīya-samvāda*, Udyoga-parvan, chapters 40-45) and focusing on its consequence in verses 321 to 325.[9]

An ordinary person works more or less, unconsciously. A spiritual person does everything with deep knowledge and awakened consciousness. He has no duty under the sun, still he remains engaged in work for the benefit of others as also to set an example. This idea has been conveyed by Sri Krishna in the third chapter, verses 20 and 22 of the *Bhagavad Gītā*.

Afterword

Now to recapitulate. Spirituality and practicality can coexist in a person. Practical life does not mean die-hard materialism, but a mature, commonsense outlook on life. As the goal is spirituality or God-realization, one who wants to lead a spiritual life in the din and bustle of the world must steer clear of all harmful influences. Sri Ramakrishna used to say echoing the scriptures that the skill by which one can realize God is the real skill [*yā lokadvaya-sādhanī caturatā sā cāturī cāturī*].

Sri Ramakrishna trained his disciples in the skill of work. When all works are done with that skill, the works are transformed into yoga. This is what Sri Krishna meant when he said: *yogah karmasu kauśalam* in the *Gītā,* chapter 2, verse 50. When even the secular work is done with this spirit by keeping the mind's gaze wide open, a wonderful transformation of consciousness takes place. In the words of Sister Nivedita: '…the workshop, the study, the farmyard, and the field are as true and fit scenes for the meeting of God with man as the cell of the monk or the door of the temple…there is no difference between service of man and worship of God, between manliness and faith, between true righteousness and spirituality.'[10]

Unless the Vedanta is brought to bear upon the plough of the peasant, the kitchen of the housewife, the management of day-to-day affairs, it is all meaningless eulogy (*arthahīna arthavāda*) and nothing else.

Sri Ramakrishna never gave an ideal that is too high to attain. To the householders he never preached total renunciation. Rather he would dissuade them from embracing monastic life if the person had family encumbrances or helpless dependants. When Keshab Sen, the eminent leader of Brahmo Samaj, said in the course of a lecture, 'O God, grant that we may be plunged in the river of Devotion and attain the Ocean of *Satchidananda,*' Sri Ramakrishna, pointing to the ladies seated behind the screen, said to Keshab in a jocular tone, 'Then what will be their fate?...So you must come out of the water from time to time.'[11] Humorous though, the statement speaks highly of the practical sense of Sri Ramakrishna.

His catholicity toward the spiritual aspirants was legendary. He never advised suppression of desires. That is like swimming against the current. His method of transforming the impulses was to 'direct the six passions to God'. Richard Schiffman, a recent biographer of Sri Ramakrishna, has expressed it with literary excellence:

> He believed in making use of whatever lay at hand. In his advice to the young woman (with deep attachment to her nephew), he had acted on the perception that affection and devotion are not ultimately separable, but are actually points on a continuum, stages in a journey of the ever-widening expansion of love. And on that sacred journey we must start from the square foot of ground on which we stand. We can't leap in a single death-defying bound to embrace the Universal Spirit. We approach on a series of rungs leading by degrees from the familiar to the Mystery without name or form. Since he knew that God pulsates within all beings as love in the heart, it was never Ramakrishna's way to renounce natural affection. Instead, he aimed to gradually expand affection beyond measure until, purified of all selfishness and narrowness, it penetrates to the immaculate boundlessness of that Love which is God.[12]

In conclusion, we must remember one thing: God-men come to create, synthesize, and restore lost glory. Just Jesus Christ said: 'I am not come to destroy, but to fulfil.'[13]

Christ's message equally applies to all trailblazers of religious history. Practical spirituality is an art of living happily in the world, to forge a bright future around the encircling gloom.

End Notes

1 Mund. Up. 1:1:5.

2 W.B. Wolfe, *How to be Happy Though Human*, Penguin Books Ltd, Middlesex, Reprint 1959, pp.344-45.

3 Śrmad Bhāgavatam, 4:29:33.

4 M, *Gospel*, Red Letter edition, Feb.2000, p.560, conversation dt.26-9-1884.

5 *Prātarnamāmi…yasminnidaṁ jagadaśeṣam aśeṣamūrtau, rajjvāṁ bhujaṅgama iva pratibhāsitaṁ vai.*

6 M, *Gospel*, Red Letter edition, Feb.2000, pp.852-3, conversations of 18-10-1885.

7 *Hitopadeśaḥ,* Ch.4, verses 109,110.

8 *Bhagavad Gītā,* Ch.18, verses 45, 46.

9 Cf. *Mahābhārata, Sanatsujātīya-samvāda,* Ed. Sukthankar, Udyoga-parvan, Chapters 40-45, verses 321 to 325.

10 CW, Vol.1, pp.xv-xvi.

11 M. *Gospel*, p.844, conversation on 1-9-1885.

12 Richard Schiffman, *Sri Ramakrishna, A Prophet for the New Age*, Paragon House, N.Y., 1st edn.1989, p.196.

13 *The Bible,* Mt.5:17.

The Genius of Avataras

OUR ESSENTIAL nature is pure, blissful *ātman*, beyond sorrow or misery. But how many of us remember this, captured as we are by delusion! The result of this forgetfulness is that we entrap ourselves in an endless vicious circle of karma, known as transmigration.

Can this situation be averted? Is there any soul who can stop this never-ending movement and come out of this circle of life and death to set an example to all the rest? Is there anybody who can act his blissful role perfectly, while remaining isolated from it like an expert actor? The answer is an emphatic yes.

In the infinite cycle of time, some rare souls take birth on this planet. They come and play with us, and like mortals they laugh and weep at times, hiding their own identity behind the façade of joy and sorrow in the drama of life. At the dénouement, they reveal their true self and depart from us with a naughty smile.

But they do not leave us empty or anchorless. Indeed, they leave a legacy behind with a sign for us to tread the path that they walked so that we may reach the same goal with our own effort, without depending on other's help. They are the salts of the earth; they are the God-men, known in Sanskrit as Avatāras (one who 'comes down' with a definite purpose).

Recognizing an Avatāra

School children sometimes enthusiastically participate in a competitive game known as 'fancy dress' in which they take various disguises and appear before the audience. If they are recognized, they become the losers; if not, they win awards. This example very much fits into the pattern of an avatāra. Since the very birth, an avatāra starts his hide-and-seek game.

Jesus took birth during the tyranny of Herod in such a secret, unheard of place that all the king's men failed to pick out the divine child. Except the three Magi from the East, none succeeded in recognizing the Saviour of mankind. Sri Krishna sometimes playfully revealed himself in various ways to his own imprisoned parents as also to his foster mother Yaśoda. But the next moment he made them forget the ecstatic vision with his childish pranks commonly seen in all children. Similar was the case with Rāma. Other than a handful of ascetics no one recognized him as God embodied. Sri Ramakrishna, in order to drive home the secret nature of an avatāra, quoted a number of stories from the pages of Hindu mythology. Said he:

> Don't you know how Rāma had to weep, stricken with grief for Sītā? Further it is said that the Lord incarnated Himself as a sow in order to kill the demon Hiranyāksha. Hiranyāksha was eventually killed, but God would not go back to His abode in heaven. He enjoyed His sow's life. He had given birth to several young ones and was rather

> happy with them. The gods said amongst themselves: 'What does this mean? The Lord does not care to return to heaven!' They all went to Śiva and laid the matter before him. Śiva came down and urged the Lord to leave the sow body and return to heaven. But the sow only suckled her young ones. Then Śiva destroyed the sow body with his trident, and the Lord came out laughing aloud and went back to His own abode.[1]

When Sri Ramakrishna was bed-ridden with the terminal illness of cancer at Cossipore garden house, one of his disciples—Swami Turiyananda—who was an ardent follower of Vedantic disciplines, remarked: 'But I don't see any disease in you; you are that blissful *ātman*. The suffering belongs to the body only.' At this remark Sri Ramakrishna broke out in a hearty laughter even amid that acute pain, saying, 'Lo! This fellow has caught me red-handed!'

During his Cossipore days, Sri Ramakrishna became so ill that he could change his side in the bed only with the help of others. His body grew emaciated. One morning, the young disciples were on a playing spree and decided to drink date juice from the garden. Holy Mother Sarada Devi, who was busy with her daily chores on the ground floor, suddenly had a glimpse of a fugitive figure like that of Sri Ramakrishna coming downstairs and hurrying towards the garden where the boys were picnicking. Unable to believe her eyes, she stood at the door of her room gazing at his disappearing footsteps, when suddenly he came back and went upstairs all by himself.

The Holy Mother went to his bedroom on the upper floor to find out what was happening. There, finding him lying in bed, she asked the reason for such strange behaviour. Sri Ramakrishna replied that he went to drive away a cobra that lived at the root of the date palm, apprehending it might harm the innocent boys.

In the *Bhagavad Gītā,* Śrī Kṛṣṇa himself announced his hiding nature. He said, 'I do not reveal myself to all, but hide myself with the veil of Māyā; the deluded world doesn't come to know Me, the unborn, the immutable.'[2]

The truth is that we all have come in disguise. But we are not aware of the fact clearly, whereas the avatāras or God-men know and remember it every moment of their life. While Rāma was searching for Sītā in the jungles, Lord Śiva and Pārvatī were watching the whole event from above. Amazed at Rāma's behaviour like a mortal, Pārvatī asked Śiva why Rāma had forgotten his real nature. Lord Śiva replied, 'Why don't you go and test him by assuming the form of Sītā?' So, in the jungle Rāma suddenly discovered his lost wealth, Sītā, standing before him. And what was his reaction to that? Rāma fell prostrate before Divine Mother, asking, 'Why Mother, do I see you alone in this desolate forest without the great Lord?'

The recorded biographies of avatāras bear testimony to the fact that they assume the role of expert actors according to the needs of the age. These roles are unique. Even in *Vivekacūḍāmaṇi*, a primer of Vedantic text, Śankarācārya mentions the actor's role, drawing analogy from life. The word for an actor is *śailūṣa* in Sanskrit. This word finds expression twice in the above text—in verses 292 and 555. There it is mentioned that as an actor discards his assumed disguise after the play, so also does the soul relinquish his attributes after knowing his true nature as the Existence-

Knowledge-Bliss absolute.

It is said that God, out of His infinite compassion for His devotees, takes human form to bless the earth. If God loves His devotees so much, then why does He hide Himself in this way, deluding the devotees?

Reasons for disguise

Every action of an avatāra is well-planned. There are a few plausible reasons for such hide-and-seek games. Firstly, all are not spiritually evolved enough to recognize an avatāra. A very few aspirants, after births of mortal existence, feel the desire to see the Lord to the exclusion of all worldly attachments. In the words of Śrī Kṛṣṇa, 'Out of thousands of people only a few aspire for perfection and of those rare few, a very small percentage come to know of me in reality.'[3]

Even if they are spiritually evolved, it is not given to all to recognize God as the all-pervading essence of everything.

Secondly, as people of the world are highly selfish, their minds are preoccupied with worldly desires. The moment an avatāra reveals himself they start pestering him only for favours and embellishments. But a God-man doesn't incarnate to pander to materialism and human weaknesses, but to awaken and kindle humankind's innate spirituality.

Thirdly, the incarnations of God, endowed with infinite power, prefer to go by the laws of nature created for the good of living entities. An avatāra always insists on individual efforts of aspirants to earn spiritual treasures, which is the most precious of all covetable objects in the world. Moreover, an avatāra aims to turn the face of aspirants towards truth, giving him only a glimpse of it, leaving him to reach realization with his own efforts.

Someone once asked Swami Brahmananda, a disciple of Sri Ramakrishna: 'Sri Ramakrishna has already endowed you with the immense spiritual treasure; then why do you still observe so much austerity and discipline?' 'To retain that which I have received,' pat came the reply.

Fourthly, it is important to separate the wheat from the chaff. People flock around a divine soul with innumerable desires, but when a critical situation occurs, they disappear into thin air.

An outstanding example of this is Sri Ramakrishna. People took him to be God, and in their judgement, God, even though in human form, should be of a pure nature, that is, free from any ailment. Unfortunately for them, Sri Ramakrishna fell prey to disease on several occasions. As an upshot of it, the number of devotees dwindled. Only those who belonged to his 'inner circle' endured forever.

This, however, was a boon in disguise. Sri Ramakrishna used this opportunity to mould the characters of the handful of would-be world movers. The days at Cossipore were halcyon days for the disciples. They were held with the firm conviction that God takes up human form and the subsequent sinister effects like disease occur only with a view to teaching humanity the secret of serving God in man.

Finally, God likes to move about playfully among his own creatures to inspect his own kingdom. Sri Ramakrishna said in this respect, 'Just as the king at times goes round his kingdom incognito and sees for himself the condition of his subjects, so also does God move about in various disguises to remain unidentified from the common gaze.' Some people take him for a fool, some say he is a plebeian, some mistake him for a brahmin, yet others think he is an emperor; and they accord either great honour or incisive insult to such noble souls. Yet he pays no heed to such attitudes and continues with his own mission on earth. God himself has proclaimed in the *Bhagavad Gītā*: 'This miraculous nature of mine is difficult to overcome. Those who take refuge in me can, however, cross its bounds.'[4]

Spilling the beans

It is a strange phenomenon that at rare moments the incarnation comes out of his sheath to proclaim his real nature to a chosen few. This real nature comes out spontaneously, defying all his desperate efforts to hide it. The case of an incarnation is just the reverse of ordinary mortals, who have to learn to hide their external forms in to have a glimpse of the divinity within. But an incarnation has to hide his real nature from common gaze with great effort.

It happened to Jesus Christ. When the Jews asked him, 'If thou be the Christ, tell us plainly.' To that Jesus answered, 'I told you and ye believed not; the works that I do in my Father's name, they bear witness of me. But ye believe not, because ye are not of my sheep…I and my Father are one.'[5] At this bold statement, it is said in the next verse that 'the Jews took up stones again to stone him.'

Śrī Kṛṣṇa proclaimed his divine glory every now and then in his gospel on the battlefield. He even went to the extent of saying that in the warp and weft of this creation, He exists in every possible form. He revealed his universal form to Arjuna, but had to retract it immediately as it frightened and confused Arjuna. Even as a child he revealed to his foster mother Yaśoda, this universal vision inside his mouth.

But Śrī Kṛṣṇa's embodiment was so much replete with

such manifestations of divine glory that often they appear normal to the readership. Not so was the case with Sri Ramakrishna. He retracted all the divine splendour and superhuman powers that manifested in him as by-products of his yogic disciplines. With great will power, Sri Ramakrishna forced his external manifestation to retreat inside. As a result, people in general failed to gauge the depth of his divinity.

Towards the end of his life, Sri Ramakrishna had foretold that before the final departure he would 'spill the beans,' that is to say, he would reveal who he was. Before that, during his stay at Dakṣineśwar he often asked his disciples a few questions: who Sri Ramakrishna was in the eyes of the person concerned; and what his relationship to Sri Ramakrishna was.

These questions he would ask only to those whom he felt belonged to his inner circle of devotees. From the answers Sri Ramakrishna received from the disciples, he could understand the inherent spiritual tendencies in them. It was not a master-disciple relationship, but an equation between a soul and a super soul. Only those who could establish such a relationship with him were entitled to get a glimpse of his divine glory in and through that human form.

Sri Ramakrishna had also given prior indication that when he would start spending nights at Calcutta, then he would eat from others' plates, and when people in general would start whispering about his divine nature, he would not live long thereafter. It exactly happened like that.

On 1 January 1886, Sri Ramakrishna unlocked the secret of his own true nature to the devotees. To some with a single touch, to others by a mere glance, he opened the lock-gate of his spiritual treasure to one and all. With a single sentence, 'Let your consciousness be awakened,' he made the devotees realize who he was and how they were related to him.

Why did he depart soon after the secret of his divinity was made public? Because with that revelation the denouement that appeared so lively would lose its charm as people would realize that the show had ended. When a person in disguise is recognized, he leaves the place. Otherwise, the hoi polloi, always bent upon getting things done for them, will rush to him for 'divine favour'—the meaning of which they do not know.

Test of genuineness

Śrīmad Bhāgavatam made a controversial comment by saying that there are innumerable avatāras (1:3:26). The purpose behind this statement was that wherever a divine manifestation is seen, God is said to be scintillating through that spark. The Advaita Vedanta does not admit the concept of avatārahood. However, the later scriptures like the *Bhagavad Gītā* and the Purānas recognized avatārahood. Unfortunately for us in the present era, each and every saint proclaims himself as an avatāra and saviour of people. Any greenhorn who succeeds in gathering a crowd of religious people around him is claimed by his disciples as an avatāra.

Consequently, this word has lost its sanctity in recent times. Our purpose is not to define an avatāra here, which is really a difficult task. But there are certain tests to ascertain the genuineness of a person posing as an avatāra.

As Arjuna has pointed out in the tenth chapter, verse 15 of the *Bhagavad Gītā* that a God-man alone knows himself best and in the right spirit—not others. Again, in the second chapter he wanted to know the signs or the hallmarks for a real knower of God—how he behaves, talks, moves about.[6]

The reply given by Śrī Kṛṣṇa stands to define such a person. But an avatāra is not just a knower of God. He is something much more than that. Sri Ramakrishna has given us the yardstick to measure the authenticity of such a soul.

The first sign is purity. One who meditates regularly on the lotus feet of God cannot but become pure himself. The Sanskrit word for foot is *pada,* which also means 'status' or 'post.' Meditating on the 'feet' means making an effort to attain that post. One who becomes merged in God becomes as pure as Him and not even a speck of impurity should linger in him.

The next sign is conviction. One who dwells in God must be one hundred per cent convinced in his faith. Even if the whole world stands against him weapons in hand at point-blank range, still his conviction of truth will remain unabated like a Socrates who, standing at the trial, said to the Athenians, 'Men of Athens, I will obey God rather than you,' and drank hemlock in preference to submitting to the opinion of the majority. Swami Vivekananda expressed this idea of conviction poetically in his conciliatory poem sent to Miss Mary Hale on 15 February 1894:

All nature wears one angry frown
To crush you out—still know, my soul,
You are Divine. March on and on,
Nor right nor left but to the goal.[7]

Once a monk claimed to Swami Śivananda that he had attained supreme realization. Swami Śivananda asked, 'Are you convinced of it?' 'Yes,' came the reply. 'Is there absolutely no doubt?' the swami asked a second time. 'Er…, I think so,' faltered the monk. 'Then you haven't realized,' declared the swami.

The third test is consistency. What a realized soul says or preaches must be in consonance with what he practices. If a saint speaks the sweetest words and the loftiest truths in broad daylight, while committing all horribly nefarious acts in the darkness of night and behind the common gaze; if his personality remains compartmentalized, he is not what he claims to be. Sri Ramakrishna would insist on testing a saint through and through before accepting him. Just as people test a silver coin of higher denomination before giving it a legal tender, a saint has to pass through such fiery ordeals.

Once one of his boy-disciples (later Swami Yogananda) suspected Sri Ramakrishna to be a split personality; but on verification, he found him to pass the acid test smilingly. But Sri Ramakrishna encouraged him saying, 'You must test the genuineness of a monk before accepting him whole-heartedly.'

Lastly, the sign of a great soul is spontaneity. His divine nature bobs up from within his being in a spontaneous manner. He is not bound to social norms and obligations, though he never refutes them. His nature is like a little boy—sometimes helplessly depending on his mother; at others moving about in a carefree manner. This spontaneity born of the integration of the self cannot be presented as a show to others. Nor can it be taught to others.

Paradoxical though it may seem, all of us are endowed with spontaneity since childhood. But with the majority this essential trait gets strangulated in our childhood trainings and by the force and influence of society.

Swami Vivekananda deplored this negative training that stunts the normal growth of the individual with his characteristic trenchant remark: 'I hate this world, this dream, this horrible nightmare, with its churches and chicaneries, its books and blackguardisms, its fair faces and false hearts, its howling righteousness on the surface and utter hollowness beneath, and, above all, its sanctified shopkeeping.'[8]

Conclusion

From the discussion on the traits of avatāras, several points have come up to the surface. First, avatāras are superhuman beings with a capacity to hide themselves. Second, their memory of divinity is spontaneous. Third, through such genius they can impart immense knowledge and training to people in the current and coming generations. Fourth, they hide their real form for the good of humanity only. Fifth, they evince spontaneity in their nature. Sixth, their acts and deeds are consistent. Seventh, they can transfer their purity to others at will. Eighth, their conviction of truth is unfaltering.

The avatāras are the human manifestations of God. Just as God can assume any form, the avatāras can take up any role they choose in keeping with the need of the time. Any role is possible for them. This is precisely the reason why Śrī Kṛṣṇa appears to be an enigmatic character to many. He assumed so many mutually contradicting roles that the common man gets confused.

The following conversations between the great playwright of Bengal, Girish Chandra Ghosh and the homœopath Dr Mahendranath Sarkar that is quoted from the *Gospel of Sri Ramakrishna* will throw more light on avatāras.

Doctor: How can I accept Rāma as an Incarnation of God? Take the example of his killing Vāli, the monkey chieftain. He hid himself behind a tree, like a thief, and murdered Vāli. This is how a man acts and not God.

Girish: But, sir, such an action is possible only for God.

Doctor: Then take the example of his sending Sītā into exile.

Girish: This too, sir, is possible only for God, not for man.[9]

Indeed, the more we try to understand an avatāra, to gauge the depth of his being, the more we get confused. Our dull intellect fails miserably to grasp the truth of an incarnation. At long last, we give up our desperate search through intellect as our heart starts singing pæans in the following tenor:

> 'O Lord, I don't know you in truth, nor do I know your real nature;
> I only bow down again and again and implore you to shower grace on me.'
> [*jānāmi tattvaṁ na hi deśikendra, kiṁ te svarūpaṁ kimu bhāvajātam /*
> *He rāmakṛṣṇa tvayi bhaktihīne, kṛpākaṭākṣaṁ kuru deva nityam //*—A hymn by Swami Abhedananda.]

End Notes

1. *The Gospel of Sri Ramakrishna*, Red Letter edition, 7 February 2000, pp 415-6
2. *B G* 7:25
3. Ibid 7:3
4. Ibid 7:14
5. *The Bible,* NT , St. John, 10:24-30
6. *B G* 2:54
7. *Complete Works,* Volume 8:163
8. *Complete Works,* Vol.5, p.73]
9. *The Gospel of Sri Ramakrishna,* Red-letter edition, 7 February 2000, p 864, conversation of 22-10-1885

Leave God to Serve God:
A Strange Concept

ON THE face of it, the title seems to be a paradox. How can one leave God aside and serve Him also? We will prove that the sentence is not a paradox but a statement of deep significance. It is a sublime idea discovered and implemented by the sages of yore.

In writing the primers on Vedanta the authors presented concepts to establish the true meaning of the *Mahāvākyas*. These concepts are called *jahallakṣaṇā* and *ajahallakṣaṇā*. They are used to capture the inherent meaning in a statement that seems meaningless or contradictory. For example, when one says, 'Go hang yourself,' he does not mean it literally; he is only expressing disapproval or dislike of something. In another example, we hear people say, 'He lives at the confluence of the river.' This is construed as 'he lives in a place near the confluence.' The first sentence is called *jahallakṣaṇā* and the second is *ajahallakṣaṇā*. While studying the scriptures, we should always look for deeper, inner meanings, rather than what appears at the surface.

Keeping this principle in mind, we should seek the inner meaning of the statement 'leave God to serve God.' What this really means is that we must train ourselves to transcend the conventional idea of worshipping God in the temple alone and should look deeper, visualizing God in all beings—not only in humankind but in all living entities.

As we evolve, we will give up the limited idea of an all-pervasive God and rediscover Him as a scintillating Presence in all living beings, more so in the suffering, fellow creatures, in the distressed.

Significantly, but strangely enough, this idea is one of the seminal concepts in our hoary scriptures. In explaining the nature of a devotee, Sri Kṛṣṇa said in chapter 12, verse 4 of the *Bhagavad Gītā* that a devotee is self-controlled, even-minded in outlook, and engaged forever in the thought of others' welfare. In the *Bhāgavatam*, the Lord said: 'I live in all beings as their inner Self'; yet people make a show of worshipping Me in still images to the neglect of that moving representation of Mine.' He said more poignantly, 'He who worships Me in images out of delusion, leaving aside that great worship in all living beings, only pours oblation on embers.'[1]

All this clearly points out the futile result of limiting God in images alone. We can overcome this futility by giving priority to the age-old Vedantic concept of all-pervasiveness of God.

Two types of meditation

Once Sri Ramakrishna made a revealing statement at Dakshineswar. He said, 'One can meditate even with eyes open. One can meditate even while talking.'[2] Similarly, on another occasion he said, closing his eyes, 'Does God exist only when the eyes are closed, and ceases to exist when the eyes are opened? The *Līlā* belongs to Him to whom the *Nitya* belongs, and the Nitya belongs to Him to whom the Līlā belongs.'[3]

These statements open new vistas in the world of religion. Sri Ramakrishna gave a more comprehensive definition than the popular notion of meditation. There are two types of meditation: one as a technique, two as a normal state of consciousness. The technique is a copy-book type, prescribing various steps from withdrawal to the final attainment—from the negative to the positive. It is practised at set times of the day and night. The intensity depends mostly on body and mind factor, state of the external nature (daybreak and twilight are the most auspicious and conducive moments for meditation when the external and internal natures work in harmony), and so on. Our scriptures prescribe methods for such meditations. But the practice may result in a struggle for attainment.

Meditation as a state of consciousness is an advancement of the copy-book type style. Once the aspirant steps into it, the revelation dawns upon him that everything from static to dynamic is saturated with that One existence in essence. It is not that the aspirant does not see the many—the manifestation of the phenomenal world. But in and through that he feels the eternal Unity of existence. The Upaniṣads are replete with such statements.[4]

Sri Ramakrishna's statements vividly convey the concept of the immanence of God. Seeing God with closed eyes implies that the devotee is aspiring to comprehend the transcendent one who is beyond all sense-perceptions.

Closed eyes symbolically represent withdrawal of all the sense-organs from the outside world. But after revelation, the same transcendent existence is seen to express itself in all manifested forms like, in Sri Ramakrishna's words, 'the material of both the terrace and the staircase leading to it.'

Strewn large in the *Gospel of Sri Ramakrishna,* these statements epitomize the philosophy behind his life and his teachings. If the One and the many are the obverse and reverse of the same reality, then all our secular works can become the means to link us with the divine. Since work is an indispensable part of our life in modern times, this theory can be successfully applied to our day-to-day life. In short, we have to divinize our everyday work.

Capacity of the mind

Meditation gives a higher direction, transcending all our cravings and urges. However, any secular work makes the mind outgoing. The question arises: how are we to keep our mind fixed in God while doing secular work? Of all the works we do, most are just mechanical and repetitive, which after some time become automatic, and do not need much concentration. With such works it is not at all difficult to keep another part of the mind fixed in divine thought.

The mind has immense capacity. It can sub-divide itself into many compartments according to its different engagements. Swami Vivekananda had this capacity in him even when he was a school-going kid. With one part of the mind he would listen to the teacher's lecture, while with another part he could tell stories to his chums. Sri Ramakrishna's conversation with a devotee throws light on the issue.

Devotee: It is extremely difficult to proceed towards God while leading the life of a householder.

Sri Ramakrishna: Why so? What about the yoga of practice? At Kamarpukur I have seen the women of the carpenter families selling flattened rice. Let me tell you how alert they are while doing their business. The pestle of the husking machine that flattens the paddy constantly falls into the hole of the mortar. The woman turns the paddy in the hole with one hand and with the other holds her baby on her lap as she nurses it. In the meantime customers arrive. The machine goes on pounding the paddy, and she carries on the bargains with the customers. She says to them, 'Pay the few pennies you owe me before you take anything more.' You see, she has all these things to do at the same time—nurse the baby, turn the paddy as the pestle pounds it, take the flattened rice out of the hole, and talk to the buyers. This is called the yoga of practice.[5]

Transmutation of work

Of course, keeping the mind fixed on God amid all engagements is a lot more difficult than we can imagine, especially when the engagement is of an intellectual type or involves more concentration and alertness than usual. But through sustained practice the awareness can be made to reach out to God.

If every piece of work can be performed with the thought that it belongs to the most beloved, every moment of our life can be transformed into bliss, not because of satisfaction in work, but on account of union with Him. However, there is really no compartmental division between work and the divine. Indeed, the work itself gets merged into the divine.

Consequently, God becomes a 24X7 'business,' rather than a being to be remembered at some fixed hours of the day, at certain times, like meditation. This is a kind of transmutation of work.

But one question may arise about dealings with evil-minded people. While it is true that God is present in everyone, it doesn't mean that a crooked fellow should be dealt with softness. This is in no way unspiritual. In fact, spirituality is too comprehensive a term to preclude anything. The common run of people nurtures peculiar ideas in the name of spirituality. They feel—and sometimes even quote from scriptures at random to bolster their statements—that a spiritual person should possess unmitigated forgiveness, tolerance, temperance and so on. But that is only one side of the picture. Examples are not lacking where highly elevated souls, even God-men fought evil 'antibodies' that tend to disintegrate society.

Sri Kṛṣṇa, who is eulogized in the *Bhāgavatam* as 'a complete representation of God in human body,' (1:3:28) displayed many such exploits. Even Rāma was no exception. But their divinity never diminished because of such activity.

The long and short of it is that even our secular activities can be divinized by changing our attitude to the work at hand, including showing evil people their place, attitude towards ourselves, and the way we look at the world.

It is then a truism to say, at an advanced stage of spiritual practice the secular merges into the sublime. Then the temple, the farm, the factory, or the laboratory—all become equally places of communion with the divine. Even the aspirant himself cannot tell when and how this strange transformation took place. The practice of mindfulness in Zen Buddhism, the 'tea ceremony' in Japan, Vipassana meditation, and all such similar practices point to the awareness of being one's own self. The real process of awareness takes place imperceptibly.

Sri Ramakrishna was a non-dualist par excellence. He was one of those extremely rare souls who came back from the topmost level of realization only to teach others to feel the immanence of God. From the Vedantic idea of immanence and transcendence of the same reality, Sri Ramakrishna made a powerful philosophy of life which may be called 'communing with the Transcendent in the form of the Immanent.'

Though it was not invented by him first, he placed this age-old idea of the Vedic harmony of life before the modern generation to fit well into its work culture. This idea was not alien even to the earlier mystics of Christianity. Jan Van Ruysbroeck, a Christian mystic of the thirteenth century, expressed this with his characteristic transparency:

> 'If you are ravished in ecstasy as highly as St. Peter or St. Paul or as anybody you like, and if you hear that a sick man is in need of hot soup, I counsel you to wake from your ecstasy and warm the soup for him. Leave God to serve God: find Him and serve Him in His members; you will lose nothing by the change....'[6]

'Don't be selfish, my child'

One day Sri Ramakrishna reproached his beloved disciple Narendranath who badgered him for an unbroken state of absorption in God. That state is ordinarily known as the highest thing to be aspired for. But Sri Ramakrishna told his disciple that there are higher stages yet. 'Shame on you!' he cried. 'I thought you were to be the great banyan tree giving shelter to thousands of tired souls. Instead, you are selfishly seeking your own well-being. Let these little things alone, my child. How can you be satisfied with so one-sided an ideal? You must be all-sided. Enjoy the Lord in all ways!'[7]

It is true that the state known as Absolute Oneness is extremely difficult and rare to attain. But having done so, the aspirant finds that the whole world of phenomena is saturated in that Oneness. The same existence is scintillating through all the manifested beings.

This is, however, the case with those who have achieved the goal. What about the vast majority who are on their way to it? For them the means has to merge in the goal. Śankarācārya, in commenting on the traits of a liberated soul in the second chapter, verse 54 of the *Bhagavad Gita,* said: 'In all spiritual contexts, the traits of an illumined person act as the means for the aspirant.' In other words, what one aspires to be a desired goal becomes the means for him. Sri Ramakrishna demonstrated this idea throughout his life.

Once Sri Ramakrishna was on a pilgrimage with a huge entourage, accompanied by Mathurānāth, the son-in-law of Rani Rasmani and heir to the huge property left by her. On their way the party halted at Deoghar to visit the Vaidyanath Dham. There Sri Ramakrishna happened upon the appalling sight of the famished, ill-nourished, poor villagers begging him piteously for a morsel of food. His sensitive heart was melted, and with tears he implored the rich Mathurānāth to feed the people.

When he demurred, pointing to the huge expenditure ahead, Sri Ramakrishna became uncompromising in his resolve and refused to move from there. 'What is the point in worshipping the stone image,' he wailed, 'neglecting the living gods moving around?' In other words, he chose to 'leave God to serve God.' He did it not to give expression to any false emotion as is generally aroused in ordinary souls; he did it from the depth of his realization of the all-pervasiveness of God.

Gaurī-Mā, a spiritually evolved, ascetic lady-devotee of Sri Ramakrishna, used to come to Dakshineswar. Finding her daring spirit of renunciation, one day Sri Ramakrishna cryptically initiated her into the service of God in the suffering womenfolk of India. He said to her playfully, 'I am pouring water, Gaurdāsi, you knead the clay.' At first, she failed to make out the implication and said, 'Why, there's no mud here; it's all gravel!' To this Sri Ramakrishna laughed out and said, 'Oh no, you couldn't catch my hint. What I meant is that the womenfolk of our country are suffering pitiably; do something to raise them.' This shows that Sri Ramakrishna used to wean his disciples, who were highly advanced in their spiritual journey, from the limited idea of worshipping God within the heart to serving God outside in so many forms.

Enjoying through renunciation

The first mantra of the *Īśāvāsyopaniṣad* beautifully expresses the concept of enjoying through renunciation. After instructing the aspirant to 'envelop everything sentient and insentient with God', the Upaniṣad reiterates, 'Enjoy through that renunciation.' This appears to be a highly paradoxical statement to a common man, for, the question immediately crops up, 'How can one enjoy and renounce simultaneously?' Śankarācārya clarified this riddle in his commentary. He said, 'It means to enjoy through detachment and not through abandonment; for, the abandonment or death of a near and dear one does not amount to nourish one's own self.'

The self, the *ātman*, has to be nourished and protected at the cost of all other worldly enjoyments. If you want to get a higher or more precious thing, you must be ready to sacrifice the lower and cheap objects of enjoyment. When the soul is assured of a more sublime enjoyment, it will naturally throw away mundane pleasures.

Meditation often gives rise to a false vanity. It so happens only when meditation is practised as a technique for relaxation and with the idea of exclusiveness. In striking contrast, realization is a unique experience of comprehensiveness. There is nothing wherein God is not. 'Whose presence makes even this inert world bubble with life like the enlivening of a rope into a snake in illusion,' goes a Sanskrit psalm. *[Parabrahma-Prātaḥsmaraṇa-stotram—Yasminnidaṁ jagadaśeṣam aśeṣamūrtau, rajvāṁ bhujaṅgama iva pratibhāsitaṁ vai]*

Idea of universal liberation

Swami Vivekananda was a champion of this concept of 'leaving God to serve God' initiated by his Master. In a large number of letters written to his brother disciples from abroad he said, 'If you want any good to come, just throw your ceremonials overboard and worship the Living God, the Man-God—every being that wears a human form—God in his universal as well as individual aspect. The universal aspect of God means this world, and worshipping it means serving it—this indeed is work, not indulging in ceremonials.'[8]

In May 1898, the dangerous epidemic of plague wreaked

havoc on Calcutta. People were fleeing for their life. Vivekananda inspected the whole situation and ordered for relief operations. The monks and the laity joined shoulders to dive in. But where were the funds to come from? Without a moment's hesitation, he said, 'Why, we shall sell the newly-bought Math grounds, if necessary! We are sannyasins; we must be ready to sleep under the trees and live on daily Bhiksha [alms] as we did before. What! Should we care for Math and possessions when by disposing of them we could relieve thousands suffering before our eyes!'[9]

This shows how passionate he was to serve the afflicted, the needy, even by abandoning the only source of comfort and shelter for so many monks. Toward the end of his life, Vivekananda told one of his disciples:

> What is the good of that spiritual practice or realization which does not benefit others, does not conduce to the well-being of people sunk in ignorance and delusion, does not help in rescuing them from the clutches of lust and wealth? Do you think, so long as one Jiva endures in bondage, you will have any liberation? So long as he is not liberated—it may take several lifetimes—you will have to be born to help him, to make him realize Brahman. Every Jiva is part of yourself—which is the rationale of all work for others. As you desire the whole-hearted good of your wife and children, knowing them to be your own, so when a like amount of love and attraction for every Jiva will awaken in you, then I shall know that Brahman is awakening in you, not a moment before. When this feeling of the all-round good of all without respect for caste or colour will awaken in your heart, then I shall know you are advancing towards the ideal.[10]

The composite motto which is the basis of all the philosophy behind the Ramakrishna movement, namely, *ātmano mokṣārtham jagad hitāya ca*, was formulated by Vivekananda keeping in mind this idea of participation in the diverse manifestation of the divine. It is only an extension of the service of God in man as exemplified by Sri Ramakrishna. Only those who have struck a balance between their meditative life and the spirit of doing good to others are eligible for this motto. Those who are either too eccentric or too extroverted cannot succeed in this endeavour under any circumstance. Just as the meaning of the phrase mentioned in the context of *Īśāvāsyopaniṣad* does not imply any negative, pessimistic type of renunciation, so also this motto does not point to any philanthropic drive at the cost of one's personal life.

Śankarācārya and work

Sri Śankarācārya is commonly assumed to have cried down the importance of work and to have given supremacy to *jñāna* over everything else. This is a wrong notion based on garbled conceptions. Śankara is quoted to have said that mere mechanical repetition of the elaborate rituals by rote cannot lead to liberation. Hence he never attempted a mutual harmony between knowledge and action (in the ritual sense) and relegated work to one corner. But a careful study of his life shows that he himself was a worker par excellence. In the short span of thirty-two years of his temporal existence what a stupendous volume of work he has done! Even he gave a sublime turn to the ritual worship by introducing the worship of five deities (*pañca-devatā*)—Gaṇeśa, Śiva, Sūrya, Nārāyaṇa, and Śakti, in addition to the worship of the

Guru—as a preliminary to the worship of any deity. Only when it came to the question of liberation direct through the performance of work, he stood adamant and declared that it was knowledge alone that led to liberation. What he meant was that work done as a means to knowledge will end up in knowledge and will disappear itself, just as clouds disappear after showering rain. The task he left as a legacy for posterity was to go beyond work through the right attitude toward work. His disciple Suresvarācārya termed it as *Naiṣkarmya-siddhi*.

Service to others should be rendered in such a spirit as will not cause one exhaustion, fatigue, or depression, nor even any sense of void within. Only those who are full within can render effective service to others.

Sri Ramakrishna and the do-gooder

Sri Ramakrishna's proposition of doing good to the afflicted and suffering people does not tally with the Buddhist view of serving others. Buddha made God otiose (serving no practical purpose) in the service to others, whereas Sri Ramakrishna made God the *raison d'être* of life, of work, and of everything. According to him, the principle of 'leave God to serve God' can be applied only to those who have drunk neck-deep of the nectar of God's bliss. But social service is easier said than done. Except for a man of Buddha's stature, it is hard to find a person who can do work for work's sake alone. Somewhere there must be lurking some ulterior motive.

And this degrades work to secular nature which Śankarācārya looked down upon as the source of bondage. Sri Ramakrishna heartily hailed those who were heard to render some kind of service to the needy people. But wherever his penetrating eyes espied the motives for name, fame, or the like, he would sternly dissuade the person from such endeavour, saying, 'First you get the vision of God, which is the prime necessity of the day, and then go on making charity as much as you can.' To another devotee he said, 'Suppose God appears before you, ready to bless you; would you ask him for a few hospitals or charitable organizations?' These words do not counter in the least his premises of 'leave God to serve God'. They rather mean to leave aside an exclusive realization to find another comprehensive existence of the Lord.

We will conclude with a quotation of Sri Ramakrishna as narrated by the renowned French litterateur, M Romain Rolland, in his biographical sketch *The Life of Swami Vivekananda and the Universal Gospel*:

> 'Come down! Come down!' Ramakrishna said in order to bring himself back from ecstasy, and he reproached himself and refused to have the happiness attained in union with God so that he might render service to others: 'O Mother, let me not attain these delights, let me remain in my normal state, so that I can be of more use to the world!'

And this very idea found expression in these passionate words of Swami Vivekananda in one of his letters to Mary Hale written from Almora:

> '...may I be born again and again and suffer thousands of miseries so that I may worship the only God that exists, the only God I believe in, the sum total of all souls—and above all, my God the wicked, my God the miserable, my God the poor of all races, of all species, is the special object of my worship.'[11]

End Notes

1 *Bhāgavatam*,3:29:21,22

2. M, *The Gospel of Sri Ramakrishna,* Red Letter edn, 2000, p.605

3. Op. cit. p.778

4. Cf. *Mund. Up*. 2:2:11

5. Op. cit. p.367

6. Quoted by Romain Rolland in *The Life of Swami Vivekananda & the Universal Gospel,* Advaita Ashrama, Calcutta, p.219 f.n.

7. R. Rolland, *The Life of Ramakrishna,* Advaita Ashrama, Calcutta, 8th edition, Oct.70, p.73

8. *Complete Works* 6:264

9. Eastern & Western Disciples, *Life of Swami Vivekananda,* Vol.2, p.328

10. *Complete Works,* Volume 7:pg 235-6

11. *Complete Works* Volume 5: pg 137

PART 2

SWAMI VIVEKANANDA THE TORCHBEARER

Swami Vivekananda:

Wisdom Applied to Human Welfare

SWAMI VIVEKANANDA was born at a time when innumerable scriptural geniuses lived not only in Bengal but all over India. Scholars used to earn their livelihood by quoting Sanskrit verses from scriptures or even composed them extempore in the courts of kings. Children grew up in environments of Sanskrit and literary culture. Even the common man had good knowledge in those subjects. Bards and poets were rewarded by the kings for their extraordinary powers of knowledge and skill in composing Sanskrit verses verbally.

More than the rich and royal, it was Sri Ramakrishna who fathomed the depth of Swami Vivekananda's knowledge and personality. Sri Ramakrishna had a typical set of values in judging a person's worth. While others would weigh a man's talent on the basis of fame that he had achieved, Sri Ramakrishna went deeper. In his assessment of Vivekananda's personality, he discovered that though he possessed those rare qualities of head and heart, he was not vain at all. He realized that Vivekananda was showered with the special grace of God.

Sri Krishna declares in the *Bhagavatam*: 'When the soul, in spite of getting a human life enriched by high birth, good stock of past karma, great youthful valour, graceful appearance, vast knowledge, and a plethora of qualities of head and heart, does not get inflated with pride, know for certain that it is my favour working there. One to whom I am the supreme goal never gets his head turned by pride born of high birth etc.'[1]

Sri Ramakrishna's analysis about Vivekananda was based on such scriptural values plus his own spiritual vision about his foremost disciple. From this it can be concluded that Swami Vivekananda's greatness in all respects was scripturally sanctioned.

Wisdom applied as soother

If one looks for outstanding feats in Swami Vivekananda's life, one gets filled with wonder at his singular effort in applying all his knowledge for the good of humankind. It would seem that the only aim of his life was to prepare a balm for soothing the centuries-old sores lingering in the body of the nation. This selfless act won him the highest rank among great sages and scholars. Indeed, it is perceived that he came as a representative of the ancient sages who had dedicated their lives in working out Mother India's problems.

He had so much potentiality in him in various fields that even a single of those could make him world famous, and yet he was not bedazzled by the brilliance of so many talents and qualities. That he did not so much as care for any praise accorded to him was a sign that his aim in life was much higher than fame and recognition. When Pandit Shankarlal of Khetri praised him for his qualities of head and heart, he expressed modesty by quoting from the *Bible*, 'None is good, save One, that is, God.'[2] and also, 'the servant is *not* worthy of the hire.'[3]

But when he experienced poverty in the prime of youth, he wondered about a God who metes out so much misery to people. What is the use of that religion which fails to wipe out the tears of the afflicted or cannot bring food to the hungry, he asked.

He was not really rebellious or doubtful about religion, but would stop only after finding the right solution. And he did it by applying all his innate resources. His desperate bid to find out, even as he was a little boy, how one's caste is lost by smoking from different pipes meant for people of different castes betrayed his inborn talent of search for truth defying all local customs. Had he been really rebellious against morbid social customs, he could have secretly switched the hookahs, breaking their proper order. Instead, he only tested the truth of the age-old custom.

It was this attitude that haunted him in his youth to know if there was a God or if He could be seen. Unlike others his quest for God was not a matter of mere childish curiosity, but a life-and-death question with which he knocked at the door of Sri Ramakrishna, and the secret of spiritual life was thrown open to him. Like Buddha, Swami Vivekananda also realized that God was not to be blamed for the misery of humankind. It was the individual that was responsible for his own actions done before.

Now, if this is a fact, then doesn't it stand to reason that one also has in reserve the results of his past good deeds waiting with the blessings and power of a thousand angels? he asked himself. And lo behold! He found his answer in the commentary of Śaṅkaracharya on the *Bhagavad Gītā*. In his lecture at New York on 26 January 1896 entitled 'Cosmos: Microcosm,' Vivekananda concluded by declaring boldly: 'Say, "this misery that I am suffering is of my own doing, and that very thing proves that it will have to be undone by me alone. That which I created, I can demolish; that which is created by someone else I shall never be able to destroy. Therefore, stand up, be bold, be strong. Take the whole responsibility on your own shoulders, and know that you are the creator of your own destiny. All the strength and succour you want is within yourselves. Therefore, make your own future. Let the dead past bury its dead."'[4]

'The infinite future is before you, and you must always remember that each word, thought, and deed lays up a store for you, and that as the bad thoughts and bad works are ready to spring upon you like tigers, so also there is the inspiring hope that the good thoughts and good deeds are ready with the power of a hundred thousand angels to defend you always and forever.'[5]

The significance of Śaṅkara's commentary is that just as the wrong actions done in the past bear bad results enduring in the present, so also good actions or virtues committed in the past must also persist in the present.[6]

Vivekananda fittingly echoed Śaṅkara's words to show to suffering humanity a clear way out of one's self-imposed misery; and also how an Advaita proponent like Śaṅkara tried to infuse courage and confidence into humanity.

When one is seen to be assailed with misery, what should be the attitude of a man of spirituality toward such souls? Should he cast a derisive smile at such a person saying, 'served him fine,' or 'I pity you ignorant fool'? No. He would place himself mentally in the other's shoes and absorb his misery as much as he could. The *Bhagavad Gītā* expresses it as *ātma-upamā*, empathy.[7]

He came to know of the death of a son of Dr Balaji Rao from a friend of his. To the friend who conveyed the news he wrote on 27 April 1893, quoting from the *Bible*, 'The Lord giveth and the Lord taketh away; blessed be the name of the Lord.'[8]

And to Balaji he wrote on 23 May 1893 again, quoting the same in full, 'Naked came I out of my mother's womb, and naked shall I return thither; the Lord gave and the Lord hath taken away; blessed be the name of the Lord.' And he continued to console him, 'Blessed are they that mourn, for they shall be comforted.'[9]

'And why? Because it is during these moments of visitations when the heart is wrung by hands which never stop for the father's cries or the mother's wail, when under the load of sorrow, dejection, and despair, the world seems to be cut off from under our feet, and when the whole horizon seems to be nothing but an impenetrable sheet of misery and utter despair—that the internal eyes open, light flashes all of a sudden, the dream vanishes, and intuitively we come face to face with the grandest mystery in nature—Existence.'[10]

Then…the shackles break… and unfettered it (soul) rises and rises until it reaches the throne of the Lord, "Where the wicked cease from troubling and the weary are at rest."[11] Vivekananda's consolation reached its peak as he broke into a soliloquy, as it were: "Lord, we know that it is the Mother's hand that is striking, and the spirit is willing but the flesh is weak".'[12]

As a result of all such afflictions, the common man is prone to become agnostic and dig his own grave. Vivekananda tries to dissuade his friend from such negative thinking and brings him to surrender to God's will. Citing Western poets, he advises, 'Ours is not to question why, Ours but to do and die.'[13]

In a letter on 16 May 1896, to Prof John Henry Wright, Harvard Professor of Greek Classics, Vivekananda expressed his sympathy at the death of his teenaged daughter Elizabeth, by weaning his mind from the ephemeral world to the Supreme God. He went on quoting from the Indian scriptures one after the other to console the afflicted soul.

'He who sees in this world of manifoldness that one support of everything, in the midst of a world of unconsciousness that one eternal consciousness, in this evanescent world that one eternal and unchangeable, unto him belongs eternal peace.'[14]

There is no other way for man buffeted by existential problems than to take refuge in God. So, he quoted aptly from the *Gītā*: 'He who rests in Me and gives up all other self-assertion and struggles, I carry to him whatever he needs.[15]

He also quoted from the Vedas: 'The four Vedas, sciences, languages, philosophy, and all other learnings are only ornamental. The real learning, the true knowledge is that which enables us to reach Him who is unchangeable in His love.'[16] And yet again, 'He is the eye of our eyes, the ear of our ears, the Soul of our souls.'[17]

In the opinion of many Western admirers, Vivekananda had much deeper knowledge of the *Bible* than many devout Christians. One finds so many rare *Bible* quotations in his lectures and letters. In his letter dated 30 April 1891 to Lala Govinda Sahay, a rich merchant of Alwar, he gave spiritual instruction, defining what true religion is. 'My children, the secret of religion lies not in theories but in practice. To be good and to do good—that is the whole of religion. "Not he that crieth Lord, Lord, but he that doeth the will of the Father".'[18]

God is like the digit 1 after which one may put as many 0's as possible, and the value will go on adding up. Vivekananda made this point clear to the merchant in his quotation from the *Bible*, 'Seek ye first the kingdom of God and all good things will be added unto you.[19] Follow God and you shall have whatever you desire by way of wealth and honour.'[20]

The nobility, erudition, and feelings of Sri Haridas Viharidas Desai, Dewan of Junagarh and opium commissioner, astonished Swamiji. He became eloquent in his praise, and wrote in exuberance of joy on 22 August 1892 quoting Bhartṛhari in the *Vairāgya-Śatakam*, "The world really is enriched by men, high-souled, noble-minded, and kind, like you; the rest are 'only abortions', as some Sanskrit poet says."[21]

Even when consoling others, he used quotations from the literati. In reply to a little poem Christina sent him, Vivekananda sent the comment, "There are thoughts that lie too deep for tears." He wrote this as a hint to indicate he could catch Christina's mental agony from it. The quotation is from William Wordsworth—from what he had read as a college student.[22]

In a letter to Mrs G W Hale in October 1899, Vivekananda imprinted in her mind that the role of work is only to awaken the soul to reality. Work is neither good nor evil. He wrote, quoting from *St. Matthew* in the *New Testament*, 'The world is evil—and will ever remain so. It is its nature, and cannot be changed.'[23]

E T Sturdy, Sanskrit scholar and member of the Theosophical Society, felt drawn to Vivekananda and started collaborating with him in propagating the Vedantic principles in England with great enthusiasm. But later on, especially after his marriage, he got divorced from the work and wrongly accused Vivekananda of leading a luxurious life. He didn't hold this against Sturdy and clearly saw that marriage had indeed proved a hell for Sturdy, and felt pity on him. He wrote to Mrs Bull on 4 April 1898 with this prayer to God, 'May He cut all his bonds—and make him free soon. Aye it is good that he is feeling the bondage—and not "hugging and kissing its spokes of agony".'[24] Interestingly, the last quotation was taken from Edwin Arnold's famous book *The Light of Asia*.[25]

Depth of feeling for others

In matters of feeling towards his fellow beings, he spoke with fullness of heart, and not with mere emotion. A letter to Mary Hale dated 9 July 1897 reveals such long pent-up desire of him: '...may I be born again and again, and suffer thousands of miseries so that I may worship the only God that exists, the only God I believe in, the sum total of all souls—and above all, my God the wicked, my God the miserable, my God the poor of all races, of all species, is the special object of my worship.'[26]

This seems to be a replica of a statement of Rantideva in the *Bhagavatam*, 'I do not ask God for salvation (the supreme goal of life), nor seek to be endowed with special eightfold powers, nor even cessation of human birth. I only want to feel the pangs of the suffering embodied souls by entering straight into their hearts so that they may get rid of their sufferings.'[27] There is another statement of the devout Prahlada in the *Bhagavatam* to the same effect: 'O Lord, sages generally concern themselves with their own salvation alone. They strive for it in solitude, without any thought for the salvation of others. But I do not desire salvation for me alone by leaving all other helpless fellows to their miserable conditions. I find no other shelter than Thee for such sufferers.'[28]

This is a very distinct and typical ideal prevalent in India since days of yore. During the Buddhist era it was named as *Bodhisattva* ideal, while among some pre-Shankarite sages like Bhartṛpra-pañca this had been coined as *Sarvamukti* ideal. Way back during the Tantric period too this ideal had been held aloft by the statement that no individual aspirant can attain final liberation until all others also get at that. Vivekananda too picked up this great idea from scriptures and preached this to the other disciples of Sri Ramakrishna to disentangle them from all ideas that reek of selfishness.

Before leaving for the West for a second time, he said in his parting address to the young monks and brahmacharins: 'To go ahead of others in salvation is wrong. One must learn sooner or later that one cannot get salvation if one does not try to seek the salvation of his brothers.'[29] In this way, he reinstated the sublime ancient principle of 'serving God in man' (*śivajñāne jīvasevā*). This idea was mooted by none else than Sri Ramakrishna. Vivekananda perceived first the sublime nature of this great saying and its usefulness in maintaining peace all over the world through brotherly feeling between different races and religious factions. So he founded the Ramakrishna organization of monks and gave its members a new motto to follow: *Atmano mokṣārthaṁ jagad hitāya ca*, meaning, 'for one's own salvation that simultaneously cater to the well-being of the world.' To many this idea may seem rather new or a unique contribution of Vivekananda. But the message of Kapila given to his mother Devahuti in the *Bhagavatam*[30] stands as clear proof that Vivekananda's feelings for humankind had a very firm scriptural sanction. Even he bolstered the concept of idol, image, or symbol worship in Hinduism, stamped in ridicule as idolatry by the missionaries of the West for ages, with the irrefutable arguments of our primary scripture, the Vedanta philosophy. The two aphorisms of the Brahma Sutra, namely, *na pratīke na hi saḥ* and *brahmadṛṣṭirutkarṣāt*[31] and the subsequent arguments in the commentaries thereof by Śaṅkara are proof enough to establish the truth behind symbol worship. Vivekananda precisely followed Śaṅkara and preached it in the simple style of his master Sri Ramakrishna.

He once said to Mrs Alice Hansbrough in San Francisco, 'You know, I may have to be born again. Because I have fallen in love with man.'[32]

He was never tired of uplifting man, no matter to what depth man had fallen. Once somebody asked him why he did not speak of sin in his talks. Vivekananda strongly retorted, 'Blessed are my sins. Through sin I have learned virtue. It is my sins, as much as my virtues that have made me what I am today. And now I am the preacher of virtue. Why do you dwell on the weak side of man's nature? Don't you know that the greatest blackguard often has some virtue that is wanting in the saint? There is only one power and that power manifests both as good and as evil.'[33] Saying this, he quoted from Vyasa's commentary on Patañjali's Yoga aphorisms, adapting the words to the present context: 'God and the devil are the same river with the water flowing in opposite directions.'[34]

This is, indeed, a graphic illustration of Vivekanana's way of applying scriptural truths for the good of mankind.

His deep feelings for the poor took a vivid form in many of his lectures. One, for instance, entitled 'My Plan of Campaign', is relevant here: 'Not a morsel of food can be eaten without depriving someone of it. This is the law; this is philosophy.'[35]

Why did he call it philosophy? Because it was preached by none else than Śaṅkaracharya in his commentary on the *Bṛhadāraṇyaka Upaniṣad*.[36] This is yet another clear evidence that even in matters of feelings for the deprived people, his outbursts were not merely emotional but based on the firm foundation of either our ancestors or the prime scriptures.

Why did Vivekananda take recourse to our scriptures in every step of life? Because till then the Hindu scriptures were repudiated by the Western world in a well-schemed campaign to disprove everything good in Hinduism, and the 'ignorant' Hindus swallowed it all. By quoting from the scriptures, he only wanted to show what a mine of strength our scriptures are.

Whenever aliens thwarted spirituality and forced in materialism, our scriptures were the first to provide succour to all without reserve. Even the Smṛtis, which were supposedly replete with diabolical injunctions, were in many instances of great benevolence to humankind. He also produced clear evidence of how some rare souls even in the Western world—like Max Müller, Rhys Davids, Maurice Bloomfield, Edwin Arnold—accepted the unparalleled teachings embedded in Hindu religion and practised by the Hindus as a way of life.[37]

On the caste problem

The compassionate Swami Vivekananda explored ways to uplift the neglected and down-trodden. But he did not rely on the mere injunctions of the Smṛti scriptures, which impose so much restrictions on people, to find solutions. Instead, he took hints from the way of life in the Vedic or Upanishadic age to address the caste problem. Quoting from the *Mahabharata,* he said that 'In the beginning of the Satya Yuga there was one caste, the Brahmins, and then by difference of occupations they went on dividing themselves into different castes.'[38]

He cherished the idea that like Satya Yuga, Brahminism alone should reign in the present age. Only he went one step further to say that 'The days of exclusive privileges and exclusive claims are gone, gone forever from the soil of India.'[39] His idea was not to bring down the Brahmins to the level of the lower caste, but to train the lower caste to rise to the level of Brahmins.

No doubt he was pained by such diabolical Injunction of *Smṛtis* as, 'If the Shudra hears the Vedas, fill his ears with molten lead, and if he remembers a line, cut his tongue out.'[40] He observed that nowhere in the Vedas it is mentioned that women or the Shudras have no right to study the Vedas. The Upanishads never differentiated between gender, social status, or caste.

Vivekananda remarked: 'Ignorance, inequality, and desire are the three causes of human misery, and each follows the other in inevitable union. Why should a man think himself above any other man, or even an animal? It is the same throughout:[41] 'Thou art the man, Thou the woman, Thou art the young man, Thou the young woman.'[42]

'The Puranas no doubt say that a certain caste has the right to such and such a recension of the Vedas. But can the servant dictate to the master? Nowadays we have put the Puranas on even a higher pedestal than the Vedas! The study of the Vedas has almost disappeared from Bengal.'

However, on careful study of the *Smṛtis* of later periods he found that the Shudras were gradually allowed to pursue the Brahminical paths if found eligible. He said further, "You will find that later on, this tone is modified a little, as for instance, 'Do not disturb the Shudras, but do not teach them higher things.'[43]

The word Brahmin had deeper implication than is commonly believed. In his lecture at Dhaka on 31 March 1901, he gave the definition of a Rishi with historical documents. 'Who are these Rishis?' asked he, and proceeded with his answer, 'Vatsyayana says, "He who has attained through proper means the direct realization of Dharma, he alone can be a Rishi even if he is a Mlechchha (one who does not practise Hinduism) by birth".[44] ...Truly speaking,... no distinction should be made with one who has realized the Truth.'[45] Saying this, Vivekananda quoted from the *Shukla-Yajur-Veda* a mantra which runs as follows: 'Let us proclaim this beneficial message to all people—to the brāhmaṇas, the kṣatriyas, the vaiśyas, the śūdras, to our own people as to the alien.'[46]

He asserted that the Brahmin caste and the Brahmanya qualities are two distinct things. The hereditary concept of Brahminhood is no more in vogue in modern times, he remarked, adding that the Brahmins have lost their caste due to admixture of blood through inter-caste marriages. He contended that one can change one's caste through meritorious acts and a change in thinking.[47] To strengthen his contention, he pointed out that Vasishtha, the enlightened sage, was born of an illegitimate union; Vyasa was born to a fisherwoman; Narada, the devout sage, was born of uncertain parentage and yet attained a high level of Rishihood.[48]

Vivekananda's proposition that so-called low-caste people could be transformed into Brahminhood, finds corroboration in Śaṅkara's commentary on the *Brahma-Sutra* where he refers to Vidura and Dharma-vyādha who were Shudra and yet reached spiritual realization.[49]

However, Vivekananda did not propose the idea of mass upliftment of lower castes to the higher, as it could lead to the degradation of a race, but he advocated the idea of *samadarśitva*, same-sightedness, preached in the *Gītā*. He often quoted in his letters and lectures: 'Even in this life, they have conquered relativity whose mind is fixed in sameness.'[50]

'But alas! They think inequality is the way to attain equality, as if they could come to right by doing wrong! This is the bane of human nature, the curse upon mankind, the root of all misery—this inequality. This is the source of all bondage, physical, mental, and spiritual. Since seeing the Lord equally existent everywhere, he injures not Self by self, and so goes to the Highest Goal.[51] This one statement contains in a few words the universal way to salvation.'[52]

To bring in a new order of life leading to goodness is a slow process that necessitates inculcation of higher culture into the general body of the race, Vivekananda affirmed. He believed in conversion that comes naturally from within, not as a compulsion. His idea was to create a sense of positive values in the people. The awakening will come as a matter of course, he concluded.

Conflict between society and religion

In reconciling the contradictory injunctions of the various Smṛtis, Vivekananda recommended returning to the Vedas. He averred, 'The Smṛtis, Puranas, Tantras—all these are acceptable only in so far as they agree with the Vedas, and wherever they are contradictory, they are to be rejected as unreliable.'[53]

Vivekananda's invaluable words in his voluminous *Complete Works* can be roughly classified in two parts; one consisting of eternal values and principles based on Vedic truths, and the other the practical application of those principles in modern life, which comprise of various injunctions and forewarnings on society and the individual.

The word 'injunction' does not mean to put shackles around the feet of individuals or society, but rather a disciplined life nourished through rigorous training and knowledge in higher values. For such a life alone is fit for freedom. Religion should be able to unfold the inherent divinity in members of society, and not add more fetters to them, especially the weaker sections.

Vivekananda cautioned that social norms and religion should not get jumbled up with one another—one should not trespass the territories of the other. In his memorable letter entitled 'What We Believe In' dated 3 March 1894 addressed to Singaravelu Mudaliar (Kidi) he made this emphatic comment: 'Religion therefore has no business to formulate social laws and insist on the difference between beings, while its aim and end is to obliterate all such fictions and monstrous differences.... Social laws were created by economic conditions under the sanction of religion. The terrible mistake of religion was to interfere in social matters, and at the same time how hypocritically it attempts to contradict itself by saying, "Social reform is not the business of religion!" True, what we want is that religion would not be a social reformer, but we insist at the same time that religion has no right to become a social law-giver, at least at the present time. Hands off! Keep yourself to your own bounds and everything would come right.'[54]

Concerned about the nationwide caste apartheid and the atrocities slammed on the lower castes, the only remedy that appealed to Vivekananda was to create awareness through education. He found that the fountain of knowledge was flowing close by, and yet people, especially of the lower class, were dying of thirst due to ignorance. In distress, he wrote to Sri Pramadadas Mitra, a great scholar of Vedanta in those days, enquiring if there is any mention in the śrutis about barring women or low-caste people from the study of the Vedas.[55] He could not get any satisfactory reply from the scholar. Vivekananda himself could not find in the śrutis any mention on the subject.

While discussing the caste problem with its pros and cons, another issue also comes up in its trail. It is the observance of one's duty or religion as per one's caste or stage of life. Vivekananda discussed it in detail in his essay 'The East & the West.'[56]

He himself raised the age-old debates of cleanliness and eating habits connected with religion and gave his view that both physical and mental cleanliness must be observed in our day-to-day dealings while carefully steering clear of any tinge of fanaticism. The body, clothes, residence, streets, food, etc. must be kept clean in deference to the injunction of Manu, '*Achara* or observance of the established rules of conduct is the first step to religion.'[57]

He was also keen to clear the air about vegetarianism. A large percentage of people, especially the Vaishnavites, feel that there cannot be any religion divorced from vegetarianism. Vivekananda pointed out to them that instances are rife in the *Ramayana*[58] and the *Mahabharata*[59] where their gods Rama and Krishna are casually taking wine and meat, while Sita Devi vows meat, rice, and a thousand jars of wine to the river-goddess, Ganga![60] The examples were to demonstrate that religion does not consist in mere observances but in being and becoming.

Giving his own verdict on the subject, he said: 'To eat meat is surely barbarous and vegetarian food is certainly purer—who can deny that? For him whose sole purpose is to lead a spiritual life, a vegetarian diet is enjoined. But he who has to steer the boat of his life with strenuous labour through the constant life-and-death struggles and the competition of this world must of necessity take meat. So long as there will be in human society such a thing as the triumph of the strong over the weak, meat is required, or some other suitable substitute for it has to be discovered; otherwise, the weak will naturally be crushed under the feet of the strong.'[61]

These words are proof of his liberal views and sympathy for one and all. His religion was all-inclusive. Vivekananda did not stop there and demonstrated further that although the principle of noninjury or *ahiṁsā* or forgiveness is one of the greatest virtues, it is not meant for all. He distinguished between two types of duties, *svadharma* (individual duty) and *jātidharma* (duty of a class). He said, that non-injury and resisting evil is a great thing, but the scriptures say, 'Thou art a householder; if anyone smites thee on thy cheek, and thou dost not return him an eye for an eye, a tooth for a tooth, thou wilt verily be a sinner.'[62] Manu also says, 'When one has come to kill you, there is no sin in killing him, even though he be a Brahmin.'[63]

How to read scriptures

In explaining the scriptures to his disciples, Vivekananda always encouraged them to assess the scriptural implications with their own intellectual resources, as one should not get influenced by others' views. Imitation of others impedes one's progress. The intellect must be free of all bias or prejudice to arrive at a right conclusion and like a honeybee one should collect honey from different scriptures and nourish oneself. This point has been mentioned in the *Bhagavatam*.[64] As a demonstration of this point, his Sanskrit letter to Swami Shuddhananda dated 1 June 1897 is given here. It was in reply to Shuddhananda's interpretation of the verse *yāvānartha udapāne* in the *Gītā* 2:46. Said he: 'The interpretation…is an old one. Does the thirst for water in living beings vanish when there is a flood around? The commentary of Śaṅkara alone should be followed.' Saying this, he proceeded to give, not one but two, interpretations of his own. The first is: 'As, even when whole tracts are flooded with water, small pools are also of great use to the thirsty, of identical use are the whole Vedas to a learned Brahmin. As even when the land is flooded, one's concern lies in the drinking water and no more; so in all the Vedas illumination alone is the concern.'

Yet Vivekananda did not stop here and gave a second interpretation of his. 'Here is another interpretation which is nearer to the meaning intended by the author: Even when the land is flooded, it is only the water which is potable and salutary, that people seek for, and no other kind. Even though the land be flooded, there are various kinds of water with different quality and properties according to soil. Likewise a skilful Brahmin too will choose from that ocean of words known as the Vedas, which is flooded with diverse courses of knowledge, that which alone will lead to liberation. And it is verily the knowledge of Brahman.'[65]

This interpretation at once reminds one of Sri Ramakrishna's allusion to a chātaka bird which never drinks any water other than raindrops.[66]

Even when the topic came to Darwinian theory of evolution, he had his own thoughts that followed only India's ancient tradition. Darwin put homo sapiens in the same category as the animal species when he defined them with threefold characteristics, namely, 1) struggle for existence, 2) survival of the fittest, and 3) natural selection. He said that even the homo sapiens is just animal within in respect of these traits. But Vivekananda refuted this view of Darwin. He cited the Yoga philosophy of Patanjali, and the still older Sankhya philosophy, pointing out that according to sage Patanjali the evolution from one species into the other takes place by means of 'infilling of nature,'[67] and not by Darwin's three characteristics.

In Vivekananda's opinion, 'Whatever may happen in the lower strata of nature's evolutions, in the higher strata at any rate, it is not true that it is only by constantly struggling against obstacles that one has to go beyond them. Rather it is observed that there the obstacles give way and a greater manifestation of the Soul takes place through education and culture, through concentration and meditation, and above all, through sacrifice.'[68] Competition for 'survival of the fittest' often impedes man's progress towards higher life. He was of the view that man is not animal by real nature, but it is human nature that is inherent in animals; and whenever all obstacles to progress are removed, out comes the real man. This point has been put in Patanjali's Yoga aphorism.[69] By the same token it can be argued that divine nature is inherent in man.

Scriptures in everyday life

When Vivekananda wrote to his dear ones, in a playful or serious mood, with melancholy or sarcasm, or to console a bereaved person, he would intersperse his communication with those precious jewels he got from the scriptures, or even literary works of writers and poets that had influenced him since childhood. In his correspondence as in his interaction with them, and his numerous talks and lectures, he tried to infuse the conviction that everyone must take refuge in God under all circumstances. At other times he also used to convey some beautiful and sublime truths about the world he learnt from the scriptures.

In his paper on Hinduism presented in the Parliament of Religions, Vivekananda quoted so aptly from Shakespeare's *Romeo and Juliet*: 'He jests at scars that never felt a wound.'[70] When he was in a playful mood, he would crack jokes at Sam, Mrs Mary Hale's only son, quoting verbatim from Charles Dickens' *Pickwick Papers*: 'Be wery careful o' vidders all your life.'[71]

Mrs Hale had picked him up from the Chicago roadside and given him shelter in her home.

Once he sent a beautiful poem in a letter dated 15 February 1895 to pacify Mrs Hale, whom he had earlier written a letter in very sharp language. After a few introductory lines of compromise to make the receiver's heart light and free, he straightaway broke into these lines:

The wounded snake its hood unfurls,
The flame stirred up doth blaze,
The desert air resounds the calls,
Of heart-struck lion's rage.
The cloud puts forth its deluge strength
When lightning cleaves its breast,
When the soul is stirred to its inmost depth,
Great ones unfold their best.

The first stanza is a neat translation of Kalidasa's *Abhijñāna-śakuntalam*.[72] And one gets amazed to learn that the second stanza is a verbatim reproduction of Śaṅkara's commentary on *Brahma Sutra*.[73]

Even in his preceding letter to her, he gave out the fire of spirituality that was burning all the while within him. When Mrs Hale stepped out of her bounds to take the role of a benefactor and advise him, he had countered her sharply through these lines: 'Manu says to the Sannyasin, "Live alone, walk alone."[74] Then again, 'Sister, do not take this amiss. But you are babies and babies must submit to be taught. You have not yet drunk of that fountain which makes "reason unreason, mortal immortal, this world a zero, and of man a God."[75] And still again, in a soliloquy, "Be still, my soul! Be alone! and the Lord is with you".'[76]

When he got the news of the betrothal of Miss Harriet Hale, the second daughter of Mrs Hale, with one Mr Woolley, his joy found expression through the lines with which sage Kanva had blessed his foster daughter Shakuntala in Kalidasa's *Abhijñāna-śakuntalam:* 'May you always enjoy the undivided love of your husband, helping him in attaining all that is desirable in this life, and when you have seen your children's children, and the drama of life is nearing its end, may you help each other in reaching that infinite ocean of Existence, Knowledge, and Bliss, at the touch of whose waters all distinctions melt away and we are all one!'[77]

Josephine MacLeod was also closely associated with Vivekananda. He looked upon her as a friend, and was full of praise for her. Her sublime purity and beauty of character reminded him of the unique description of Kalidasa in his memorable epic *Abhijñāna-śakuntalam*. He wrote to Miss MacLeod on 7 October 1896 quoting those beautiful lines translated by Monier Williams: 'Man's all-wise maker, wishing to create a faultless form, whose matchless symmetry should far transcend creation's choicest works, did cull together by his mighty will, and garner up in his eternal mind, a bright assemblage of all lovely things, and then, as in a picture, fashioned them into one perfect and ideal form. Such the divine, the wondrous prototype, whence her fair shape was moulded into being.'[78]

Christina Greenstidel was another lady whom Vivekananda looked upon as his foster daughter. She came of a very poor family and was most of her life afflicted with worldly troubles. In his letters to her, he used to console her with his rich stock of scriptural knowledge. His letter dated 4 March 1900 to her[79] read: 'We are like cattle driven to the slaughter-house—hastily nibbling a bite of grass on the roadside as they are driven along under the whip.' It is an exact reference from *Srimad Bhagavatam*.[80]

When in her letters, Vivekananda perceived a shade of despondence, he immediately gave her an antidote of the message of our scriptures as a source of encouragement:

'Disease and misfortune come to do us good in the long run, although at the time we feel that we are submerged for ever. "I am the infinite blue sky; the clouds may gather over me, but I am the same infinite blue".'[81]

In another letter of 6 July 1901, Vivekananda tried to boost up her downcast spirit by quoting from one of the Sanskrit literary works which mentions that a great man's heart never changes, come what may. 'Even the mountains will fly, the fire will be cooled, yet the heart of the great will never change.'[82]

To his disciple Sister Nivedita, Vivekananda wrote on 3 November 1897, quoting from *Uttara-rāma-caritam* of Bhavabhuti, as an encouragement, 'Hard as steel and soft as a flower.'[83]

In a tone of melancholy he wrote to his brother-disciple Swami Brahmananda on 11 October 1897, quoting from another literary work of the same Bhavabhuti, 'Certainly there will be born one equal to me.'[84] And to the same brother-disciple he wrote with exuberant emotion on 20 May 1897 by way of a promise, in the tone of Hanuman in the *Ramayana*, 'O Rama, so long as the story of your life goes round on the earth, I am present there.'[85]

Another letter written to Mrs G W Hale dated 23 October 1899 betrays a clear Advaitic attitude on pleasure and pain in life. Like an adept commentator, Vivekananda drew parallel illustration from life. It runs thus: 'Pleasure and pain are both feeling, not willing. They are only processes which convey to the mind excitements or motives of action. The real positive action is the willing, or to work, of the mind—begun when the sensation has been taken in (pleasure and pain); thus the real is neither pleasure nor pain. It has no connection with either—quite different from either. The barking of the dog awakens his master to guard against a thief or receive his dearest friend. It does not follow, therefore, that the dog and his master are of the same nature or have any degree of kinship. The feelings of pleasure or pain similarly awaken the soul to activity, without any kinship at all. The soul is beyond pain, beyond pleasure, sufficient in its own nature. And no hell can punish it, nor any heaven can please it.'[86]

Śaṅkara also discusses in his commentary on *Bṛhadaraṇyaka Upaniṣad* this point of happiness and misery being mere perceptions and not will power.[87]

In a letter to Sturdy dated 9 August 1895, he beautifully gives expression to his liberal feelings for humanity at large. 'What is India, or England, or America to us? We are the servants of that God who by the ignorant is called MAN.'[88] There is a quotation in the *Bible, New Testament, Acts of the Apostles*, 17:23 [Whom therefore ye ignorantly worship, him declare I unto you], and he has echoed it so fittingly with his concept of divinity in man. Again, in the very next sentence he continues the idea by bringing in reference from the *Bhagavatam*, 'He who pours water at the root, does he not water the whole tree?'[89]

To Mrs Sarah Chapman Bull, he writes in a letter dated 11 April 1895, 'Streams will be in the desert and the beggar will have plenty, if He wills it. He seeth the sparrow's fall.' This quotation derives its source from the *Bible*, *New Testament*, *Matthew*, 10:29. Shakespeare also writes in Hamlet, 'There's a special providence in the fall of a sparrow.'[90] In another letter to the same lady, Vivekananda writes in grief due to the recent defection of Landsberg, and quoting from the *Ramayana*, writes, 'All conjunctions are for subsequent disjunction.'[91]

And last but not the least were his instructions and warnings to his disciple Nivedita, who had a legendary will power and determination of a lioness. When she, after long deliberation, decided to come to India to work for Indian women, Vivekananda, though delighted beyond measure, forewarned her about the new environment she would find herself in.

Then he wrote her these remarkable lines: 'If you are really ready to take the world's burden, take it by all means. But do not let us hear your groans and curses. Do not frighten us with your sufferings, so that we come to feel we were better off with our own burdens. The man who really takes the burden blesses the world and goes his own way. He has not a word of condemnation, a word of criticism, not because there was no evil but that he has taken it on his own shoulders willingly, voluntarily. It is the Saviour who should "go his way rejoicing, and not the saved".'[92]

He concluded the letter with a quotation from the *Bible (Matthews)*, presenting it in his inimitable style: 'Come ye that are heavily laden[93] and lay all your burden on me, and then do whatever you like and be happy and forget that I ever existed.'

Art of interpreting scriptures

Vivekananda was very fond of free translation of Sanskrit scriptural texts. In order to make the meanings easily understandable by the Western audience or the common listener, he would prefer a free rendering of the Sanskrit texts, especially those with complicated structures. In all spiritual texts in India, the Sanskrit language has been kept as simple as possible, as terse as an aphorism, while the ideas conveyed are so vast, sublime, as well as deep. So many schools of philosophy have developed to interpret the texts in different ways. In striking contrast, Sanskrit literature conveys very little and simple ideas wrapped in gorgeous language, jargons, and adorned with adjectives.

Vivekananda had keenly watched the proclivity of Hindu scriptures to come straight to the point in question. So, he happily adopted this simple style of the scriptures to give palpably sublime ideas to his listeners. Throughout the full set of *Complete Works* we find that he embellishes the ideas inherent in scriptures in the simplest style, adapting them to the current context and making them easily comprehensible. In his Karma-yoga lectures he wanted people to work like a king and not like a slave; and knowing that the idea of duty stands in their way, he repudiated duty by quoting from the *Aṣṭāvakra-Saṁhitā*: 'In this tremendous fiery furnace where the fire of duty scorches everybody, drink this cup of nectar and be happy.'[94]

To emphasize this point, he quoted the very same lines in many places in his letters also. In a letter dated August 1895, to his ardent follower and propagator of Vedanta, Alasinga Perumal, he wrote, 'Duty is the curse of the *Sansari* (householder), not for the *Sannyasin*.' To Christina again, he wrote, 'Duty is the midday sun whose fierce rays are burning the very vitals of humanity.'[95] Speaking on the *Secret of Work,* Vivekananda said, quoting from the *Mahabharata*, 'Ignorance is death, knowledge is life.'[96] In the same lecture, he quoted from Kapila's *Sāṅkhya-Kārikā*, translating in his own style, "The whole of nature is for the soul, not the soul for nature."[97]

In the lecture entitled 'Non attachment is Self-abnegation', he quoted from *Mahābhārata*, 'The Action one has done cannot be destroyed until it has borne fruit.'[98]

In the same lecture, he interpreted a verse in the fourth chapter of the *Gītā*, 'He who in good action sees that there is something evil in it, and in the midst of evil sees that there is something good in it somewhere, has known the secret of work.'[99]

Again, he says in the same lecture,[100] 'We cannot breathe or live without injuring others.'[101] Though he referred to the *Bhagavad Gītā* here, the verse quoted is from the *Mahabharata*. Vivekananda continues, 'Every bit of the food we eat is taken away from another's mouth.' He echoes Śaṅkara's commentary on the *Bṛhadāraṇyaka Upaniṣad* here.[102] In the same lecture, he dwelt on the natures of people in the world and classified them according to king Bhartṛhari and in story-telling language, says: 'You will find various classes of men in this world. First, there are the God-men, whose self-abnegation is complete, and who do only good to others even at the sacrifice of their own lives. These are the highest of men.... Then there are the good men who do good to others so long as it does not injure themselves. And there is a third class who, to do good to themselves, injure others. It is said by a Sanskrit poet that there is a fourth unnameable class of people who injure others merely for injury's sake.'[103]

The aspirant in the path of Karma-yoga, after making substantial progress, experiences a subjective change; and accordingly, the objective world view also changes to him. He said this in the same lecture. 'As soon as this seeming self has gone, the whole world, which at first appears to us to be filled with evil, will appear to be heaven itself and full of blessedness. Its very atmosphere will be blessed. Every human face there will be good.'[104] This reference has been borrowed from the *Bhagavatam*.

In his lecture, 'Freedom', he gave a beautiful interpretation of the *Kaṭhopaniṣad*. Said he, 'If we give up our attachment to this little universe of the senses and of the mind, we shall be free immediately.'[105]

He gives a new rendering on verse 9 of the *Gītā*, 'Misery comes through attachment, not through work,' he says.[106]

He also praised Sarah C Bull and Rajah Ajit Singh of Khetri who, in his words, 'were so silent that it was only when the result came that people could infer that they were working. "Just as we infer a past life by the results in the present".'[107] One is awe-stricken to note Vivekananda relating two such characters to a literary work of the famous poet Kalidasa. The only answer to this riddle is that spiritual persons relate everything, including mundane experience, to spiritual life, while the worldly persons relate everything, however spiritual, to their petty worldly gain. There lies the difference.

Dignity of women

When Vivekananda went to the West, he felt extremely happy to see the honour and freedom accorded to women. The womenfolk were enjoying life to the maximum degree, and their education and cultural achievements in various fields were legendary. Vivekananda observed that they did everything from household chores to shopping, going to office apace with men. They controlled social and civic duties, ran schools and colleges.

What is more, he was helped there in every way by the ladies for every bit of official work—arranging for his lectures, taking him to the market, and doing everything for his comfort and convenience. Seeing such a manifestation of culture and education in them, he was immediately reminded of the ill-fated condition of women in India. He wrote to Haripada Mitra of Belgaum on 28 December 1893, 'It is indeed true that "the Goddess Herself lives in the houses of virtuous men as Lakshmi".'[108]

Their happy condition reminded Vivekananda of what Manu, the law-giver, had said: 'The gods bless those families where women are happy and well treated.'[109]

When he observed that women are not married before twenty or twenty-five years, he felt grieved at the early marriage system forced by Indian society. Here, too, he narrated the injunction of *Mahanirvana Tantra*: 'Daughters should be supported and educated with as much care and attention as the sons.'[110] Once Indumati Mitra, his disciple wrote to him a letter, and concluded it with the words 'Indumati Dasi.' The word 'Dasi' means maid-servant. In reply, Vivekananda rebuked her for writing that, because according to the law-giver Manu each caste must hold on to the dignity enjoined for it.[111]

The lady in question belonged to the Kshatriya or warrior caste, and so she should look upon herself with dignity proper to her own caste. In another letter to his brother-disciple Swami Ramakrishnananda dated mid-January 1894, he again sang paeans of grace about the women in the West. '*Tvaṁ śrīs-tvam-īśvarī tvaṁ hrīḥ*—Thou art the Goddess of Fortune, Thou art the supreme Goddess, Thou art Modesty.'[112]

Again, *Yā devī sarvabhūteṣu śaktirupeṇa saṁsthitā*—The Goddess who resides in all beings as Power.[113] *Tvaṁ strī tvaṁ pumānasi tvaṁ kumāra uta vā kumārī*—Thou art the woman,

Thou art the man, Thou art the boy and the girl as well' (*Śvetāśvatara Upaniṣad*, 4:3).[114] Vivekananda's pure mind was strung to the divine tune in such a way that he knew like a real poet the art of appreciating beauty for beauty's sake.

In the next letter dated 28 February 1894, to his disciple, Rajah Ajit Singh Bahadur, the Maharaja of Khetri, he again wrote about the women in lofty depiction, 'How many beautiful homes I have seen, how many mothers whose purity of character, whose unselfish love for their children are beyond expression, how many daughters and pure maidens, "pure as the icicle on Diana's temple".'[115]

Even while speaking on the social custom like marriage or a maid's selection of husband, Vivekananda would display his skill in citing from epics composed by Indian literati. In praising the bright side of the young maidens in America, he once wrote to his friend Manmathanath Bhattacharya on 5 September 1894: 'The unmarried girls are exceedingly good, because their future is bright; so why should they behave like a cow desiring a bull (*vṛṣasyantīva gau*)?'[116] The reference under question is from the works of Bhatti in *Rāvaṇavadha*.

Speaking of the sympathy and grace American women had showered on him, Vivekananda would often wax poetic in emotion. To the king of Khetri, he started his letter with the praise of women: 'It is not the building that makes the home, but it is the wife that makes it.'[117]

The reason for such a comment was his lofty regards for the American women about whom earlier he had only very poor knowledge based on hearsay. But after a year's experience in America his ideas underwent a radical change. So he wrote 'American women! A hundred lives would not be sufficient to pay my deep debt of gratitude to you! I have not words enough to express my gratitude to you.' Saying this, he cited an 'oriental hyperbole' used by Pushpadanta, the author of the memorable eulogy *Śiva-mahimnaḥ-stotra*, 'If the Indian Ocean were an inkstand, the highest mountain of the Himalaya the pen, the earth the scroll and time itself the writer, still it will not express my gratitude to you!'[118]

Spiritual knowledge through scriptures

Vivekananda's spiritual stature attained its peak during his sojourn in the Thousand Island Park, New York. He revealed himself as the ideal Guru, ideal preacher, a chosen commander from birth, to just a dozen of his selected disciples and admirers. It is said that he also attained the culmination of spiritual consciousness here below a tree—a rare state of meditation wrongly conceived as death by those present on the spot. It was through the 'Inspired Talks at Thousand Island Park' that his deep knowledge and incredible feats of scriptural and literary knowledge came to be revealed to his listeners.

On the very first day, Vivekananda opened the chapter on St John in the *Bible*. In the very first verse he pointed out how Christianity considers the Word as identified with God. Then he proceeded to declare that the first five verses of St John, being full of the profoundest philosophy, gave the whole essence of Christianity. Next, he showed the parallels in the Vedanta philosophy and said, 'The Perfect never becomes imperfect. It is in the darkness, but is not affected by the darkness. God's mercy goes to all, but is not affected by man's wickedness. The sun is not affected by any disease of our eyes which may make us see it distortedly.[119]

In the twenty-ninth verse, 'taketh away the sin of the

world'[120] means that Christ would show us the way to become perfect. God became Christ to show man his true nature, that we too are God. We are human coverings over the Divine; but as the divine Man, Christ and we are one.'[121]

It was, indeed, a unique way of comparing notes to make a deep impression in the minds of listeners, so as to wean them from the clutches of the wrong concept about the goal of spiritual life. So he said, 'After learning not to be disturbed by evil, we have to learn not to be made happy by good. We must find that we are beyond both evil and good; we must study their adjustment and see that they are both necessary.'[122]

He also showed how, even in Christianity, religion begins with fear and later evolves into pure, untarnished love. Quoting successively from the Old and New Testaments, he gave a proof of this statement. 'Human religion begins with fear. "The fear of the Lord is the beginning of wisdom".'[123] But later comes the higher idea. "Perfect love casteth out fear".'[124]

On another day, Vivekananda took up the aphorisms of Narada on devotion and said, quoting from the *Bhagavatam*, 'Extreme love and highest knowledge are one.'[125]

He warned the aspirants on the path, quoting from the Bhakti aphorisms, not to engage in vain arguments about God. He clearly declared, 'Theorising about God will not do.'[126] This is another example of his distinct way of interpretation. In eulogising the great power of transformation through holy company, Vivekananda would be beyond himself in joy. He said, 'The company of these children of light is very hard to get; five minutes in their company will change a whole life;[127] and if you really want it enough, one will come to you. The presence of those who love God makes a place holy, "such is the glory of the children of the Lord".'[128]

'They are He; and when they speak, their words are scriptures. The place where they have been becomes filled with their vibrations, and those going there feel them and have a tendency to become holy also.'[129]

While elucidating Patañjali's Yoga Aphorisms, Vivekananda interpreted the third aphorism in the first chapter with the words: 'When the (mind) waves are stilled, all is one: "a spectator without a spectacle".'[130]

His explanation of the *Bhagavad Gītā* was also as unique as the Yoga aphorisms. Equating this world with its adhering tendency, he gave the remedy to get out of it after the way shown in the *Bhagavad Gītā*: 'He from whom blight and delusion have fallen, he who has conquered the evils of association, he alone is *azad* (free).'[131] Still another example of his incredibly simple translation of a very oft-quoted verse of the *Gītā* is the second half of a verse in the sixth chapter: 'Getting whom, mountain high misery has no power to move the soul.'[132] What happens to the individual soul when after long and repeated striving it attains to its real stature, the Atman? Vivekananda gave the answer as a finale to his two-month-long discourse at Thousand Island Park: 'All dross has been burned out and there remains "flame without heat and without smoke".'(*Kathopanishad*)[133]

We now come to some more scriptural references worth mentioning in this context. Vivekananda rendered them in English with such aptitude that it becomes difficult to find out the reference even when the source is mentioned. From an unpublished note of a lecture 'What is Religion' delivered in New York Vedanta Society on 24 June 1900, he was quoted to have said, 'Manu says, salvation is for all, save only for a traitor.' The verse in question says: "Those Brahmanas (hypocrites) who act like herons, and those who display the characteristics of cats, fall in consequence into (the hell called) *Andhatāmisra*."[134] Obviously Vivekananda took only the essential meaning of the verse.

In a letter on 18 July1896, to his disciple, American writer and philanthropist Sarah C Bull, he wrote, quoting from the *Bhagavad Gītā*: 'He who works unattached to persons and giving up the fruits of work is a genuine worker.'[135] This also is another free style of rendering that he used. In his lecture on the Sāṅkhya philosophy, he quoted from the *Gītā*: 'When thou goest beyond the heard and the hearing, the thought and the thinking, then alone wilt thou come to truth.'[136] This is a typically free rendering of the *Bhagavad Gītā*. Again, he quoted from the same book: 'Go thou beyond the scriptures, because they teach only up to nature, up to the three qualities.'[137]

In his lecture, titled 'The Goal' in San Francisco on 27 March 1900, he quoted from the *Imitation of Christ*: 'Silence ye teachers of the world. Silence ye books. Lord, Thou alone speak and Thy servant listeneth.'[138]

While explaining the hymn of creation called *Nāsadīya Sūktam* in his lecture titled 'Vedic Religious Ideals' delivered in London, he compared its sublime beauty with some of the contemporary poets, Indian and Western alike.[139] The portion of the hymn saying: 'Gloom existed first, hidden in gloom,'[140] was compared with Kalidasa's epic *Meghadūtam* which expresses darkness as: 'Darkness which can be penetrated with a needle.'[141] Then he brought in Milton's work to show the Western way of citing the simile of darkness. 'No light, but rather darkness visible.'[142]

In this way, Vivekananda proved the sublimeness of Vedic descriptions vis-à-vis world literature. In his opinion, the Vedic ways of picturing God, nature, or the universe are as poetical as lyrical and sublime. He cited this sentence in support of his statement. 'He ushers the beautiful morning.'[143] His translation of the Rig-vedic hymn also bears mention here. 'He alone existed in the beginning; He is the one Lord of all that exists; He supports this universe; He who is the author of souls, He who is the author of strength, whom all the gods worship, whose shadow is life, whose shadow is death; whom else shall we worship? Whose glory the snow-tops of the Himalayas declare, whose glory the oceans with all their waters proclaim.'[144]

During his lectures, Vivekananda never kept notes, but used his mythical memory that supplied to him in an incessant flow all that was fitting for the topic. It is impossible to gauge the power of that flow. Even while writing letters, he never kept any scriptural books by his side. In fact, his references are so variegated over a wide range of source books that one fails to find them out. His flow of thought being legendary, it cannot but be accepted that he unravelled his power of *medhā* (wisdom) spontaneously, to the audience or the addressees of his letters.

This chapter has a twofold purpose.

First, it aims at igniting that desire to explore in serious thinkers and researchers of Swami Vivekananda's life, works, and legacy. Second, its objective is to inspire all admirers of Swami Vivekananda, high and low, to feel from the depth of their hearts for that section of our countrymen who are struggling against all odds to stand on their own. Let

Vivekananda's burning words keep blazing forever in the hearts of all: 'I bequeath to you, young men, this sympathy, this struggle for the poor, the ignorant, the oppressed.'[145]

End Notes

1. *Śrīmad Bhāgavatam*, 8:22:25-7.
2. *Luke*, 18:19.
3. Ibid, 10:7 [For the labourer is worthy of his hire].
4. Henry Wadsworth Longfellow, *A Psalm of Life*, St. 6; see also *Matthew* 8: 22 ('Let the dead bury their dead.').
5. *Complete Works* volume 2, page 225.
6. *yathā pūrvopāttānāṁ duritānām anārabdhaphalānāṁ sambhavaḥ tathā puṇyānām api anārabdhaphalānāṁ syāt sambhavaḥ.*—Vide Śaṅkara's commentary on the *Gītā*, 18:66.
7. *Gītā*, 6:32 *[ātmaupamyena sarvatra samaṁ paśyati yo'rjuna...]*
8. *Old Testament, Job*, 1:21.
9. *Matthew,* 5:4.
10. *Complete Works* volume 4, page 347.
11. *Bible, Old Testament, Job,* 3.17. (There the wicked cease from troubling; and there the weary be at rest.)

12. *Matthew*, 26:41; *Mark* 14:38.

13. Adapted from Lord A. Tennyson, *The Charge of the Light Brigade* (1854): '*Their's not to reason why,/Their's but to do and die.*'

14. *Kaṭhopaniṣad*, 2:2:13.

15. *Gītā,* 9:22.

16. *Muṇḍakopaniṣad*, 1:1:5.

17. *Kenopaniṣad*, 1:2.

18. *Matthew* 7.21

19. *Matthew*, 6.33; *Luke*, 12.31.

20. *Complete Works* volume 6, page 245.

21. *Vairāgyaśatakam* of Bhartṛhari, verse 45.

22. William Wordsworth, *Ode (Intimations of Immortality)* 1803-06, stanza 11.

23. 'Which of you by taking thought can add one cubit unto his stature?'—*Matthew*, 6:27.

24. *Complete Works* volume 9, page 99.

25. Edwin Arnold in the *Light of Asia*: (Book the Eighth).

26. *Complete Works* volume 5, page137.

27. *Bhāgavatam*, 9:21:12.

28. Ibid, 7:9:44.

29. *Complete Works* volume 3, page 415.

30. *Srīmad Bhāgavatam,* 3:29:21-27.

31. *Brahma-Sūtra*, 4:1:4-5.

32. Marie Louise Burke, Swami Vivekananda in the *West: New Discoveries*, Advaita Ashrama, 4th edn, 1992, Vol.6, p.79.

33. Op. cit., Vol.5, pp.158-9. Also see *Reminiscences of Swami Atulananda*, Prabuddha Bharata, April 1918, pp.85-6.

34. Ibid, Vol.5, pp.158-9. Cf. *citta-nadī ubhayato vāhinī; vahati kalyāṇāya vahati papaya ca*... Vyāsa's commentary on P.Y.S.1:12.

35. *Complete Works* volume 3, page182.

36. *na param apīḍayitvā grasitum api śakyate*—Śaṅkara's commentary on *Bṛhadāraṇyaka* Upanishad.1:5:2.

37. Swamiji's letter to Mrs. G W Hale dt.1 July 1894, in *Complete Works* volume 9 pages 24-5.

38. *Complete Works*, Advaita Ashrama, 12th reprint, 1979, Vol.3, p.293. The *Mahābhārata* reference is from Sukthankar's Cr. Edn., 12:181:10.

39. Ibid, Vol.3, p.294.

40. *Gautama-dharma-sūtra*, 12:4.

41. *Complete Works* volume 4, page 321.

42. Śvetāśvatara *Upaniṣad*, 4:3.

43. *Manu-smṛti*, 4.80.

44. *Nyāya-bhāṣyam* of Vātsyāyana, see his commentary to the aphorism, āptopadeśaḥ śabdaḥ of Gautama.

45. *Complete Works* volume 3, page 424.

46. Śukla-Yajur-*Veda*, 26:2.

47. *Complete Works* volume 5, pages 376-77 (Conversations with Priyanath Sinha) in this context.

48. *Complete Works* volume 3, page 456-7.

49. *Brahma Sūtra*,1:3:38.

50. *Gītā*, 5:19; *Complete Works* volume 4:321.

51. *Gītā*, 13:28.

52. *Complete Works* volume 4:322.

53. *Complete Works* volume 3:457. Cf. *Gautama Dharmasūtra* 61 and *Jābāla-smṛtiḥ*

54. *Complete Works* volume 4:351.

55 Swamiji's letter dt.7 Aug.1889 to Pramadadas Mitra.

56. *Complete Works* volume 5:441-537.

57. *Manu* 1:108.

58 *Rāmāyaṇa* of Vālmīki, *Uttara-kāṇḍam*, 7.45.20,21.

59 *ubhau madhvāsavakṣībāvubhau candana-rūṣitau*—'(I saw) both of them (Krishna and Arjuna) drunk with *Madhvasava* (sweet spirituous liquor made from honey),' .—Sukthankar, *Mahābhārata,* Cr. Edn., *Udyoga-parvan*, 5.58.5.

60. *surāghaṭa-sahasreṇa māṁsabhūtaudanena ca, yakṣye tvāṁ prayatā devi purīṁ punarupāgatā.*—(*Rāmāyaṇa*, Ayodhyā-kāṇḍam, Ch.2, verse 89).

61. *Complete Works* volume 5:485.

62. Cf. The *Bible, N.T. Matthew,* 5:38, 39. CW 5:448.

63. Manu, 8.350..

64. *aṇubhyaś ca mahadbhyaś ca śāstrebhyaḥ kuśalo naraḥ /sarvataḥ sāram ādadyāt puṣpebhya iva ṣaṭpadaḥ //*—11:8:10.

65. *Complete Works* volume 6:398.

66. 'M'., *Gospel of Sri Ramakrishna*, tr. Nikhilananda, SRK Math, Chennai, 2000, conversations on p.201, 312 and 344.

67. *jātyantara-pariṇāmaḥ prakṛtyāpūrāt*—Patanjali Yoga Sutras, 4:2.

68. *Complete Works* volume 7:153.

69. *nimittam aprayojakaṁ prakṛtīnāṁ varaṇabhedastu tataḥ kṣetrikavat*—*PatanjaliYoga Sutras*, 4:3.

70. Shakespeare, *Romeo & Juliet*, II:ii:1.

71. Charles Dickens, *Pickwick Papers*, Chapter 20.

72. Kalidasa's *Abhijñāna-śakuntalam*—Act 6.

73. Śaṅkara's commentary on the *Brahma Sutra*, 4:3:3.

74. Manu-smṛtiḥ, 6:42.

75. *Brihadaranyaka Upanishad* 4:3:22

76. Be still and know that I am God, The *Bible*, *Old Testament, Psalms*, 46:10.

77. Kalidasa's *Abhijñāna-śakuntalam,* Act 4, verse 20. *Complete Works*, volume 6, page 373 (letter dated 17 September 1896).

78. *Abhijñāna-śakuntalam* by Kalidasa, 2:9.

79. Wrongly addressed to Sister Nivedita in extant edition.

80. Cf. *Śrīmad Bhāgavatam*, 11.10.20

81. *Upadeśa-sāhasrī*, *Śaṅkarācārya, Ch.14, verse 50.*

82. *Subhāṣita-Ratnabhāṇḍāgāram*, Prakaraṇa 2, Sajjana-praśaṁsā, verse 222 (Original source *Vikramacaritam,* 249).

83. *Uttara-rāma-caritam,* 2:7

84. Mālatimādhava (*utpatsyate'sti mama ko'pi samānadharmā, kālo hyayaṁ niravadhir vipulā ca pṛthvī*).

85. Vālmīki-*Rāmāyaṇa,* Uttarakāṇḍaḥ, Ch.108, verse 36.

86. *Complete Works* volume 9, page 98.

87 Śaṅkara's commentary on *Brihadaranyaka Upanishad.* 1:4:7.

88. *Complete Works* volume 8, page 349.

89. *Bhāgavatam*, 4:31:14, and 8:9:29.

90. Shakespeare, *Hamlet*, V:ii:232.

91. *Rāmāyaṇa,* Ayodhyā kāṇḍa (2), Ch.98, verse 16.

92. (According to some versions it is Ch.105)92. The *Bible, NewTestament, Acts*, 8:39.

93. Cf. *Matthew*, 11:28.

94. *Complete Works* volume 1, page 101. See *Aṣṭāvakra-Saṁhitā,* 18:3 Also, Op. cit.1:7.

95. *Complete Works* volume6, page 417 (dated 27 August 1898, wrongly addressed to Nivedita).

96. Sukthankar, *Mahābhārata,* Cr. Edn., 5:42:4.

97. *Sāṅkhya-kārikā,* 56.

98. *Mahābhārata*, 3:200:5.

99. *Gītā,* 4:18.

100. *Complete Works* volume 1, page 80.

101. *Mahābhārata*, 3:199:27.

102. Śaṅkara's commentary on *Brihadaranyaka Upanishad* 1:5:2.

103. Bhartṛhari, *Nītiśatakam,* verse 65.

104. *Bhagavatam*, 9:19:15.

105. *Ka.Up.*2:3:14.

106. *Bhagavad Gita* 3:9.

107. *Complete Works* volume 5, page 92; Kalidasa, *Raghuvaṁśam,* 1:20

108. The allusion is to *Devī māhātmyam,* Ch.4, verse 5

109. *Manu-smṛtiḥ*, Ch.3, verse 56.

110. *Mahānirvāṇa-Tantra*, Ch.8, verse 47.

111. Cf. *Manu-smṛtiḥ*, 2:31-2.

112. *Devī māhātmyam*, Ch.1, verse 79.

113. Ibid, Ch.5, verse 32.

114. *Śvetāśvatara Upaniṣad,* 4:3.

115. *Complete Works*, volume 6, page 248. Also, Shakespeare, Coriolanus (1608), Act 5, Scene 3, 1.65. (Chaste as the icicle/ that's curdled by the frost from purest snow,/And hangs on Dian's temple.)

116. *Bhaṭṭikāvyam,* 4:30.

117. Pañcatantram, *Tantra 3 (Kākolūkīyam)*, Story 7, verse 147; and *Tantra 4 (Labdhapraṇāśam),* Story 11, verse 58. And *Mahābhārata*, Cr. Edn. by Sukthankar, Śāntiparvan, Vol.12, Ch.142, verse 4, Star passage No.364/3.

118 *asita-giri-samaṁ syāt kajjvalaṁ sindhu-pātre, sura-taru-vara-śākhā lekhanī patram urvī/likhati yadi gṛhītvā sāradā sarva-kālaṁ, tadapi tava guṇānām īśa pāraṁ na yāti//*—Stanza 32.

119. *Kaṭhopaniṣad*, 2.2.11.

120. The *Bible, New Testament, St. John*, 1.29.

121. *Complete Works*, volume 7, page 3.

122. Ibid, p.4.

123. The *Bible, Old Testament The Proverbs* 9.10

124. The First Epistle General of John 4.18.

125. *Śrīmad Bhāgavatam,* 11.32.32.

126. *Nārada-Bhakti-Sūtra*, 74.

127. Op. cit.,39. *[mahatsaṅgastu durlabho'gamyo'moghaśca]* Also, *Śaṅkarācārya in Mohamudgara*, verse 4.

128. Cf. *Bhagavatam,* 1.7.10

129. Op. cit., 69

130. Patanjali's *Yoga Sutras,* 1:3.

131. *Bhagavad Gītā*, 15:5.

132. Bhagavad Gita, 6:22.

133. *Kaṭha Upanishad.* 2.1.13, Also, *Śvetāśvatara Up. 6.19.*

134. *Manu-smṛtih,* 4:197

135. *Gītā*, 6:1

136. *Complete Works*, volume 2 page 449. *Bhagavad Gītā*, 2:52.

137. Ibid. *Bhagavad Gītā,* 2:45.

138. *Complete Works*, volume 2, page 473. 'Let all teachers hold their peace; let all creatures be silent in your sight; do you alone speak to me.' Thomas à Kempis, *Imitation of Christ*, Book I, Ch.3, §2.

139. *Complete Works*, volume 1, page 351.

140. *Ṛg-veda*, 10:129:3.

141. Kālidāsa, *Meghadūtam,* Pūrvamegha, 37.

142. Milton, *Paradise Lost*, Book 1, Line 63.

143. *Ṛg-veda,* 1.124.1; Also, *uvāsoṣā ucchācca nu devī jīrā rathānām.*—Op. cit., 1.48.3.

144. *Ṛg-veda,* 10.121.1,2,4.

145. *Complete Works*, volume 5, page 17.

In Vivekananda's Footsteps

WHEN ONE walks along the sea beach, one leaves temporary marks of footsteps on the sand. Soon they are washed off by the incessant waves. Not so, however, is the case with great souls. They walk freely down the corridors of time, leaving indelible footmarks which no deluge can wipe out. Those footprints are followed by posterity through generations to create a new era in history. Sri Ramakrishna and Swami Vivekananda were two such pioneers. People the world over continue to follow in their footsteps.

The holy organization, founded by Sri Ramakrishna and nurtured by Swami Vivekananda and his brother-disciples in succession, is more than a century old, paving its path through thick and thin, facing numerous ordeals, even crises, yet inspiring people to steadfastly strive for their own liberation.

The organization helped society to come out of its cocoon of age-old superstition and mend itself for a better life of understanding and awareness. People in many spheres are learning to stand on their own feet, discovering their inner self and the joy within, through a number of effective measures proposed by the monks.

People are being transformed through proper education aimed at restoring the lost confidence in them. Through various projects the Order has succeeded in alleviating the conditions of the poor and afflicted people all over India. The organization's multifarious activities has won praise from the people.

As pointed out by Vivekananda on several occasions—as also by Swami Saradananda in the first convention of the Ramakrishna Math and Mission—a new establishment develops in three phases, namely opposition, indifference, and acceptance. Through the combined honest efforts of the leaders who were spiritual stalwarts, the Order has already overcome the two initial bottlenecks faced by all new organizations. And now the third and most important phase—acceptance—is on.

Vivekananda had said this is the most dangerous, and hence critical, period in the progress of an order. As soon as praises are showered on its members, they lose sight of the uphill path ahead of them out of a false sense of security, and fall into the ditch of their vanity or feeling of supremacy over other groups.

In the *Kenopanishad,* the Supreme Lord had to appear in disguise before the devas—specially qualified persons of higher level—to break off their masks of egoistic revelry when they appropriated to themselves all the credits in overpowering the demons through their own prowess. Each of them tried in succession to burn or blow off a mere piece of straw at the behest of the stranger; but failing miserably in their attempts, they came to their senses.[1] This allegory points to the need for spiritual travellers to stop at times to take stock of their real progress, and take a retrospective view from time to time, analysing successes and failures, actions and reactions in the remote and recent past.

Even a lion in its onward journey sometimes turns back for its own security. Our ancient teachers have coined the word *simhāvalokanam* in Sanskrit, meaning, to look back, to have an account of one's credits and defaults. This Sanskrit word is equally applicable to an individual or a group. Without this precautionary measure, man runs the risk of turning into a frog in the well.

Enigmatic world teachers

In the march of time, India has seen innumerable world teachers, men of superhuman character. It is believed that they come for the redemption of humanity whenever virtue declines and vice rules the roost. But their teachings as also their lives convey such far-reaching messages that seem incomprehensible to ordinary minds. Sri Rama is looked upon as God incarnate, and yet many of his actions and teachings appear paradoxical. Even his all-time companion Lakshman felt irritated at his queer behaviour at times. But there was the noble Hanuman who remained ever-obedient to Rama, and never questioned his acts. And it was this Hanuman who lived to spread the message of Rama long after he left this earth. He was considered the greatest scholar and devotee of all time.

All the more enigmatic was Sri Krishna's character. Even great savants failed to gauge the depth of his personality. So, he brought with him Vidura, Uddhava, and a few such souls on whom he conferred the power of understanding his character. In later period, the all-renouncing Shukadeva recognized him in the right perspective. While he was narrating the life story of Sri Krishna to Parikshit, a descendant of the Pandavas, within a short period of seven days, the listener raised the question on the character of Krishna who engaged himself in amorous dance with others' wives on a moonlit night and asked Shukadeva intriguingly, 'What good will it bring to the human mind?' Shukadeva gave a significant brief reply which applies to incarnations in all ages and climes. Said he, 'In the lives of incarnations some exceptions are also found at times. Yet they are not tainted by the evil effects of such acts, since they are as pure as blazing fire that reduces to ashes everything that falls into it.'[2]

Like the great incarnations of the Ramayana and Mahabharata eras, other great souls also brought with them some persons of extraordinary spiritual achievement, to disseminate their teachings. Thus, Sri Ramakrishna brought with him Swami Vivekananda to fulfil a definite purpose. Only a Vivekananda could perceive in the right perspective the vastness and profound nature of Sri Ramakrishna's teachings. All others found them very difficult to grasp.

Sri Ramakrishna more often than not used to say that the chief aim of human life is to realize God. To emphasize this statement he said to a close disciple, 'If God appears before you ready to confer boons, will you ask for a few hospitals and charity homes or ask for devotion at His holy feet?' Again, on another occasion he said before a group of devotees in matters of being compassionate to others, 'Who are you to have mercy on others, insignificant creature that you are? Instead, serve others with an attitude of worship to Shiva.' To many this may appear as a highly enigmatic statement, because many questions may crop up from it.

'Why should one have mercy on others without striving for one's own liberation, which is the aim of life?' 'Will such acts not cause bondages for the aspirant?' 'Serving others means subservience to others' commands; does it not impede spiritual progress?'

'When one sees God in others, one becomes identified with Him, and no more remains fit to serve Him in the afflicted people; and when one goes to serve others without realizing God first, there is every chance of being caught up in the mesh of Maya. What is the way out of this riddle?'

Swami Vivekananda came forward to resolve all the conflicts in this context. He built up a new and unique philosophy on this wonderful statement of Sri Ramakrishna. He showed through irrefutable arguments that the statement can be equally effective both to a spiritual aspirant and a realized soul, and at the same time it also caters to the amelioration of society. So, he made this statement the motto of the Ramakrishna organization of monks: *Atmano mokṣārthaṁ jagad-hitaya ca*—for one's own liberation and the well-being of the world. And this also suggests the way of coordination between the monks and the householders. As it was in ancient times, both may stretch out their hands and contribute their mites in the welfare of each other.

In implementing this, he felt that the monks must first come out of their age-old idea of sitting in a cave, spending their whole life in austerity. Sri Ramakrishna bade Swami Vivekananda to unite all the energies of the other disciples through an all-embracing love, so that they did not fritter their spiritual energies, and apply themselves wholeheartedly to the welfare of others as a means to their spiritual goal.

This was indeed a new concept, of which Sri Ramakrishna

was the propagator. He handed over this onerous responsibility to his fittest disciple, Swami Vivekananda, who was merged neck-deep in spirituality, and wanted to remain immersed in it forever. But Sri Ramakrishna subdued him with his infinite, incomparable love. Thus, a new concept sprouted in a new era in which the monks came out of their closets in forests or mountain caves and employed themselves heart and soul in the service of the poor and afflicted humankind.

The intriguing question

After Sri Ramakrishna passed away, Swami Vivekananda felt an inner urge to know the real India in depth. To know a nation it is necessary to go to the common masses, to meet them in their shanties and ploughing fields, to love and sympathize with them. In other words, one has to identify oneself with them. Vivekananda did exactly that. He being a benevolent monk the common people opened their hearts to him. He went on discovering newer and newer truths of India. The elite of India were amazed by his extraordinary, all-round talents.

Vivekananda, having established his credentials as a spiritual guru, left for the USA to speak on Hinduism in the forthcoming Parliament of Religions. In a while, he reached the peak of success and became a world figure. But all the while, the words of Sri Ramkrishna kept ringing in his ears. He was fascinated to see the people of that country working with a common interest in an organized way, and remarked to Mrs Lyon of Chicago that he had had the greatest temptation of his life in America. It was Organization.[3]

Even during his itinerant days in India, he observed in some parts of Northwest India a monk serving the poor and the needy with the necessities of their lives all by himself. He built schools, hospitals, group-feeding inns and so on. Vivekananda depicted the picture in glowing terms in a letter to his Madras disciples:

> The ever-travelling Tyāgis of the various orders, Daśanāmīs or Vairāgīs or Panthīs bring religion to everybody's door, and the cost is only a bit of bread. And how noble and disinterested most of them are! There is one *Sannyasin* belonging to the *Kachu Panthis* or independents who has been instrumental in the establishing of hundreds of schools and charitable asylums all over Rajputana. He has opened hospitals in forests, and thrown iron bridges over the gorges in the Himalayas, and this man never touches a coin with his hands, has no earthly possession except a blanket, which has given him the nick name of the 'blanket Swami', and begs his bread from door to door. I have never known him taking a whole dinner from one house, lest it should be a tax on the householder. And he is only one amongst many. Do you think that so long as these Gods on earth live in India and protect the 'Religion Eternal' with the impenetrable rampart of such godly characters, the old religion will die?[4]

Simultaneously the idea assailed him that if a monk without much literary basis can do so much singlehanded, how much more could be done by the well-read monastic disciples of Sri Ramakrishna by forming themselves into a group? Vivekananda's concept was much more deep-rooted than what he saw outside. His idea was to make people stand on their own through proper training, to be with them in their weal and woe, and to equip them to fight against all onslaughts of poverty and other social evils. He felt that so much selfless service could only be done by the renouncing monks and not by the householders. Then how would the householders benefit from such a method? Yes, it would be a twofold benefit: They would be spiritually lifted through association with the monks, and in exchange they would contribute their mites in the noble cause to earn the merits of good works.

Vivekananda expressed this idea in a letter dated 24 January 1894 to his Madras disciples and admirers: 'My whole ambition in life is to set in motion a machinery which will bring noble ideas to the door of everybody, and then men or women, they will settle their own fate. Let them know what our forefathers have thought and other nations have thought on the most momentous questions of life. Let them see what others are doing now especially, and let them decide. We are to put the chemicals together; the crystallization would be done by nature according to her laws.'[5]

With this end in view, Vivekananda founded the great organization and named it after his master, Sri Ramakrishna. On 1 May 1897, before a group of householders and monastic disciples of Sri Ramakrishna, he presented the topic in a convincing manner: 'From my travels in various countries I have come to the conclusion that without organization nothing great and permanent can be done. But in a country like India, at our present stage of development, it does not seem to me well advised to start an organization on a democratic basis in which every member has an equal voice, and decisions are arrived at by a majority of the votes of the community.... When with the spread of education we learn to sacrifice, to stand above our individual interests and concerns, for the good of the community or the nation at large, then it will be possible to work on a democratic basis. Taking this into consideration, we should have for our organization at present a Director whose orders everyone should obey. Then, in the fullness of time, it will be guided by the opinion and consent of the members.'[6]

Here the second sentence raises a significant question, especially in the Indian context: 'How far are we abreast with other nations in the context of democracy?' This is the first necessary condition Vivekananda put before us. To be within the fold of an organization means to grasp the real meaning of democracy and to practise it. To enjoy the freedom of monastic right does never mean to extract the maximum privileges from it, but to contribute maximum service to the community one belongs to. The moment even a tinge of self-interest creeps into the mind of an individual, it starts destroying his inner system like a bug in a computer.

Vivekananda was well aware of all these pitfalls through his extensive experience all over the world. So, he wanted the members of this new organization to be divested of this virus. On the eve of his second departure for the West (19 June 1899) he addressed the Swamis and Brahmacharins assembled before him in an inspiring tone: 'In our country, the old idea is to sit in a cave and meditate and die. To go ahead of others in salvation is wrong. One must learn sooner or later that one cannot get salvation if one does not try to seek the salvation of his brothers. You must try to combine in your life immense idealism with immense practicality. The next thing to remember is that the aim of this institution is to make men...You must stand on your own feet. You must have this new method—the method of man-making. The true man is he who is strong as strength itself and yet possesses a woman's heart; though it may seem a little paradoxical—you must possess these apparently conflicting virtues.'[7]

These are some of the ideas of a democratic society. Monks are often heard to quote these lines from scriptures—*Nistraiguṇye pathi vicaratāṁ ko vidhiḥ kniṣedhaḥ*—with the ulterior motive of avoiding responsibilities or obligations of their duties. But ironically, Vivekananda preached just the reverse of it. He said that spiritual life begins when one takes up all responsibilities of his actions on oneself and stops passing the buck to others. In fact, our hoary ancestors have warned us against such falls. Sureshwaracharya, for one, clearly stated in *Naiṣkarmya-siddhi* that even a realized soul has no right to exercise his whimsical, unethical desires; and if he does so, he will end up identifying himself with the dog that eats defiled, impure food.[8] Freedom of monks, especially those belonging to a group, does not imply licence to do anything in any way they like. Instead, they must be ready to accept the responsibility for each of their moves.

On organized religion

Two contrary ideas intrigued Vivekananda during this time. One was the formation of an organization and the other was the fear of it being reduced to a new sect. Vivekananda often used to quote a Sanskrit verse from the *Hitopadeśa*, a primer on moral and ethical values for children, which means, grass blades, though very tender, can be twined into a rope which becomes strong enough to hold back a mad elephant.[9] Spirituality forms the vital force that has to be applied in a unified form to uplift this country. Vivekananda had noted that this tremendous energy was not being applied to its fullest potential. He felt that though the monks of

India wield tremendous power, this may also lead to greed followed by exploitation after a few generations. Hence, a bridge needed to be erected between spiritual and secular powers; in other words, he wanted to establish a bridge of mutual bonds between the monks and the householders. With this idea in mind, Vivekananda made a very bold statement which may appear contradictory on the face of it, but after reading between the lines one wonders about the greatness of Vivekananda even in points of impartiality.

In his lecture entitled 'My Life and Mission' delivered in California, he blurted out: 'I must tell you that I am not a great believer in monastic systems. They have great merits, and also great defects. There should be a perfect balance between the monastics and the householders. But monasticism has absorbed all the power in India...Now, that is bad, so much power, even in the hands of good men—although these monastics have been the bulwark of the people. They stand between priestcraft and knowledge. They are the centres of knowledge and reform.... But all the same so much power is not good there; better methods should be worked out...What we can do is just to transform it, give it another form. This tremendous power in the hands of the roving Sannyasins of India has got to be transformed, and it will raise the masses up.'[10]

Vivekananda said this on 27 January 1900, that is, about two and a half years after founding the Ramakrishna Mission Association on 1 May 1897. Then again, in his lecture on the *Bhagavad Gita* at San Francisco he said, 'We start a religion and make a set of dogmas and betray the goal of mankind and treat everyone as having the same nature. No two persons have the same mind or the same body. No two persons have the same religion. If you want to be religious, enter not the gate of any organized religions. They do a hundred times more evil than good, because they stop the growth of each one's individual development. Study everything, but keep your own seat firm. If you take my advice, do not put your neck into the trap. The moment they try to put their noose on you, get your neck out and go somewhere else. As the bee culling honey from many flowers remains free, not bound by any flower, be not bound…Enter not the door of any organized religion. Religion is only between you and your God, and no third person must come between you.'[11]

How can these two ideas be reconciled with his act of founding the Organization? Even initially Vivekananda himself was in a dilemma. So, he sought the valued opinion of Nag Mahashay, a great devotee of Sri Ramakrishna, when he came to meet him at Belur Math sometime in the beginning of 1899: 'Is the starting of these Maths and Ashramas etc. a step in the right direction?' And Nag Mahashay, an embodiment of humility that he was, replied with full conviction: 'I am an insignificant being, what do I understand? Whatever you do, I know for a certainty, will conduce to the well-being of the world.'

Again Vivekananda expressed doubts about all the works he initiated: 'I do not fully understand whether what I am doing is right or not. At particular times I feel a great inclination to work in a certain direction, and I work according to that. Whether it is for good or evil, I cannot understand.' Nag Mahashay's brief reply was: 'Well, Sri Ramakrishna said, "The treasure is now locked. Therefore, he does not let you know fully. The moment you know it, your play of human life will be at an end."'[12]

Framing of rules

Vivekananda pondered over the pros and cons of this concept of organized life. His experience and learning from history gave him insights into the dark side of organized life, which he described in another lecture in San Francisco: 'The moment you form yourselves into an organization, you begin to hate everybody outside of that organization. When you join an organization you are putting bonds upon yourself, you are limiting your own freedom. Why should you form yourselves into an order having rules and regulations thus limiting everyone as to his independent action? If one breaks a law of an Order or society, he is hated by the rest. What right has anyone to lay down rules and laws governing others? Such laws are not laws at all. If it were a law, it could not be broken. The fact that these so-called laws are broken shows clearly they are not laws.'[13]

So, while framing a number of rules for members of his newly founded organization, he made this point clear to everyone. Those rules stand as sentries to protect every spiritual aspirant belonging to the fold of our Order, and may be treated as moral codes of conduct like *Manu-smṛti* and similar other scriptures of India. In his letter dated 3 March 1894 to Kidi, his Madras devotee, Vivekananda wrote explicitly: 'For a religion to be effective, enthusiasm is necessary. At the same time we must try to avoid the danger of multiplying creeds. We avoid that by being a non-sectarian sect, at the same time having all the advantages of a sect and the broadness of a universal religion.'[14]

Again, 'We reject none, neither theist, nor pantheist, monist, polytheist, or agnostic, or atheist; but the only condition of being a disciple is modelling a character at once the broadest and the most intense. Nor do we insist upon particular codes of morality as to conduct, or character, or eating and drinking, except so far as it injures others.'[15]

In order to give a concrete form to this principle, Vivekananda jotted down the following mandatory rules for the monastic members:

1) Know partiality to be the chief cause of all evil. That is to say, if you show towards any one more love than towards somebody else, rest assured, you will be sowing the seeds of future troubles.
2) If anybody comes to you to speak ill of any of his brothers, refuse to listen to him in toto. It is a great sin to listen even. In that lies the germ of future troubles.
3) Moreover, bear with everyone's shortcomings. Forgive offences by the million. And if you love all unselfishly, all will by degrees come to love one another. As soon as they fully understand that the interests of one depend upon those of others, every one of them will give up jealousy. To do something conjointly is not in our very national character. Therefore you must try to inaugurate that spirit with the utmost care, and wait patiently.
4) All of you have infinite strength—how long does it take you to have sway on petty factionalism, jealousy, or egotistic ideas? The moment such propensity comes, resign yourselves to the Lord! Just make over your body and mind to His work, and all troubles will be at an end forever.[16]
5) It shall be wholly forbidden to huddle together in a room and chat the whole day away, with any number of outsiders coming and joining in the gossip.
6) Tale-bearing, caballing, or scandal-mongering should be altogether eschewed.[17]

Apart from these, Vivekananda's instructions come down to us through his instructions to intimate friends, disciples, and admirers also. From those instructions one gets a few definitions of real management and can also guess his intention to protect the members from the evils of an organization. A few of them, strewn in his letters, are:

1) Skilful management lies in giving every man work after his own heart. (Letter to Swami Brahmananda, 17 July 1898)
2) The term organization means division of labour. Each does his own part, and all the parts taken together express an ideal of harmony. (Letter to brother-disciples, summer 1894)
3) Take care how you trample on the least rights of others. Many a huge ship has drowned in that whirlpool. Remember, perfect devotion minus its bigotry—this is what we have got to show. (Letter to Ramakrishnananda, 19 March 1894, V.6, p.285)
4) As long as the idea of faction will remain, the attitude of disgust towards the disciples of Paramahamsa will also linger, the desire to interfere in their work will crop up so long, and the quarrels will go on increasing only. [Letter to Balaram Bose dt.14 Feb.1890 (As per original document in Archives, Belur Math)] How can one preach the catholic ideas of Ramakrishna Paramahamsa and form sects at the same time? (Letter to Ramakrishnananda, Sept., 1894 according to the original document in Archives, Belur Math)
5) No one ever succeeded in keeping society in good humour and at the same time did great works. One must work as the dictate comes from within, and then if it is right and

good, society is bound to veer round, perhaps centuries after one is dead and gone. (Letter to Mrs Sarah C Bull, dt 21 March 1895)

6) If a man does not have interest in a thing he will not work whole-heartedly; all should be made to understand that everyone has a share in the work and property, and a voice in the management. Give a responsible position to everyone alternately, but keep a watchful eye so that you can control when necessary; thus only can men be trained for the work. We Indians suffer from a great defect, viz we cannot make a permanent organization—and the reason is that we never like to share power with others and never think of what will come after we are gone. (Letter to Sw Brahmananda dt 1 August 1898)
7) We will do nothing ourselves and will scoff at others who try to do something—this is the bane that has brought about our downfall as a nation. Want of sympathy and lack of enthusiasm are at the root of all misery, and you must therefore give these two up. Who but the Lord knows what potentialities there are in particular individuals—let all have opportunities, and leave the rest to the Lord. It is indeed very difficult to have an equal love for all, but without it there is no *mukti*. (Letter to Yogananda, 24-1-1896)
8) You must not throw cold water on anybody's project. Give up criticism altogether. Help all as long as you find they are doing all right, and in cases where they seem to be going wrong, show them their mistakes gently. It is criticizing each other that is at the root of all ruin. That is the secret of breaking down organizations. 'What does he know?' 'What can you do?'—such comments

accompanied by a derisive smile—these are the main factors of all dissensions. (Letter to Brahmananda & others, End 1895)

9) He who knows how to obey knows how to command. Learn obedience first. Among these Western nations with such a high spirit of independence, the spirit of obedience is equally strong. We are all of us self-important—that never brings about success. Great enterprise, boundless courage, tremendous energy, and, above all, perfect obedience—these are the only traits that lead to individual and national regeneration. These traits are altogether lacking in us. (Letter to Akhandananda, 13-11-1895)

10) Our nation is totally lacking in the faculty of organization. It is this one drawback which produces all sorts of evil. Five persons cannot at all join hands together to accomplish a common end. The first requisite for organization is obedience—not doing a little bit of work only when I feel so disposed, and then let it go to the dogs. This kind of work is of no avail. We must have plodding industry and perseverance. (Letter to Swami Akhandananda, October 1895)

11) The only way of getting our divine nature manifested is by helping others to do the same. If there is inequality in nature, still there must be equal chance for all—or if greater for some and for some less—the weaker should be given more chance than the strong. (Letter to Brahmananda, January 1895)

12) Know that talking ill of others in private is a great sin. You must wholly renounce it. Many things may occur in the mind, but to speak it out expressly makes a mountain

of a molehill. Everything ends if somebody swallows it within. (Letter to Ramakrishnananda, 11 April 1895)

13) We must not join any sect, but we must sympathize and work with each. (Letter to Alasinga, 11 July, 1894, CW5.37)

14) You will have to take charge of the whole movement, not as a leader, but as a servant, do you understand? Do you know, the least show of leading destroys everything by rousing jealousy? (Letter to Alasinga, 31 Aug 1894)

15) It is not at all necessary that all should have the same faith in our Lord as we have, but we want to unite all the powers of goodness against all the powers of evil. (Letter to Ramakrishnananda, 19 March 1894)

16) A great sin with Sannyasins is the vanity of monasticism.… One must make no distinction between householders and Sannyasins—then only one is a true Sannyasin. (Letter to Ramakrishnananda, 19 March1894)

17) All combined efforts in India sink under the weight of one iniquity—we have not yet developed strict business principles. Business is business, in the highest sense, and no friendship—or as the Hindu proverb says 'eye-shame'—should be there. One should keep the clearest account of everything in one's charge—and never, never apply the funds intended for one thing to any other use whatsoever—even if one starves the next moment. This is business integrity. Next, energy unfailing. Whatever you do let that be your worship for the time. (Letter to Dr Nanjunda Rao, dt 26 August 1896)

18) Some people do the best work when led. Not everyone is born to lead. The best leader, however, is one who 'leads like the baby.' The baby, though apparently depending on

> everyone, is the king of the household. At least, to my thinking, that is the secret. It is the power of expressing one's love and appreciation and sympathy for others, that enables one person to succeed better in spreading the idea than others. A leader must be impersonal. (Letter to Sister Nivedita dt 1 October 1897)

The distinct features of the Ramakrishna Order are, its liberal and broad outlook on other religions, lack of factionalism, jealousy, backbiting and so on. It is only by following these guidelines that the Order can be made into 'a sect without the evils of sectarianism.'

Vivekananda presented this idea in picturesque style in his lecture entitled 'The Way to the Realization of a Universal Religion: Not only toleration, for so-called toleration is often blasphemy, and I do not believe in it. I believe in acceptance. Why should I tolerate? Toleration means that I think that you are wrong and I am just allowing you to live…I accept all religions that were in the past, and worship with them all; I worship God with every one of them, in whatever form they worship Him…Not only shall I do all these, but I shall keep my heart open for all that may come in the future.

'Is God's book finished? The *Bible*, the Vedas, the *Quran*, and all other sacred books are but so many pages, and an infinite number of pages remain yet to be unfolded. I would leave it open for all of them. We stand in the present, but open ourselves to the infinite future. We take in all that has been in the past, enjoy the light of the present, and open every window of the heart for all that will come in the future.'[18]

Leadership, obedience and freedom

Vivekananda advised all the members of the Order not to harbour any desire to lead others. He said, 'Do not try to lead your brethren, but serve them. The brutal mania for leading has sunk many a great ship in the waters of life. Take care especially of that, that is, be unselfish even unto death, and work.'[19] He wrote further, 'Do you know, the least show of leading destroys everything by rousing jealousy?'[20] This means a perfect leader should be a perfect blend of a lion's courage and a lamb's meekness. In other words, in points of dominating others he should be the last person, humble and meek; but given the responsibility to lead the rank under critical situations, he should bear the brunt of all onslaughts like a lion, the king of the jungle.

To make the point further clear, he cited another example from the pages of Indian history, showing the root cause of failure of Indian soldiers in the Sepoy Mutiny. He said in a humorous tone: 'An English friend of mine, named General Strong, was in India during the Sepoy Mutiny. He used to tell many stories about it. One day, in the course of conversation, I asked him how it was that the sepoys who had enough of guns, ammunition, and provision at their disposal, and were also trained veterans, came to suffer such a defeat. He replied that the leaders among them, instead of advancing forward, only kept shouting from a safe position in the rear, "Fight on, brave lads," and so forth; but unless the commanding officer goes ahead and faces death, the rank and file will never fight with heart. It is the same in every branch. "A captain must sacrifice his head," they say.[21]

If you can lay down your life for a cause, then only you can be a leader. But we all want to be leaders without making the necessary sacrifice. And the result is zero—nobody listens to us!'[22]

Another necessary quality for leadership is strength of character. In his Raja-yoga lectures Vivekananda pointed out to his students, 'The majority of sects will be transient, and last only as bubbles because the leaders are not usually men of character. Perfect love, the heart never reacting, this is what builds character. There is no allegiance possible where there is no character in the leader, and perfect purity ensures the most lasting allegiance and confidence.'[23]

Nobody will dare to disobey a leader whose character is made of such noble qualities. Then the very question of obedience will become irrelevant.

However, obedience can only be followed as long as it does not lower the self-respect of a person. The desire to become free is latent in every individual, and hence no one likes to become a puppet in others' hands in the name of obedience. Especially those whose conscience has awakened a little find it painful to obey. On the other hand, obedience never becomes a source of conflict, nor creates a gulf in mutual relationship where true love finds expression in the dealings among the members. When Vivekananda wrote to his brother-disciples such words as, 'The first thing needed is obedience. You must be ready to plunge into fire,'[24] 'Organization is power, and the secret of this is obedience,'[25] what did he actually mean by obedience here?

That obedience does not mean a slavish, unconditional subservience to a particular individual. It is an expression of surrendering one's own whimsical desires to a sublime, noble ideal. A really mature person can become at once 'free as the air, and as obedient as this plant and the dog,' as Vivekananda put it.[26]

It is in the name of this very ideal that people assemble under the same banner having thrown overboard all their home and hearth, kith and kin, and desires for name and fame, because even their hearts blood becomes insignificant, the sacrifice of their lives becomes meaningful, on the altar of that noble ideal.

Whenever a large crowd of youths form into a group centring around a leader, it should be kept in mind that they have surrendered themselves to the ideal represented by that man, and not to the individual in flesh and blood. Unfortunately, in almost all such cases obedience stands to mean as becoming a puppet in the hands of a leader who is full of power-mongering and selfishness. The phrase 'unconditional obedience' is a slogan raised only by those shrewd leaders. In this context also, Vivekananda's comments are valid: 'If it is finally settled that the path of human welfare is forever chalked out by these omniscient men, society naturally fears its own destruction if the least deviation be made from the boundary line of the path, and so it tries to compel all men through rigid laws and threats of punishment to follow that path with unconditional obedience. If society succeeds in imposing such obedience to itself by confining all men within the narrow groove of these paths, then the destiny of mankind becomes no better than that of a machine....In course of time, for want of proper use, all activity is given up, all originality is lost, a sort of *Tāmasika* dreamy lifelessness hovers over the whole nation, and headlong it goes down and down.'[27]

What happens when an individual member of a society or an organization surrenders his aspirations to this so-called obedience? He moves away from his own soul which, finding no outlet to express its own joyful nature, gives expression to its yearning through anger, malice, antagonism, roguish behaviour, and so on. Once Mr Leon Landsberg (later Swami Kripananda), an American monastic disciple of Swami Vivekananda, wrote a letter to Mrs Sarah Chapman Bull (Dhiramata, as Vivekananda called her) with some complaints born out of his own misunderstanding in points of obedience. In reply Mrs Bull tersely and unequivocally wrote to him, 'Vivekananda asks obedience of his students, only to those ideals they voluntarily assume, not to his teachings, if I understand him.'[28] In other words, she vouched for Vivekananda's idea of obedience to a principle rather than an individual. When one obeys the principle rather than the individual, it helps spiritual growth. On the other hand, blind obedience to an individual leader may eventually cause loss of one's own individuality.

One may ask how it is possible to reach a principle without having recourse to an individual. And pat comes Vivekananda's reply: 'Obedience and respect cannot be enforced by word of command; neither can they be exacted. It depends upon the man, upon his loving nature and exalted character. None can resist true love and greatness.'[29]

One whose life is founded on the firm bedrock of love and truth will certainly win the respect and unconditional love of others even unasked; he need not have to impose any rule or command to exact obedience. On the contrary, those who enforce laws in their desperate attempt to keep other members under control are actually under a sway of mental aberration termed 'necrophilia' by western psychologists. People possessed by this attitude evince a strong tendency to destroy their opponents; but they cannot actually do so in fear of the law breathing heavily down their neck. Hence, they take recourse to tricky ways of turning their subordinates into slaves.

Now, it is as clear as broad daylight that Vivekananda was the harbinger of freedom, and hence could not preach such personal obedience to people. In his discourse on 'Law and Freedom' he emphatically said: 'I disagree with the idea that freedom is obedience to the laws of nature. I do not understand what it means. According to the history of human progress, it is disobedience to nature that has constituted that progress. It may be said that the conquest of lower laws was through the higher. But even there, the conquering mind was only trying to be free; and as soon as it found that the struggle was also through law, it wanted to conquer that also. So the ideal was freedom in every case. The trees never disobey law. I never saw a cow steal. An oyster never told a lie. Yet they are not greater than man. This life is a tremendous assertion of freedom; and this obedience to law, carried far enough, would make us simply matter—either in society or in politics, or in religion. Too many laws are a sure sign of death.'[30]

In a letter to Swami Brahmananda dated 11 October 1897, Vivekananda wrote: 'To me cringing, fawning, whining, degrading inertia and hell are one and the same thing.'[31]

Even in his voyage to the West for the second time, he was delighted to see the crew members, a large number of them Bengalees, working so cheerfully and with an attitude of fearlessness. He wrote in his 'memoirs': 'Seeing these Bengali lascars, coalmen, servants, and boys at work, the feeling of despair with regard to my countrymen…was abated… how fearless, yet docile! That cringing, sycophant attitude common to 'natives' even the sweepers do not possess.'[32]

These lines bear clear evidence that Vivekananda never liked cringing, slavish obedience.

Holy Mother on obedience

In Holy Mother Sarada Devi's opinion, obedience to a principle or one's spiritual teacher (guru) can be made unconditional without much trouble. The problem comes when authorized superiors other than the spiritual teacher come in between with all their sophistry to make a slave of the innocent aspirant. Even sometimes the spiritual teacher also, out of his earthly, base desires, exploits the innocent disciple. One has to be on guard against such atrocities.

Once two American ladies approached the Holy Mother with a significant question: When the spiritual teacher belongs to the opposite sex how far should one obey him in all matters? Now, as a matter of fact, the spiritual teacher of the Holy Mother was none else than her own husband, Sri Ramakrishna. Hence, she was never assailed by such a problem in her life. Yet she gave a bold answer: 'In spiritual matters alone you should follow your teacher's instructions unconditionally, but not in worldly matters.'

This answer clearly cautions against exploitation in the name of spiritual ministration. In her own life, she would disobey or disapprove Sri Ramakrishna's instructions on worldly matters wherever they seemed unjustified to her. Once Sri Ramakrishna, a great taskmaster to his monastic disciples in the making, came to know that a disciple had taken two or three extra pieces of bread at supper, far beyond what he had earlier stipulated for him; he forbade the Holy Mother to allow him do so in the future. But she was not a person to be ordered around concerning such matters and replied to the master sharply: 'Why are you worrying just because he has eaten two extra pieces of bread? I am looking after these children. I do not want you to criticize them about food.'

She never hesitated to speak the blunt truth to her husband when the occasion demanded it. At one time the kitchen at Kamarpukur badly needed repair and the master was asked to pay the expense. But he said, 'We do not live there; let them somehow manage it.' 'How selfish!' Sarada Devi said at once.[33]

On another occasion, when she was asked by Sri Ramakrishna to be a little parsimonious in the matter of giving away things to the devotees, her motherly feeling of charity got hurt. She abruptly left the room, leaving Sri Ramakrishna in great distress at her rigid silence.

Pros and cons of organized life

Organized life has both bright and dark aspects. One of the bright sides is that it helps its members to come out of a crude condition to a substantially cultured and developed state of life through discipline, study, common interest, and mutual love. The members also grow confidence in their abilities by shouldering responsible jobs by degrees. It also enriches the members with a sense of security. Yet there are dark sides of life in organizations.

In a letter to the Maharaja of Khetri, dated 9 July 1985, Vivekananda had written: 'Each work has to pass through three stages—ridicule, opposition, and then acceptance. Each man who thinks ahead of his time is sure to be misunderstood. So, opposition and persecution are welcome, only I have to be steady and pure and must have immense faith in God, and all these will vanish.'[34]

Firstly, the members may mistake the security enjoyed in the Order for a worldly security and start thinking that they may do whatever they like without fear. True security comes out of self-surrender to God alone, and not from the support of some powerful members of the organization.

The second dark aspect of an organized spiritual life is the common tendency of every member of a society to pull down every other member to the average level. All the talents and creative genius get stifled amid this average way of life.

The third dark aspect of an organization is that its members usually look down upon others with a 'holier-than-thou', 'more competent-than-thou' or such other attitudes. It is very good to develop confidence, but that should not come by lowering others' dignity. One who is well aware of his own capacities and limitations will also have a right assessment of others' good qualities. He will treat others with dignity and, above all, will have full faith in divine dispensation. This proclamation of the divine Mother should always ring in his ears— 'I do uplift him whom I wish; I raise him to the status of Brahmā, or a seer, or one excelling in talents; I confer power on him.'[35] Then he will learn to give freedom to others. No idea of power-mongering or envy towards others will find any place in his heart. Vivekananda wrote in a letter, 'None deserves liberty who is not ready to give liberty.'[36]

Again, 'Liberty is the first condition of growth. Man must have liberty to think and speak so long as he does not injure others.'[37]

The fourth dark side is to ostracize a member out of sheer personal grudge. In modern English 'mobbing' is the term used for such attitude.

Jealousy in renunciates

Vivekananda was vociferous in denouncing jealousy among the members. He poignantly pointed out that jealousy only betrays one's weakness; it is a ridiculously desperate attempt to raise oneself at the cost of others. Jealousy doesn't afflict the talented and knowledgeable. In an Order there is no room for individual preference. No post can remain occupied forever by an individual; to leave the post voluntarily and willingly for others after a certain period indicates a wholesome mental attitude.

Vivekananda demonstrated this teaching in his own life by resigning from the topmost rank of president of the whole Order to make room for his beloved brother-disciple Swami Brahmananda. And after that event he sent an attendant to the newly ordained president begging for a few petty coins needed to ferry across the Ganga. Even one of the reasons of his giving up the body was to allow smaller personalities to come up and express themselves freely. Smaller plants cannot grow around a huge banyan or a peepul tree. What a sky-high greatness Vivekananda had!

In a letter to Swami Ramakrishnananda, he expressed his deep concern over this weakness of the Indian mind: 'Let all give up party-spirit and jealousy, and unite in action. A universal religion cannot be set up through party faction…If all understand one day for one minute that he only rises whom He raises, and he falls whom He brings down, then all trouble is at an end. But there is that egotism—hollow in itself, and without the power to move a finger; how ludicrous of it to say, "I won't let anyone rise!" That jealousy, that absence of conjoint action, is the very nature of enslaved nations. But we must try to shake it off. The terrible jealousy is characteristic of us.'[38]

Swami Vivekananda had foretold that the ideas propagated by the holy organization will last for fifteen hundred years. With the far-sightedness of a seer, he could also see that this Order, in its onward march, will suffer from some setback after a few generations due to the laxity of the members to hold on to its norms. This is but natural. Even Shankaracharya has vouched for this fact in his introductory commentary to the *Bhagavad Gita*.[39]

But Vivekananda also foresaw that every downfall is immediately followed by another rise. So he gave out to posterity some practical hints as an antidote. One has nothing to fear if one holds on steadfastly to norms and rules. The choice is one's own.

End Notes

1. *Kenopanishad*, chapters 3 and 4.
2. *Bhagavatam*, 10:33:30.
3. Cf. Marie Louise Burke, *Swami Vivekananda in the West: New Discoveries*, Advaita Ashrama, Kolkata, 4th edn., June 1992, Vol. 1, p.155.
4. The *Complete Works of Swami Vivekananda*, (Hereafter CW) Advaita Ashrama, Mayavati Memorial edn., 1978, Vol.4, pp.338-39.
5. *Complete Works of Swami Vivekananda* Vol.5, pp.29.
6. The Eastern & Western Disciples, *Life of Swami Vivekananda*, (Hereafter Life) Advaita Ashrama, Vol.2, §34, p.247.
7. *Complete Works of Swami Vivekananda* Vol.3, pp.447-48.
8 *Naiṣkarmya-siddhiḥ*, Ch.4, Verse
9. *Hitopadeshaḥ*, Mitralabhaḥ, Story 1, Verse 35.
10. *Complete Works of Swami Vivekananda*, June 1977 edn.,Vol.8, pp.89-90.
11. *Complete Works of Swami Vivekananda*, March 1977 edn.,Vol.1, pp.473-74.
12. *Complete Works of Swami Vivekananda*, Vol.7, p.187.
13. Marie Louise Burke, *Swami Vivekananda in the West, New Discoveries* (Hereafter ND), Advaita Ashrama, Mayavati, Vol.6, p.216, Rhode Hammel Notes, VSNC.
14. *Complete Works of Swami Vivekananda*, Vol.4, p.356.
15. Ibid, p.357.

16. Letter to brother-disciples dt. Summer 1895. Source: Belur Math Archives.
17. *Complete Works of Swami Vivekananda*, Vol.6, p.322. [Letter to brother-disciples dt.27 April 1896]
18. *Complete Works of Swami Vivekananda*, April 2011, Vol.2, p.374.
19. *Complete Works of Swami Vivekananda*, July 1979 edn., Vol.5, p.36.
20. *Complete Works of Swami Vivekananda*, July 1979 edn., Vol.5, p.41.
21. The sentence refers to a Hindi adage: *Sirdār to sardār. Sardār* means a leader, and sir means head.
22. *Complete Works of Swami Vivekananda*, June 1979 edn., Vol.7, pp.325-26.
23. *Complete Works of Swami Vivekananda*, February 1978, Vol.6, p.135.
24. *Complete Works of Swami Vivekananda*, February 1978 edn., Vol.6, p.322.
25. *Complete Works of Swami Vivekananda*, February 1978 edn., Vol.6, p.364.
26. *Complete Works of Swami Vivekananda*, Vol.3, p.448.
27. *Complete Works of Swami Vivekananda*, January 1978 edn.,Vol.4, pp.434-36.
28. ND, Vol.6, pp.254-55.
29. Eastern and Western Disciples, *The Life of Swami Vivekananda,* Advaita Ashrama, Mayavati, Vol.2, p.569.
30. *Complete Works of Swami Vivekananda*, March 1977 edn, Vol.1, p.287.
31. *Complete Works of Swami Vivekananda*, Vol.8, p.432.
32. *Complete Works of Swami Vivekananda*, Vol.7, p.325.
33. Nikhilananda, *Holy Mother, Ramakrishna-Vivekananda Center*, New York, 2nd printing, 1982, pp.72-3.

34. *Complete Works of Swami Vivekananda*, April 1979 edn., Vol.5, p.91.

35. Vide *Ṛg-vedīya Devī Sūktam*

36. *Complete Works of Swami Vivekananda*, January 1978 edn.,Vol.4, p.368.

37. *Complete Works of Swami Vivekananda*, January 1978 edn.,Vol.4, pp.267-68.

38. *Complete Works of Swami Vivekananda*, February 1978 edn., Vol.6, pp.285-86.

39. *dīrgheṇa kālena anuṣṭātṛṛṇāṁ kāmodbhavāt hīyamānavivekavijñāna-hetukena adharmeṇa abhibhūyamāne dharme...*

Vivekananda's Catchphrase:
Love of Death

ON THE eve of his second voyage to the West in June 1899, Swami Vivekananda gave a brief but deep and meaningful speech to the young sannyasins of the Ramakrishna Order. Presenting a revolutionary definition of renunciation, his telling address set the young sannyasins thinking and bequeathed posterity a new perspective. The *Complete Works* list Vivekananda's words in Volume 3, page 446:

> There is no time to deliver a long discourse on 'Renunciation', but I shall very briefly characterise it as the love of death. Worldly people love life. The Sannyasin is to love death. Are we to commit suicide then? Far from it. For suicides are not lovers of death, as it is often seen that when a man trying to commit suicide fails, he never attempts it for a second time. What is the love of death then? We must die, that is certain; let us die then for a good cause. Let all our actions—eating, drinking, and everything that we do—tend towards the sacrifice of our self. You nourish your body by eating. What good is there in doing that if you do not hold it as a sacrifice to the

> well-being of others? You nourish your minds by reading books. There is no good in doing that unless you hold it also as a sacrifice to the whole world. For the whole world is one; you are rated a very insignificant part of it, and therefore it is right for you that you should serve your millions of brothers rather than aggrandise this little self.

At first sight, such a definition of renunciation may raise many eyebrows, as it seems divergent from the conventional view. But Vivekananda's sagacious vision only echoed the true sense of sacrifice. In order to differentiate the idea of renunciation from conventional *sannyāsa* (Sanskrit word for a life of sacrifice), Sri Krishna coined two words, *tyāga* and *sannyāsa* in the *Bhagavad Gita*, Chapter 18. Gautama Buddha exemplified in his own life what he preached—selfless service to humanity by monks. Significantly, the *Hitopadeśa*, a primer on the art of happy living, states clearly that when death is inevitable, it is better to sacrifice oneself for a noble cause. (Chapter 3, Verse 100)

What the scriptures say

Why should one love death? Death is the very antithesis of life, the negation of an affirmation. The very idea of death hits us at the core of our being, because no one seems to love his own extinction. We all like to bask in the light of life. Of the four sights that drove the young prince Gautama mad, one was the vision of death—the inevitable, unavoidable, irrefutable truth of the world. Why, then, did Vivekananda place such a 'horrible' ideal before posterity? To put the question in another way, what is the secret behind this love of death?

To answer this question, we have to recall two stories from our scriptures. One is of the prodigious Nachiketas in the *Kaṭhopaniṣad.* He went straight to the abode of the king of death and asked him in the face about the existence beyond death. The other story, narrated in the *Mahābhārata, Devī-Bhāgavata*, and *Brahmavaivarta-purana,* depicts an austere and chaste wife, Sāvitrī, following the king of death who took away the soul of her prematurely dead husband. The stories show that death, terrible as it may look to the ordinary soul, opens the secret gates of life to the truly aspiring soul with a sharp and pure intellect born out of chastity.

The two well-known stories from our scriptures reveal that even death can be encountered face to face. This point may seem hollow in the face of the alarming increase in modern times in terrorism, human bombs, suicide squads and, above all, the tendency to bring an end to life at the slightest provocation. All these clearly tell us the stories of desperate bids to stake young and innocent lives. Either through indoctrination, brainwashing, overt or covert authoritarianism, innocent people are decoyed into gory acts of violence leading to death. People with vested interests play childish games with death without knowing the grave consequences. Such people may be classified under necrophiles (lovers of death) as opposed to biophiles (lovers of life).

According to the eminent German psychologist Erich Fromm, suicidal persons nurture in their hearts revengeful motives when their self-esteem is shattered by insult or injury in any way. In contrast, the person living a productive life, even when hurt or insulted, does not feel the need to hold fast to the *lex talionis*: (law of retaliation) 'an eye for an eye, a tooth for a tooth'. (Erich Fromm, *The Heart of Man*,

Harper & Row Publishers Inc, NY, 1st Perennial Library edn, 1971, p 21)

Such examples of death encounters and experiences may be termed 'reactive violence' or 'revengeful violence' of the unproductive person.

Necrophilia

This is characteristic human behaviour patterns directed against life. Psychologically it may also be called 'death instinct.' People of this nature love to talk glibly on sickness, decay, dirt, death, burial, corpse, destruction and all such destructive things. The idea and sight of death excites them. They like to dwell in the past and brood over past deeds without launching into any tangible solution. They also like to force, control, dominate, and humiliate others just because these drives imply, according to them, killing. They have a peculiar tendency to convert even living things into inorganic, inert, mechanical objects that have no sign of life. They feel drawn to darkness, instead of light, night instead of day, death instead of life. Even people with creative genius may be plagued with this trait.

A necrophile may adopt a host of methods as handy alternatives to killing others: by denying hope to people, not recognising talents in others, being insensitive to others, shielding the beloved one against the dangers of life, deliberately humiliating others, by a studied neglect whipped at the person whom one does not like, and so on.

If man is essentially pure and beaming with life, how do such traits of 'death' instinct develop in him? There may be many reasons for this. We run the risk of developing this necrophilic attitude to life, if we grow up in bondage amid pessimistic, negative-minded, fault-finding, hyper-critical, detracting people whose main task seems to be to belittle others at any cost; we are surrounded by people who cut a poor figure with their lifeless, depressive, frightful bearing; we are forced by authority to a mechanical, routine life of rote learning; most of our energy is wasted in defending ourselves against physical and psychological attacks, that is, in fighting against starvation, poverty, deprivation, social injustice; and above all, if our freedom is threatened every now and then.

We are, then, unable to relate ourselves meaningfully to life. Some foolish people try to take a short cut to escape from life by means of either suicide or homicide. Little do they know that things are going to be worse with them and that they will have to start life again from where they left. Life is eternal and one cannot win over it just by evading it by such suicidal acts. We have to learn through experiences, mostly bitter and exacting, and come to grips with life to win the battle and be happy.

Biophilia

This means love of life and is diametrically opposite to necrophilia. It is an attitude toward life marked by a positive outlook, freedom of thought, word, and deed, controlled and organized life, sympathy for others and readiness to help with a smiling face, absence of complaint, jealousy, grievance, even under trying circumstances, and above all, a spiritual bearing. Biophilia also implies inner harmony and strength. The most remarkable feature in people of this type is that they neither want to avoid responsibility nor do they run away from trying circumstances. They utilize all opportunities for the attainment of higher values of life.

When Swami Vivekananda was in the West, he always wore a happy look. The conventional idea of the people was that a monk was a wizened ascetic with a grave face that never knows a smile. Seeing Vivekananda's appearance diametrically opposite, someone asked him, 'How do you maintain that blissful bearing under all circumstances?' The immediate reply was, 'We are the children of immortality; how can we be grave?'

Clinging to life

There is still a third kind of attitude to life, namely, a desperate attempt to hold fast to life. In Sanskrit language, this is known as *abhiniveśa.* This is nothing but existential fear born in the mind out of many painful experiences of death. Since death for an ignorant person is the opposite of life, the idea of death always threatens his existence. *Abhiniveśa* is neither necrophilia nor Biophilia. Such attitude comes to one who does not know that birth and death are like high and low tides of the same stream of eternal life. According to Indian scriptures there are six phases in life known in Sanskrit as *ṣaḍ-vikāras*—birth, existence, growth, maturity, decay, and death.

From this standpoint, death is just a change of phase. After death, the soul does not cease to exist. It takes up another body and experiences the pleasures and pains of life again. This process continues until the soul frees itself of all attachments to life and its modifications with the dawning of true knowledge.

The immense fear that is observed among people of so-called lower class is found even in learned persons. So, this clinging to life may well be termed as 'fear of death' in contrast to 'love of death.' According to Patañjali, the founder of Yoga philosophy, this inordinate fear forms one of the five 'miseries' (*kleśāḥ)* of life, and can be got rid of only in the depth of meditation as mentioned in *Patanjali Yoga Sutras*.

Evading life

There are several types among people who evade reality. One is hesitation at a distance from the battlefront. Those who are brought up in conducive surroundings, being patted on the back since childhood for every little or insignificant deed, display such a trait. Such people break in the face of the slightest challenge from the outside world. Arjuna, for one, experienced this hesitation when he realized all of a sudden that he had to fight out his beloved relatives and respected elders in the impending battle of Kurukshetra. So, he lost his wits and took shelter in Lord Krishna. All the external signs of nervousness that Arjuna developed and spoke out to Krishna point to this trait only. The first chapter of the *Bhagavad Gita* has been named *Arjuna-Viṣāda-Yoga* after the melancholy that had engulfed Arjuna then.

The next sign of evasion is marked by a detour from the mainstream of reality. This is a clever way of evading a problem which one fails to solve. This policy, popularly known as 'red herring principle,' is aimed at diverting one's attention to some other unimportant work, and rationalising such actions. Arjuna proposed a life of a recluse for himself in preference to the impending fratricide and genocide. This is one of the tricks of mental patients to hoodwink others. The symptoms characterized by migraine, high blood pressure, nervous stomach, fatigue, stuttering, and so on are clear indications in most cases about the inability of the person to cope with a problem or a situation, which leads to such ailments.

Another clear sign of such flight from reality is to assume the role of a helpless child who always wants others to do something for him. Our present-day civilization abounds with such people. Their sole motive is to wean the attention of the doctor away from the point at issue to themselves. The last technique of evasion of reality is the destruction of oneself, known commonly as 'suicide.'

Encountering death

Evasion from life is poles apart from the cool-headed encounter with death. But what will the modern man do under the circumstances, given the helpless plight enveloping him in the workaday world? Sri Ramakrishna gave a categorical answer to this great riddle of life in his inimitable way.

One day, Mani Mallick, a rich devotee from Calcutta, came to Dakshineswar straight from the cremation ground, after he finished the rites of his only son who died at a premature age. The shock being too much for the aged man to bear, he sought solace in the holy company of Sri Ramakrishna. Surrounded as usual by devotees, Sri Ramakrishna quietly listened to the hapless news without twitching a nerve, while the other devotees, in their vain efforts to console the bereaved father, waxed philosophic and reeled off sermons about the inevitability of death. Suddenly, Sri Ramakrishna went into a spiritual mood and stood up, bursting forth into a song with deep spiritual fervour. The tenor of it runs as follows:

> *To arms! To arms! Oh man, death invades thy home in battle array. Get up into the chariot of faith, and arm thyself with the quiver of wisdom. Draw the mighty bow and hurl, hurl the divine arrow, the holy name of the Mother!*

All along Sri Ramakrishna was possessed, as it were, by an inscrutable power. The song ended, and, as he calmed down, Sri Ramakrishna narrated to the devotees his own experience under similar plight. He saw his beloved nephew passing away—the soul leaving the sheath to merge in the Whole—and he felt a great joy. But when the cremators returned in the evening, with all his non-dualistic identification he felt his heart being wrung like a wet towel at the void created in the heart by the death of his nephew. So, he mused: 'If such is the condition of a person like me who is bereft of all worldly ties, what could be the depth of pain for the people of the world? In other words, Sri Ramakrishna, instead of looking down upon the poor creatures wallowing in the mire of the world, placed himself in empathy at par with the sufferer, and relieved him of his misery.

Encountering death, the terminating reality, is no child's play. It presupposes a lot of preparation and discipline. Without a good stock of spiritual weapons and shields of good past impressions called *samskāras,* this encounter ends up only in tragedy, leaving the soul at the mercy of fate. Even Swami Vivekananda, who vociferously inspired his followers to 'love death,' was at his wits' end when, during one of his earlier visits to Dakshineswar, Sri Ramakrishna 'touched' him to show the truth behind all manifestations.

Much later, he spoke out his personal experience in this way: 'With my eyes open I saw the walls and everything in the room whirling and vanishing into nothingness. The whole universe and my own individuality were at the same time almost lost in a nameless void, which swallowed up everything that is. I was terrified and believed I was face to face with death.' R Rolland records this in *The Life of Sri*

Ramakrishna published by Advaita Ashrama, Calcutta, in the eighth edition in 1970.

And as a reaction to such terrible experience of the unknown mystery of the universe, the young Naren cried out in fear. 'Oh, what are you doing? I have my parents at home.' It is true that in his later life this very fear of death was transformed into love of death. But he had miles yet to go before he reached that state.

Sri Ramakrishna used to say that grief pushes aside all such concepts as God and the like. People see their near and dear ones die helplessly defying all medical efforts. They cry pitiably, and are consoled in return by the rest of the family members or friends. They again forget about it all, wipe out their tears, and jump headlong into the world of newer attractions. But death stalks them again and takes them unawares. Very few wake up to the irrevocable reality called death. This irony of life was marked by the Pāṇḍava king Yudhiṣthira as the greatest wonder of life. In answer to a question as to what is the most astonishing fact of life, he said: 'Every day finds so many souls setting sail for the abode of death; yet those that are left behind take themselves to be immortal. What can be of a greater astonishment in life?'

Dr Viktor E Frankl, a Jewish psychologist, witnessed the gruelling experience of a day-to-day encounter with death when he was held captive along with other prisoners of war in the Nazi concentration camp during the Second World War. Each day, a number of captives would be taken to the gas chamber—a veritable abode of death. Nobody knew whose turn would come next. But even amid that bleak surrounding, Dr Frankl did not give up and went on serving people whole-heartedly, while secretly recording his everyday experience, looking straight in the face of death.

When a person realizes that everything does not come to an end with death; when he knows for certain that life is eternal and death is just a change of state like childhood, adolescence, youth, and so on, he realizes for the first time that all his experiences gathered over so many lives were just a passing show, just as a few cloudlets blown away by the wind cover the blazing sun for a while, and then resume their journey to an unknown destination. It is then that he starts seeing 'the Changeless amid all changes, the Consciousness of all conscious beings, the One amidst the many, that dispenses the desired objects to all.' (*Kaṭhopaniṣad*, 2:2:13)

Conclusion

To love God one should have a bracing attitude about life as well as death. According to the Hindu faith, God has an infinite number of forms which can be broadly classified into two groups: the benign and the terrible. Most people love to see God in a benign form, showering blessings on the devotees. But the all-renouncing monks should not stop there. One must dare to see the destructive form of God with the same calmness as he would welcome the benign aspect. The truth of it is that without being desperate and pure to the core of our being, one cannot have a complete vision of God.

Truth is immanent in everything around us. We fail to realize it due to our blocked mindset. Instead of floating on the surface of things, we must go deep into the essence to discover that everything, both sentient and insentient, is enlivened by the presence of God. Just as even dumb animals communicate with each other by various signs and gestures, similarly there is every moment a communication going on in the whole of nature—external as well as internal. If we can listen carefully to that 'still small voice' within, we can palpably feel our identity with the universe in every bit of our dealings with the outside world.

Then all the pettiness of the mind like hatred, jealousy, and selfishness, will disappear and oneness with others will automatically lead to doing good for people at every moment, at every opportunity. The by-product of such love is a calm bearing of mind and the right use of emotion which otherwise blurs our vision of truth. With that calmness even death can be faced and its secret will be revealed to us.

Vivekananda expressed this idea spontaneously in a poem entitled *Kali, the Mother*.

Who dares misery love,
And hug the form of Death,
Dance in destruction's dance,
To him the Mother comes.

The poem is available in volume 4 of the *Complete Works* on page 384; Also see *The Complete Works of Sister Nivedita*, Advaita Ashrama, Calcutta, 4th impression, Jan.1975, Vol.1, page 95.

PART 3

How to be Spiritual in Daily Life

Human Values in Stories

A MASTER and a disciple were walking a long distance in the sun. Tired beyond measure, both rested awhile under the bower of a roadside tree. Both were hungry. The master, after a careful search in his bundle, discovered a couple of coins, handed them over to the disciple, and asked him to go and fetch something from a roadside grocer's shop to appease their hunger. The disciple returned after a long time with one 5 kg bag of puffed rice in one hand and another 5 kg pot of sweetmeats in the other. His joy knew no bounds, for, a glutton as he was, it was a veritable heaven as the costly sweetmeats and cheap puffed rice were available for equal price. But the master, immediately on hearing the whole story, lifted his bundle and beckoned the disciple to follow him if he valued his own life. He could not be deceived so easily as he saw through it all and smelt a rat.

The story gives the moral that there must be the right estimation of values in human life. What is meant by value? Man does not live by bread alone. He has higher and higher needs of life. One need gets fulfilled and he strives for another.

But to get any wish fulfilled, and to hold it on lifelong, one has to pay a price. The higher and difficult the goal is, the more price is fixed for it, and the more struggle one has to undergo. This price is known as value. In spiritual context there may be innumerable values. They are like stepping stones leading to the goal of human life. Some of the higher values in human life are *ahiṁsā* (harmlessness), *satya* (truth), *asteya* (non-covetousness) and so on. The list is quite long. If anyone wants to reach the higher goals of his life, he will always have to abandon the lower goals and dwell on certain higher values. The inherent urge for higher values guides a man upward in pursuing higher goals.

Analogy and illustration

Right from the dawn of human civilization, the word 'truth' has been applied to mean God. The Upanishads never tired of eulogising truth in various terms. There are two contexts in which the word truth has been applied; one, as a means, like *satyena labhyastapasâ hyeṣa ātmā; satyameva jayate, nânṛtam*; and again, in such lines as *satyaṁ jnânamanantaṁ brahma; ṛtaṁ satyaṁ paraṁ brahma*, truth has been placed as the goal which is God Himself. Sri Ramakrishna has said that in this Kali Yuga truth is the thing one should aspire and strive for. He also said that one who always speaks truth is sitting in the lap of God. Here one may be faced with a dilemma. Is truth a quality or a state?

The answer is, it is both. This means that in order to attain the goal of life, which is truth, one has to be truthful in his pursuit. In fact, the use of the same word truth to mean the goal as well as the path is an age-old tradition in the Indian spiritual context. If you practise truthfulness as a way to become perfect, after reaching perfection, you will not behave untruthfully. You cannot help being truthful. This was uniquely represented in the teachings of Sri Ramakrishna such as, 'An expert dancer never makes a wrong step.'

According to the Vedic seers, truth has two dimensions; one is the absolute and the other is the relative. The absolute dimension is expressed as harmony and peace everywhere, and is called *ṛtam* in Sanskrit. The relative dimension has five levels of existence: physical, vital, mental, intellectual, and blissful. In each of these five levels, truth expresses itself in a particular way.

For example, when we live in the physical level, the truth relating to our body holds good, and trimming and grooming the body, survival of the fittest are the laws of truth prevalent there. When we dwell on the pranic level, the former truth becomes less significant and some higher form of truth corresponding to the higher level expresses itself. We become more concerned with the subtle forces working in and around us. In this way, as we go higher, the lower levels of truth become relegated, or even cease to function in us. Such relative truths are called *satyam*. When we say *satyameva jayate, nânṛtam*, we must know that it is spoken of both the absolute and relative truths expressed in the phenomenal existence.

Sometimes we find that the truth that holds good under a particular circumstance does not do so under a different condition. This anomaly in truth need not unsettle our understanding. It will just suffice if we know that the levels of understanding in the two cases were different. If we want to find our truth we must not stop anywhere on the road until we reach the final truth. If, on the other hand, we become amazed by the glamorous truths of the lower level, our growth will become stunted there. This fact has been graphically exemplified in the following story given in the *Chhandogya Upanishad.*

Once Prajāpati, the creator god, uttered these words to demonstrate the Self: 'It is free from sin, old age, death, sorrow, hunger and thirst. One must seek for this Self and know it in depth. The person who has known the Self attains all worlds and all desires.' Hearing such inspiring words, his two disciples, Indra and Virochana, the chiefs of the gods and demons felt fascinated as both of them had the desire to win all the worlds. So, they approached Prajāpati, the creator god, with humility, and requested him to teach the secret of the Self. Prajāpati acceded to the proposal and made them observe chastity for thirty-two years as a preliminary discipline.

After that rigorous discipline, one day he suddenly enquired, 'Why are you here? What do you want?' Both the disciples replied, 'We are here to know the truth of the Self.' Then Prajāpati only said, 'That which is seen in the eyes is the Self. This Self is immortal and fearless. It is Brahman.'

The disciples asked, 'Sir, what is that which we see when we look into the clear water or in a mirror?' Prajāpati replied, 'The Self is seen in all these. Look at your image in a vessel full of water. What do you see?' 'We see the reflection of ourselves,' they replied. 'Now go and dress yourselves well with fineries and come here.'

They did so, and then again at Prajāpati's bidding they looked at their reflection and found their images also adorned. Prajapati expected that the disciples would wake up to a serious thought after seeing the change in their reflections. But none of them was pure enough to call forth that question from within.

So he said, 'That is the immortal Self called Brahman.' He saw that the students' capacity of understanding, that is known in modern times as IQ, did not come to the right standard. So he did not proceed further. This was typically the Indian traditional system of teaching in days of yore. The teacher won't launch into a deeper study until the student evoked the query from within. So in this case the students became satisfied and wended their way home. The teacher smiled. He said to himself, 'If they construe the teaching in this way by taking this body as the be-all and end-all of life, they will be lost.'

And it actually happened with Virochana, the king of demons. He went back to his own people and spread the message: 'The body is the Self; so take care of this body as much as you can.' Thus the demons, in their pursuit of Self-knowledge, ended up in taking care of and nourishing the body only, leaving aside all ideas of sacrifice and austerity. Even today if a person does not have charity, feeling for others, respect for superiors, he is looked upon as a demon.

But Indra did not feel satisfied with the answer. Some doubt arose in his mind as to the changing nature of the body. So he again went back to the teacher and humbly approached him with his question. The great teacher became pleased. He bade the disciple observe chastity for another thirty-two years. Thereafter, one day he gave his sermon, 'The Self experienced in the Dream State is the real Self.' Indra became once again seemingly satisfied and set out on his return journey. But no! Soon he realized he did not get the right answer. His analytic mind, made still purer by virtue of chastity, was repelled.

Again he approached the teacher, and this time also he was welcomed with a prerequisite of thirty-two more years of pure life. When the period came to a close, the teacher gave him even a subtler truth. He said that the Self in deep sleep is the real Self. But even that answer did not dispel Indra's doubts forever. So he again returned to the teacher, and completed five more years of living in the holy company of the guru. At long last the guru was pleased with his disciple's insatiable thirst for the highest knowledge. So he gave his final sermon on the untainted, immutable truth.

There are so many things happening before our eyes in our day-to-day life. We seldom take care of them. From our very childhood we are used to hear innumerable stories. How few among us can take the right lesson to improve our way of life? Here lies the strong line of demarcation between the common man and a prophet. A great soul is he who can take lessons from the most commonplace happenings of his daily life. This is particularly so since God is immanent in everything, according to Vedantic teaching.

When the one and the many are not different, every expression in nature must be speaking of God alone. In the Vedic age, our rishis saw that universal harmony everywhere around and named it *ṛtam*. They took lessons from everything and learned to live in communion with nature. Their daily experiences served them as divine commands. He is the truly wise person who can transform even the most mundane experience as an impetus to rise higher in spiritual life. Śaṅkarācārya was one such seer; so was Ramana Maharshi; and more so was Sri Ramakrishna. That is why they could give so apt examples connected with life to illustrate such intricate truths of the spiritual world. One becomes astonished to think how spontaneously these people arrived at a great truth from even the most commonplace examples of life. A seer or prophet is he who can convert the most crude, banal worldly topic into the highest spiritual discussion. Contrarily, the worldly person pulls down even the spiritual chats to the mundane level.

Search for truth

The purer the capacity of our understanding, the higher the truth we realize. Our pursuit of truth depends on our degree of understanding. But all the same, we should not stop searching for truth. How should we conduct our search for truth? Our teachers say that the search should be steadfast and one-pointed. According to Swami Vivekananda we should 'stop not till the goal is reached.' After we achieve an immediate goal, we should launch the next search for a higher goal. This way it will go on till we arrive at the ultimate goal of life. Depending on the bearings of each individual the immediate goals may vary, but the final goal remains the same for all.

Sri Ramakrishna used to tell a beautiful story about the pursuit of truth:

> A poor woodcutter earned his livelihood by chopping wood in the deep forest. Once on his way to the woods he met a holy man, who learnt that the poor fellow could hardly keep the wolf from his door. He took pity on the simple woodcutter and, before leaving when the poor man sought holy advice from him, he only said, 'My child, go forward; don't stop until you've reached the goal.'

The words worked a miracle for the woodcutter. The next

day he felt inclined to go deeper into the woods. As he did so, he found himself in a forest of sandalwood trees. He was overjoyed. That fetched him a fortune and his condition improved. But again, after some time he remembered, 'Why, the holy man didn't ask me to stop. Let me go deeper in the forest tomorrow.' He mustered up courage, set out for a journey into the unknown on the very next morning.

The new venture brought him before a mine of silver. His joy knew no bounds. He became richer and mentally thanked the holy man for the valuable advice. Some time passed in this way. Then again some force from within prodded him to embark on a deeper search as he remembered the holy man's advice. This time he crossed the inaccessible depths and found a gold mine. His financial status also grew by leaps and bounds. But no! The holy man's advice kept ringing in his ears and gave him no rest. So again he launched another search and went forward to find thereafter diamond mines, and so on. Think of the amount of wealth the poor woodcutter amassed by following the simple advice of the holy man—'Go forward.'

It should be kept in mind that this story is told on the pursuit of truth and not of riches as the story may suggest. Even in the competitive world the law of truth operates. For instance, if one wants to earn money, one must know the secrets of it—how to go ahead of others in competition and so on. It won't do just to step aside from the competitive field and look forward to God's grace saying it is bad to elbow out others by immoral means.

In short, in each level of existence the corresponding truth comes into operation and you have either to live it through or just ignore it in order to go to a higher level. This seldom happens. Most of us become jealous of others' achievements and blame either God or our stars for all the misfortune or failure. So, when it is said, 'Truth alone triumphs,' the word truth should be construed as 'truth for a particular level of understanding.' If we know this secret we will never blame God for our failures and will know decidedly that anybody who really seeks truth gets it.

Ahiṁsā or harmlessness

Another high value of human life is *ahiṁsā*, which means complete absence of harmful thoughts with respect to others. It is a common observation that we do not have ill feeling towards others as long as we are not harmed. It is like a condition set by us. So long as things go well, even a coward can evince spectacular feats of *ahiṁsā* towards others. But that is not the test of real harmlessness. Harmlessness is a very difficult practice, indeed.

In this world there are people who practise the great quality *ahiṁsā*. Why should we not do harm to others even when they do so to us? The great Buddha gave a most fitting reply. He said, 'Because anger cannot win over anger; fire cannot extinguish fire.' By doing harm to others as a tit-for-tat policy, we only perpetuate sorrow in this world. When Jesus Christ said, 'If someone slaps you on your left cheek, produce the other cheek also,' he pointed to the practice of this great quality of harmlessness.

From the Vedantic standpoint, by doing harm to others we actually do harm to ourselves only; because the Self is immanent in all beings. Great souls come from time to time to teach us this great truth in various ways. They strive their utmost to bring about peace and harmony everywhere in nature since they know it only too well that the state of harmony and peace is the original state of equilibrium in nature, which has to be re-established from time to time.

When the Buddha was a young boy, his father sent him and his cousin brother to expert teachers for learning archery, weaponry, among other aggressive things. Gautama learnt it all appreciably well in a very short time, but refused to aim at any living being. One day, as he was resting in the royal garden lost in his own thoughts, suddenly he got startled to hear the fluttering of the wings of a poor bird pierced by an arrow shot by his cousin brother.

Gautama spared no time in treating the wounded bird which slowly recovered due to the loving motherly care of Gautama. In the meantime, the cousin came running with the bow and arrows in his hand and found the game bird he was seeking so long ensconced comfortably in the cosy lap of Gautama. In an angry mood, the boy demanded the bird which he shot. But Gautama calmly refused, saying that the poor creature took shelter in him, so he would protect the bird at all costs. The cousin went post-haste to king Shuddhodana, Gautama's father and sought justice. Gautama was also summoned. Defending his point, Gautama asked his father, 'Who has the right to keep the bird, father, one who tries to take its life, or one who saves its life?' The great king was bewildered and had to give his verdict in favour of his son.

The next story is from the life of Sri Ramakrishna. He was then working as a priest in the Kali temple of Dakshineswar. By virtue of his unfathomable spiritual bearing he was held in high esteem by Mathuranath Biswas, the son-in-law of Rani Rasmani. Rich as he was, Mathuranath spared no pains to keep Sri Ramakrishna comfortable and would not pay the least heed to the useless complaints of the detractors against Sri Ramakrishna. This made many other priests of the temple jealous of him. They thought the young priest of Kali temple must have cast a magic spell on Mathuranath. One evening, as Sri Ramakrishna was sitting alone, lost in the thought of Divine Mother in a semi-ecstatic mood, another old priest came to him and started pushing him from behind, saying, 'Tell me, you devil of a priest, what spell you have cast on the Babu!' Absorbed as he was in that mood, Sri Ramakrishna could hardly hear any word and continued to be silent. This infuriated the priest who, impatient with the silence of Sri Ramakrishna, kicked him hard and left the place in a hurry.

The pain of the kick awoke Sri Ramakrishna who came back to the worldly plane and found the priest running away. What was his reaction to that sort of atrocity? He kept mum over the whole matter, knowing fully well that once Mathuranath came to know of it he would not only sack the poor priest but might even kill him in a fit of anger. This was one of the prominent examples of Sri Ramakrishna's quality to forgive and practise harmlessness. We can forgive others only when we harbour no ill feeling against the other person.

This harmlessness is a quality to be practised by those who want to achieve the higher goals of life as human beings. Like other austerities, harmlessness is also to be exercised even in the mental plane. It will not do just to keep from killing animals for the sake of enjoyment. We must also learn how to keep ourselves completely free from even harmful thoughts about others. Before we do any harm to others physically, the wave comes in the mind taking the form of harmful thought. This has to be recognized and nipped in the bud long before it comes to the surface. When one gets completely established in deactivating harmful thoughts even in a seed state, one is said to be perfect in the practice of *ahiṁsā.*

Patañjali in his Yoga aphorisms has clearly given the result of being perfect in the pursuit of such higher values of life as *ahiṁsā, satya, asteya, brahmacharya, aparigraha, śaucha, santoṣa*, and others. According to him, even wild and ferocious animals lose their aggressiveness against sworn enemies when they come in proximity of one who has perfected himself in *ahiṁsā.* Tailanga Swami, the great saint from Andhra, who was a master in Hatha-Yoga, lived in the deep forest in order to keep away from the company of worldly people.

One day, a king entered the forest in a hunting spree and shot a tiger. But the wounded tiger disappeared behind the woods. The king chased it hard and suddenly found the game sitting before a sage in a mood of surrender and whining. The sage was lovingly touching the tiger's whole body with his hand. As the king's presence diverted the sage's attention, he rebuked the king for his cruel act and bade him to give up killing animals just for pleasure. The perplexed king fell at his feet and went back with a full heart.

Swami Samartha Ramadasa was also a soul of great spiritual achievements. He was so established in harmlessness that animals, both meek and ferocious, used to sit around him quietly in the deep forest. It was Shivaji who discovered him in such a condition in the forest and realized that the holy man was the fittest person to become his guru.

Epilogue

Right from the Vedic period the style of exemplifying and story-telling has come down to us. In the Vedas the absolute truth has been preached in various ways and approached from various angles. The infinite, ultimate Reality cannot be limited by saying that it is of such and such pattern. Our rishis were great enough to give a comprehensive idea of the Reality. In the earlier parts of the Vedas, there are so many sacrifices mentioned. These aim at bringing about certain results. In the later part of the Vedas, it is mentioned that those sacrifices are also part and parcel of truth but there is a higher truth than that, and the Vedas proceeded to depict that higher truth. This way they went on showing the aspirant higher and higher paths for the ultimate Truth.

Once we reach the higher truth, the lower truth becomes insignificant. Suppose you are ascending a hill and on the way met with a sudden and heavy storm. You struggle hard to get over that and with great effort succeed in reaching the summit where the fury of the storm is not felt. Standing there, you observe the raging storm, ready to uproot the trees below. Perhaps you will enjoy the beauty of the scene so happily from atop the hill. But just a few moments ago you felt so afraid when you were taken over by the storm.

This is exactly what we feel when we reach the higher goals of life. From the higher pedestal, we observe other people floundering and suffering in agony in the lower levels of existence. We feel great compassion and perhaps stretch out our hands to help them. But we never criticize them for their folly, because we vividly remember our struggles under that condition.

In the *Bhagavad Gita* it has been clearly mentioned in the third chapter that the really wise man should not create unsettlement of understanding in people who are engaged in action with attachment. Rather, the wise men should engage themselves in detached actions to set an example before those people.

The Vedas and the Upanishads speak of the Absolute Truth in various ways. For ordinary people it is difficult to conceive those subtle ideas. The compassionate rishis knew this very well. That is why from time to time they formulated such stories as the *Ramayana* or the *Mahabharata* or the Puranas which convey certain truths or higher values of life in concrete form. This is just to show the people of lower understanding that those ideals and truths are translatable in human life and practicable. This is why, not only in India but the world over, people hold the *Ramayana* and the *Mahabharata* in such high esteem. Higher truths have value to the common people only when they can be brought to the ordinary plane of existence.

Pray to God that we had many more such stories to invigorate us and make us proud of our ourselves, the nation and the world.

Old Is Cold Or Gold?

SINCE THE mid-seventeenth century a Greek word, euthanasia, was coined, and absorbed later in the English language. Euthanasia is a painless way of bringing about death. When people suffer from terminal and painful diseases, this process may be used to relieve them of all suffering forever. In earlier days, it used to be chiefly applied to old or injured pet animals to end their suffering. But in recent times, an alarmingly increasing number of the populace has started choosing euthanasia, the largest percentage of them being old people.

Ugly beautification campaigns

Newspapers and journals often give an account of the horrible consequences that follow surgical operations like liposuction, eyelid surgery, plastic surgery and other procedures resorted to by people, desperate to look good, and stay young and attractive. Despite the dangers, including untimely deaths during or after surgery, the cosmetic industry is booming.

The craze for looking young even in old age is prevalent

in countries the world over. The older generation join the younger ones in their exhibitionism, as is evident in parks and sidewalks of cities. They want to shun old age. But with all their honest attempts, old age stalks them and pounces upon them with its sinister effects when the time comes.

With the invasion of such frivolity people depend on false values and eventually end up feeling lonely and uncared for. Is not death a better alternative to such unbearable suffering?

The king-turned-sage Bhartṛhari has given a picturesque account of the plight of man under such helpless conditions. In his *One Hundred Verses on Detachment* he says: 'The face is attacked with lines of wrinkle, the head is painted grey, the limbs become loose, yet thirst alone gets rejuvenated!' [verse 8]

Is old age the greatest curse of human life? After working like a machine all through youth is it all the reward man deserves? Should he die in the harness like a spent, worn-out bullock? Is there no way out of this predicament? Can one not live happily at the fag-end of one's life to say boldly in the tenor of Swami Vivekananda: 'I am glad I was born, glad I suffered so, glad I made big blunders, glad to enter peace.'(*Complete Works*, volume 6, page 432)

Before we try to find out plausible answers to these important questions, we must probe why humans fear old age.

Causes of aversion

Every child makes a hero of his father or any other familiar 'big guy' and dreams of the day when he himself will reach that age of maturity to boss over others. The child grows up through adolescence and youth to a mature adult. His responsibilities increase, he starts tasting the bitter and sweet fruits of life and his childhood dreams shatter. He starts wishing he had never grown old. Why does he feel so?

The first reason is the fear of responsibility. With advanced age man has to wield more and more responsibility. To grow old is not just to have some extra rights but to understand and recognize others' rights too. Most adults like to pass the buck to others with one or the other excuse whenever their authority is questioned. With the dawn of adulthood man starts experiencing, along with the bright side of life, the dark faces of it also. He starts getting glimpses of the results of his past actions, which he should rather not have done. There goes a sardonic Sanskrit verse—'Man wants to enjoy the result of virtuous actions but refrains from exercising them; on the other hand, he does not like to suffer the consequences of his bad actions; yet he deliberately and arduously engages himself in evil actions.' This is a paradox of human life leading to tragedy in advanced age.

The second reason is non-acceptance of the sixfold changing system called life. Hindu philosophy defines life as a constantly flowing stream with six phases: birth, existence, growth, maturity, decay, and death. If we accept birth, we have to accept the other five also. Generally speaking, this seldom happens. We rejoice at birth but cannot bear the sight of demise of our near and dear ones. Likewise, when we grow old, instead of accepting it as a passing phase we desperately shun it and try to look young with make up or a facelift. But mere avoidance or pretence cannot rid us of the cold clutch of a truth. King Yudhiṣthira defined this truth as the strangest fact. In reply to the question of a demi-god (*yakṣa*) he said: 'A large number of people go to the abode of death every day, while those who are still left behind feel they are immortal. What can be a stranger fact?'

The third reason is the fear of insecurity. In old age, man feels helpless like a newborn child. He feels the earth is slipping below his feet. He feels lonely, and more so when he is either a widower or a divorcee. And whenever man is lonely and helpless, he is simultaneously assailed by the spectre of his many unknown and forgotten faces which he carefully repressed so long with the quackish antidote of workaholism. This feeling of loneliness gives rise to monotony and laziness. In order to avoid this, man has devised certain techniques of killing time aimlessly.

Sri Ramakrishna poignantly speaks of this tendency of old people to while away their energy in his characteristic simple style: 'The bound souls never think of God. If they get any leisure they indulge in idle gossip and foolish talk, or they engage in fruitless talk. If you ask one of them the reason, he answers, "Oh, I cannot keep still; so I am making a hedge." When time hangs heavy on their hands they perhaps start playing cards.' (*The Gospel of Sri Ramakrishna*, Red letter edn, Feb. 2000, page 87)

The fourth reason is the inability to hold on to one's higher identity. Man has to assert his true identity under all circumstances. He can seek his higher identity to find there all security and shelter. But ironically enough, most people never attempt to do this and instead seek justice from the unjust world. It needs extraordinary courage and manliness to seek solace in one's higher self in times of trouble, not to speak of persisting in finding God within oneself.

As a fifth reason it can be said that the desire for enjoyment of life sneaks out of youth and adulthood into old age. Sage Patañjali calls it *bhogavāsanā*. It is compared to the flaming tongues of fire which will never get satiated and go on increasing in strength with more objects of enjoyment. The *Viṣṇu-purāṇa* records such a statement supposed to have been uttered by king Yayāti at the fag end of his life of sensual enjoyment. Said he: 'Desire can never be satiated by enjoyment; like oblation poured into the fire-flame, it goes on increasing indefinitely.'

The solution

Old age comes slowly and imperceptibly into our life. In the vanity of youth people often forget that all of them are inevitably going to experience that state called old age. So, people should learn to live in the present. Most of the time we live either in the past or plan for the future. To live in the present one must practise mindfulness every moment of life. Being mindful is to be aware of a continuous state of consciousness. Besides, if we want to rectify our misdeeds or mistakes in the past or to make a glorious future, we can do it at the very present moment. Postponing things for the future is not the sign of a mature personality. To learn to live in the present, we should take a cue from American poet Henry Wadsworth Longfellow's poem *A Psalm of Life*:

Trust no Future, howe'er pleasant!
Let the dead Past bury its dead!
Act, ——act in the living Present!
Heart within, and God o'erhead!

We can conquer all, including old age by being a lover of God. As Brother Lawrence has put it, practise the presence of God.

In order to practise this, the first task is to chuck the old bogey of worry for the past or future. Dr Norman Vincent Peale has personified worry in his unique style of fantasy in his book, *The New Art of Living*, first published by William Heinemann Ltd in 1987: 'He has sunken cheeks and a shifting, anxious look in his deep-set eyes. He is a cadaverous old fellow with icy fingers and a cold, clammy breath. He is sitting there with you even though he knows how you abhor him. You have allowed him to think he is your master, and he exercises his authority to the full. After a while you will go to bed and the old fellow will shamble into your bedroom with you. He will sit there and keep you awake for a long time, and after a troubled sleep, when you awaken in the morning, the first thing to greet you will be the sardonic face of Old Man Worry.'

In the second place, we must learn to accept the changes of life. From the cradle to the funeral pyre, life is a state of continuous changes. If we live every phase of our life mindfully by utilising the opportunities in each phase then all our vanity of youth and contempt of old age will hang its head in shame. Keeping in mind this fact of inevitability of all the six phases of life Buddha said, 'The vanity of youth should be conquered by the thought of old age.'

This never means that one should become a hardcore pessimist. Facts of life must be accepted as they are, without a tinge of worry for any personal loss or gain. Śrī Śankarācārya has put this idea graphically in his celebrated hymn, *Śivāparādha-kṣamāpaṇa-stotram*: 'O Lord, with the passage of time the life shortens and youth decays; days gone never come back—time is the all-devourer; fortune is as fickle as the ripples on the water and life is momentary like the lightning. Therefore, Thou refuge of all! Protect me who seeks refuge in Thee.' (Verse 13)

The sense of security in old age can be restored in three

ways: i) by developing a mature outlook on life ii) by learning to face all situations in life, and iii) by making genuine friends.

The first, maturity in life lies in the art of living with others as also with oneself. Society turns its back upon the aging person who is no more capable of keeping pace with fast-moving society. Under such situations instead of getting affected, the senior person should explore higher dimensions of his personality. The history of the world bristles with people who, in their sixties, seventies, or eighties, have not only contributed richly to the world's culture but also have cultivated sufficient awareness and interest in their inner world to make their life a delight.

By the time a man is sixty, he must know about his reserved source or treasury in the depth of his being, his capacities and limitations. Again, to a mature person success is not synonymous with happiness. His happiness does not wax or wane with public applause or calumny, monetary income or loss. He also knows that beyond his body and mind there is another existence that endures beyond death.

The second way to face life is to escape from fear. The eminent English novelist Gilbert Keith Chesterton (1894-1936), when asked to say something clever if not wise, said, 'If I had only one sermon to preach, it would be a sermon against fear.' Fear is the very negation of one's existence. In the *Complete Works*, volume 3, you will find that Swami Vivekananda, who was never tired of speaking of strength of the soul, of strength which finds repeated occurrence in the Upaniṣads, said, 'The moment you fear, you are nobody.'

Fear can best be dispelled by facing the cause of it boldly. Everything in this world is fraught with fear. Man has financial fear, fear of ill health, old age, unknown future, and what not. Bhartṛhari comes to suggest a solution to all fears in a celebrated verse of the *Vairāgya-śatakam*: 'In enjoyment there is the fear of illness, in vanity of lineage the fear of fall, in wealth the fear of the hostile king; in honour the fear of humiliation; in power the fear of enemies; in beauty, the fear of old age; in scholarship, the fear of opponents; in virtue, the fear of scandal-mongers; in body, the fear of death. Indeed everything in the world is fraught with fear; detachment alone is without a tinge of fear.' (Verse 31)

The third way of restoring security in old age is by making friends, which besides being an art of living, is a great help to aging people who want to keep loneliness at arm's length. It is not merely an art but also a wonderful science of analysing human nature. Each individual is of a particular bent and the process of friendship implies an interpersonal relationship in which one's own ego gets less priority. All through the history of the world there was never a time when kindness, unselfishness, and consideration for others were not considered essential qualities.

Almost all the religions preach the same truth to mankind, namely, doing good to others. To cite a few examples, the Purāṇas say, 'Do not do to others what you wouldn't like to be done to yourself.' The *Bible (St. Matthew 7:12)* says, 'All things whatsoever ye would that men should do to you, do ye even so to them.' Confucious says, 'What you do not wish done to yourself, do not do to others.' Mohammed says, 'A man's true wealth is the good he does in this world.' Again, in the *Old Testament* we find: 'Thou shalt love thy neighbour as thyself.' Swami Vivekananda coordinated all these and said aphoristically, 'Unselfishness is more paying, only people have not the patience to practise it.'

For man to discover and hold on to his higher identity, he must understand himself in the right perspective, and be able to listen to his inner voice, his inner feelings. This means that he must identify and evaluate his emotions correctly. When man is overpowered by feelings of frustration and anger, the general tendency is to suppress these emotions for fear of social calumny. But the emotions boomerang on him when he is at home and he vents them on the family members.

This happens due to the denial of those drives. That is why it is suggested that one should go to a solitary place from time to time and listen to one's inner voice. Above all, this 'holding on to the higher human dimension or God' paves the way for deep faith. Man boldly continues his spiritual journey amidst the encircling gloom with redoubled enthusiasm and vigour. With the dawn of faith his fear leaves him once and for all. Swami Vivekananda expresses this idea in the lines of his famous poem entitled *In Search of God* published in volume 7 of the *Complete Works.*

When dire calamity seizes me
The heart seems weak and faint,
All nature seems to crush me down
With laws that never bend,
Meseems I hear Thee whispering sweet
My love, 'I am near, I am near,'
My heart gets strong, with Thee my love
A thousand deaths no fear....

Growing old gracefully

Old age is the fulfilment and consummation of life. With age comes wisdom and understanding. Man actually starts living after sixty. Youth is dominated by unconscious drives.

People feel they are enjoying life while the fact is that they are being enjoyed by nature. The delusion that youth, beauty and virility are meant for enjoyment gets shattered sooner than expected. It is only after sixty that man starts to become clearly aware of the forces acting in and out of him. At that age though the body is not suited for violent exercises, man can enjoy health much better than in youth; though the peak performance of work no more remains, the mind continues to be sound. And the beauty of character emerges more shiningly from the mature person than the beauty of youth from youngsters.

In the field of learning the desire for more and deeper knowledge replaces the youth's uncritical thirst for learning. The mind, intellect, emotion, and will start coordinating each other in a harmonious way. Spiritual far-sightedness grows in old people, resulting in wisdom, peace of mind, and a high degree of tolerance. The faculty of true love can now be exercised as completely divorced from the idea of sex and as an expression of the unity of all existence. As a logical consequence, detachment widens the horizon of love to one and all.

History abounds with examples of very old people with excellent intellectual powers. A few of them are cited here: The sons of Sophocles tried to move the court against him declaring him incompetent when he was ninety. But the old man refuted the charge by reading to the judges from the fresh manuscript of his latest tragedy, *Oedipus at Colonus,* and the sons were rebuked by the judge for their action.

The blind musician George Frideric Handel composed his *Messiah* at 74. Cornaro wrote a treatise on life and death when he was ninety-five. Michelangelo Buonarroti, the great Italian artist-architect-poet (1475-1564), was still producing masterpieces at eighty-nine. Johann Wolfgang von Goethe, the German poet-cum-dramatist (1749-1832), completed the second part of *Faust* when he was eighty-two. Longfellow was still writing immortal poetry after he was seventy.

Walter Pitkin pointed out in his book *Life Begins At Forty* that nine-tenths of the world's best work has been done by older people, well past their prime. Apart from these, examples are not lacking where people master languages, start a new venture at a quite ripe age. It is relevant to quote a few lines from Marcus Tullius Cicero, one of the greatest orators and statesmen of Rome, who wrote at the ripe age of eighty-four in one of his most enduring works, *de Senectute*, in the following refrain:

> As I like a young man in whom there is something of the old, so I like an old man in whom there is something of the young; and he who follows this maxim will possibly be an old man in body, but he will never be an old man in mind. Intelligence, reflection, and judgement reside in old men...Age, especially an honoured old age, has so great authority that this is of more value than all the pleasures of the youth. Old age is the consummation of life, just as of a play...The harvest of old age is the recollection and abundance of blessings previously secured.

Man cannot hold back his chronological age, but he can very well hold on to his spirit at all costs. No one can snatch away his spirit from him unless he himself wills it.

Conclusion

To make life a success and worth living, the family and society, whenever necessary, must lend a helping hand. The 'good Samaritans' should be around to demonstrate that old age is not a liability but rather an asset. The mature elder must also learn to bear pain and suffering. Father Eugene C Kennedy, in his book *The Pain of Being Human,* points out very clearly this aspect of life. Decrying the need for tranquilizers or drugs to reduce physical pain, he says:

> There is a place in life for the experience of pain, not for its own sake, but because it burns the dross off a man in a way that nothing else can. Man estranged from pain will hardly be the figure we have known all through history. He will be like a child overmedicated against the infant diseases so that he never builds up a strong inner immunity against them; the man who never learns to live with pain only makes himself more vulnerable to it. I am not defending the large measure of unnecessary suffering that is found everywhere in life…I refer to the inevitable sufferings of life, the pains that shape our existence, the pains that must be faced because they cannot be fended off.

Millions of dollars are being spent by people all over the world after masseurs, beauty experts, plastic surgeons and others in the desperate bid to look young. Old people should rather learn the secrets of growing old gracefully. The leisure gaps of old age should be filled up with creative hobbies, mature counselling to youngsters on their asking, and innocent jokes. And above all, the ceaseless practice of the presence of God in the core of our being can make our life a precious jewel.

One point must always be remembered. True, old is not cold but gold; but as pure gold has to be blended with a modicum of dross, that is, base metal, to make it usable, so also the vigour and enthusiasm of youth must be mixed in right proportion with the wisdom and maturity of old age. Neither should old people boast of their superiority nor should the youth sneer at senescence. Don't the sweet waters of all rivers become saline on merging with the ocean? The ocean is the father and the river the son, though both are recognized by the common name 'water.' They are the two phases in the same cycle.

Forgive and Forget

RĀVAṆA, STRICKEN with grief at the death of his son Indrajeet at the hands of Lakhḥsmaṇa, appeared in battle array before Rāma to settle the issue. But the mental shock made him tired and weak. This did not elude the eyes of Rāma. The embodiment of mercy that he was, Rāma ordered his arch-rival, who abducted his beloved wife Sītā, to go back and rest until he regained his strength and vigour, and then come back for the decisive battle. This was an example of forgiving the enemy. The brave kings of yore were said to possess this distinct, legendary quality of forgiveness.

In striking contrast, in a fierce battle between Arjuna and Karṇa, when the wheel of Karṇa's chariot stuck in the mud, he begged of Arjuna for a few moments of cease-fire. Arjuna wanted to comply, but Śrī Kṛṣṇa instigated and prodded him to vanquish the enemy at that unguarded condition. The outcome is known to all. Karṇa succumbed to the fatal injury on his back. In other words, forgiveness was not accorded to Karṇa.

Śrīmad Bhāgavatam narrates the story of king Parikṣit,

the descendant of the Pāṇḍava clan. Once he went out on a hunting spree in a forest. After a wild chase he became tired and overcome with thirst and hunger. A while later he espied a hermitage in which the sage Śamīka was sitting, lost in ecstasy. The king's repeated calls met with no response. Impatient with the sage, the king collected a dead snake from the vicinity, hung it round the neck of the meditating sage, and left the place in a huff.

The sage had a young son who had gone outdoors on an errand. On his return he was grieved to see the humiliating sight. Meanwhile, his father came back to normal consciousness and innocently asked the reason for his son's wrath. When his son angrily told him of the king's offence, sage Śamīka only stuck to the noble virtue of forgiveness. But before the father could warn him, the enraged son had spat out his curse: 'The king will no more see the light of the earth after seven days. He will be fatally bitten by a venomous snake.' Here the father forgave but the son did not. The author of the *Bhāgavatam* beautifully depicted and concluded this epoch-making event in just a couple of verses with these comments:

iti putrakṛtāghena so'nutapto mahāmuniḥ /
svayam viprakṛto rājñā naivāghaṁ tadacintayat //
prāyaśaḥ sādhavo loke parairdvandveṣu yojitāḥ /
na vyathanti na hṛṣyanti yata ātmā'guṇāśrayaḥ //

Thus the sage regretted on hearing the enraged curse of his son; yet he never dwelt on the wrong done to him by the king (Parikṣit). It is quite frequent that in this world there are holy men who do not feel miserable or happy at the contradictory behaviours from others. To them the *ātman* is free from all attributes of nature or *prakṛti. (Bhāgavatam 1:8:49,50)*

Sri Ramakrishna's shadow companion Hriday had served him a lot. But in later days, he became puffed up with vanity and every now and then hurled insolent comments at Sri Ramakrishna. Once the offence crossed the limit of his tolerance. Yet Sri Ramakrishna reviled him not. Months later, as ill luck would have it, Hriday incurred the wrath of the temple authority on some other ground and was dismissed from the temple forever. One day, a repentant Hriday came to his senses and went to Dakshineswar to meet Sri Ramakrishna. As he was refused entry in the temple precincts, Sri Ramakrishna himself went to the gate and asked about his welfare. The poor repentant Hriday fell flat at his feet, crying aloud. Sri Ramakrishna consoled him, and in mercy his eyes also became flooded with tears. In other words, he forgave his tormentor.

These stories are outstanding examples of forgiveness while others are exceptions. These examples give rise to certain pertinent questions. To put it in the poet's language: 'to forgive or not to forgive; that is the question.' Our great epics and scriptures must guide us in the way of living. And in all our interpersonal dealings one of the important points is, 'when to forgive and when not.' These apparently conflicting stories may confuse us. At times in our life, we forgive others; but they revile us in return. Naturally the question comes: should we have rather not forgiven? Was it a mistake to forgive?

The phrase 'forgive and forget' has, of late, become almost a cliché. Most parents, with a view to settling certain issues, and in fear of losing peace, advise their children to 'forgive and forget.' But ironically enough, when their turn comes to forgive and forget, they miserably fail to hold aloft their maxim.

Why we fail to forgive

The first reason for failing to forgive is man's weakness. Weak persons can never forgive others. Within their hearts they nurture the deep-seated sense of deprivation. To forgive others one has to be stronger than others. Vivekananda said that only that person who can hit back, has the capacity to forgive. This was precisely the reason why he was so vociferous on developing inner strength first. His concept of education was to restore the lost confidence to the race. For a weakling the only logical course of action will be to grudge, backbite, or complain perpetually.

A young man once approached Vivekananda and divulged his desire to become a monk. Seeing his emaciated structure, Vivekananda understood his incapability; so he asked, 'Can you tell lies? Can you steal?' These scandalised boy answered in the negative, at which Vivekananda said, 'You must become strong enough to do these acts deliberately before you think of coming to monastic life.' In other words, he insisted that strength, and not weakness, should be the prerequisite to monastic life.

The second reason for failing to forgive is the deep-seated feeling of hatred for others. This may be rooted in a humiliating insult from others or come from being victimised by evil-minded people or from suppression by superiors or a powerful authority. A large number of the world's populace harbour, in psychological parlance, a typical instinct in them known as death instinct. It expresses itself in unreasonable domination over others, suppression of others' talents, causing humiliation to others, and so on. This trait may also be triggered off by the persons in power through their studied neglect, refusal to recognize others' talents, and in many other ways. For such people with 'death instinct,' even forgiving others implies conditional forgiveness. The other name for this is making slaves of others. These people use such highfalutin words such as 'obedience like a dog,' 'unconditional obedience,' only to deceive naive people. They want their subordinates to do everything at their whimsical command, in return for some physical comforts and false sense of security from the world.

Most of their victims give in just for the sake of the little comforts of life they get. But those who cannot be content with such petty achievements will treat such superiors as the sworn enemy of mankind. Far from forgiving, these oppressed people, out of deep hatred, will seek every opportunity to upset their opponents.

As a third reason it can be said that when we feel hurt at others' adverse comments or behaviour, we go on reliving the experience by repeatedly remembering it or narrating it to others. Each time we remember, the impulses that should have come out at the time of its happening, bubble up in the mind making it a slave of the impulse. A lot of our energy gets dissipated in this way. The pictures associated with the memory go on adding impulses each time we relive it. At last it takes the form of a huge wave and hooks our will which, thus enslaved by the wrongly directed mental waves, makes a *samkalpa* (resolve) to take revenge. An enslaved will cannot forgive others. To forgive in the right spirit one needs to be a master of the will.

Once a disciple Peter asked Jesus Christ, 'Lord, how often shall I forgive my brother who has sinned against me?' He gave a significant reply: 'Seventy times seven.' (Matthew,18:21-22) Why did he say so? Because though, perhaps, the sin was committed only once, we go on mentally reliving the offence umpteenth times. This is not only meaningless but also harmful on a subjective basis. A monk, while bathing in a river happened to see a young lady helplessly blown away by the current and crying out for help. He swam to her and rescued her. The news spread with some aspersion on the monk. He was summoned to a group of his brother monks and was challenged for his breach of monastic conduct. But the monk rejoined indifferently with this remark, 'I have left the woman on the bank, while you are carrying her still in your heart!'

Why are we not able to digest the hurts inflicted on us by others? It is because we fail to make our heart large enough to merge all such petty feelings into it. And in order to make our heart spacious enough to contain others' feelings, we must know the art of loving others. It is the lack of mature love that forces us to recoil from forgiving others. This, then, is the fourth reason for our failure to forgive.

The fifth reason is our inability to hold fast to our human identity. On analysis it is found that people take advantage of our foolishness or lack of knowledge in certain worldly affairs. The fact is that people take the upper hand with us not for our goodness—the inherent asset of all of us—but for our foolishness. One is hit on one's vulnerable point only.

So, instead of howling at others' misdemeanours, if we concentrate more on patching the chinks in our armour, if we take just the needed lesson from our bitter experiences and insist on holding more to our human identity, forgiveness will stop to be a cause of conflict in us. By 'holding on to human identity' we can take the correct lesson from our failures. Śrī Śankara, in his comments on the 63rd verse of the second chapter of the *Bhagavad Gītā*, clearly states that man can hold on to his human identity only as long as he can distinguish between what ought to be done and what ought not be done in a particular situation. Lack of this discrimination renders him unfit to be called a man.

In the long course of evolution, man has succeeded in differentiating himself from all other species; he has come out of his animal sheath and is lording over other lower species. But how far has he truly succeeded in establishing his human identity? If you want to be rooted in your distinction as a human being, you must be cautious about vying for supremacy and such other 'drawbacks' of human life. The tendency to go ahead of others is like a canker in human civilization. It is to a large extent responsible for our inability to forgive others. This is the sixth reason why we are incapable of forgiving.

The last reason is our inability to forgive ourselves. Sounds strange? Indeed, many people, with all their good qualities, foster deep hatred for themselves since childhood. This is not an inherent trait. Rather, such traits are thrust upon people by the other members of the family by way of negative, pessimistic training, sharp criticism at slightest lapse or inadvertence, loud laughter at others' failure, cornering or expressly boycotting of one person by all others as a single unit, or making one the butt of ridicule of all others. All these drives stunt the mental growth of a child who develops self-hatred as an outcome of all these horrible experiences.

One who does not love oneself, but fosters deep self-hatred within, cannot be expected to forgive others under any circumstance. This is the most important of all the factors and, unfortunately enough, modern society bristles with people of this sort.

Fields of exception

Forgiving is, indeed, a great quality. However, there are certain fields where 'forgive and forget' must not be applied if at all we value human development and love human beings. The world is badly in need of people with blazing characters who may live in the world but do not become of the world.

The first is the area of children and youngsters. They have no mind of their own; it is all an unconscious flow of vital forces acting in and through their persons. Every moment they go on identifying themselves with the surroundings. This is no fault on their part. Yet they should be taught to struggle against the stream—rather than floating with the current or conforming to the ways of majority—right from childhood. When they commit something evil out of ignorance, imitate bad gestures, covet others' possessions or feel unreasonably jealous of others, they must be dissuaded by their parents or guardians in a way that is conducive to their all-round development. This seldom happens. Parents either feel emotionally upset at such off-track movement of their ward or remain callously indifferent to such harmful behaviour on the plea of love.

As a matter of fact, many parents are not themselves groomed up properly from their childhood; so they are not clearly aware of every inch of the path of life. Very few people will whole-heartedly accept this fact. But mere acceptance or rejection cannot disprove a truth. The long and short of it is that children and youngsters must be made aware of the facts of both good and evil and their difference under a backdrop of high human values. Without a clear knowledge of the difference between good and evil, man cannot transcend them or even grow in life.

Most of the tragedies and stunted growth in human life may be traced to ignorance of the ideas of good and evil and their distinction. Moreover, if by lethargy or indulgence of habit, youngsters repeatedly do the same offence, they must be dealt with sternly and firmly. The purpose is not to intimidate them but just to put them on the right track. The affectionate mother may sometimes have to spank the unreasonably importunate child. She is not called a cruel mother or devoid of forgiveness on that score.

The second is the working field. Our working places are replete with men and women of the ever-changing type. Their hearts are set to crass selfishness. Examples are not lacking where the colleague, with a veneer of sweet speech, cooks accounts in such a way that the boss, even though suspicious of the breach of trust of the colleague, feels either shy or nervous to approach the accused. Well has it been said by a great thinker of the West in satiric terms: 'Lord, save me from my friends; I shall take care of my enemies!'

Last of all, we must be very frank with our own self. Our mind must be forcibly weaned from all types of harmful indulgence. We must learn to say an emphatic 'no' to our own mind. This, however, is more easily said than done. The mind, by nature, is like a child; it has no sense of good or bad until 'someone' points it out. This someone, again, is the person himself. So the task is all the more difficult, though not impossible.

Forgive, don't forget

'To err is human, to forgive divine,' goes the saying. But judging by human standards it seems that if to err is human, to forgive also is human. Forgiving implies inner strength. It has been found that when two animals fight with each other for supremacy, and one of them accepts defeat, the loser makes a gesture by falling flat on the ground. The winner then stomps away in pride, forgiving his enemy. What holds true for the animal world should also apply all the more in human relations of understanding.

But human society is a complex network of a wide variety of people with angularities and idiosyncrasies. The animals invariably abide by the jungle law; whoever violates it must be punished. Not so, however, with human species. When one forgives another, the person forgiven may also turn hostile against the forgiver and revile him at an opportune moment. Indeed, man sometimes behaves in a strangely chimerical manner. Judging by certain behaviour it becomes difficult to define humanity. Why do people behave in such a queer way? We get no plausible answer except that the suppressed *samskāras* come up in that way.

But the problem before us remains whether to forgive or not. The great power of forgiveness should be showered on those alone who seek forgiveness, not as a slave but with the implicit determination to change themselves, if forgiven. Those who display a slavish nature and beg pardon for every detected fault are found later to become more crooked by nature. They cut a poor figure as far as humanness is concerned. And it is these people who are more dangerous than animals. They will seek every opportunity to overturn the person who forgave them. This class of people comprises even the power-wielders whom Sri Ramakrishna equated with snakes. 'M' writes in *The Gospel of Sri Ramakrishna* that Sri Ramakrishna warned, 'Some people have the nature of a snake: they will bite you without warning. You have to discriminate a great deal in order to avoid the bite; otherwise your passion will be stirred up to such an extent that you will feel like doing injury in return.'

When the question of forgiving such types of people arises, one has to be very wary so as not to take any false step. If forgive we must, we must not forget. We must learn to shield ourselves from the crooked person. The great battle of Kurukshetra in the *Mahābhārata* taught us how to remain awake in the midst of battle and even during night sleep.

'This world is like a gymnasium,' said Vivekananda. Here we come to strengthen our soul from incessant attacks of alien forces. There goes a saying that the world can best be enjoyed by the strong—*vīrabhogyā vasundharā.* The weak will crumble under so many adverse forces. Only the strong can forgive. Only a strong man knows how much to hit back, because he has full control over his strength and power. Again, the really strong and brave has a creative bent in him. It is he who knows how to make use of the available and reserved resources.

Conclusion

We have seen that there are people, the weaklings, who flatly ask for pardon when caught red-handed with their harmful intentions. But when relieved of charges, they again attack through some other loopholes in an exceptionally shrewd manner. We should rather not forgive such people. Indian history has been stained by such traitors.

There are, however, another kind of people who may not verbally beg pardon but whose mute gesture and face will tell you in clear terms that they are full of remorse for their wrongs. Not only so, their attitude will speak of their readiness to change. Such people should, of necessity, be forgiven. The queen of England was once approached for mercy by some convicts on whom the Apex court had slammed a death sentence. Her Majesty pardoned them. The upshot was, in later years they completely changed themselves so much so that they adorned the posts of personal body-guards of Her Majesty!

Great men do forgive us every now and then. They do not dwell on our shortcomings. Rather, they make us feel repentant at our trespasses through their purity and strength of character. Those who do not understand such great men through their own intellect are really hapless creatures. Such people only try to torture those great souls, and as a result, heaven's curse descends on them.

Jesus Christ was tortured and convicted, and people sentenced him to death for all the good he did to humankind. How did Christ react to that verdict? That is really important and unparalleled. He prayed, 'Father, forgive them; for they know not what they do.' (Luke, 23:34) Jesus did not utter these words out of helplessness or any weakness. Rather he spoke out of fullness, out of his bounty of love.

There is still among us a rare class of people who know only to forgive, who can give love for no return. They are brave enough to go to any length for doing good to others. They are the salt of the earth. The wind carries the fragrance of their character. What little goodness we still find in the world can be ascribed to their contribution. They never hesitate to forgive and help us notwithstanding our failures and lapses.

These people never cared for the black spots on other persons. Their unconditional grace flowed spontaneously in a perennial stream. It is such people who can really forgive; others only do a mockery in the name of forgiveness.

Bhartṛhari has classed them in his hundred verses on ethics as 'well-wishers of all the three *worlds' (tribhuvanamupakāra-śreṇibhiḥ prīṇayantaḥ).*

In our daily interpersonal dealings, clashes are unavoidable. Still, we must forge ahead with our human dignity and emerge victorious. We should not nurture the wounds of hurts by bearing malice against the wrong-doers; for, that will degrade us and not the bad persons. We must become sensitive to others' feelings.

Let us remember that there are still some good people in the world who tolerate and forgive us; we should neither ignore nor undermine their importance.

The Eternal Dance of Śiva

AN ETERNAL rhythm is playing ceaselessly in the universe, Pandit Birju Maharaj once said. Before he commenced his performance, the renowned dance maestro indulged in some philosophical talk. Knowingly or unknowingly we are all dancing to that rhythm. At times we move away from it, only to come back to the original rhythm before long. The various modulations and ramifications of rhythm in a ballet demonstrate this phenomenon.

There's an uncanny link between real life and dance. As we look at our lives, we discover a rhythmic play similar to dance. Our joys and sorrows, passions and emotions, love and hate, work and meditation seem like dramatic dance performances, as we navigate our journey to eternity. To some, this path is pleasant, perhaps strewn with flowers, while to others it is painful and thorny. Some like to take a shortcut by travelling in a straight line—perhaps in the line of least resistance—to reach quickly to the end, yet others may make a detour. But sooner or later, all will come back to the central line to join the rhythm of life. In the theory of sound or light this type of motion is graphically expressed as a transverse wave or a pendulum movement.

The Vedic seers in India discovered this eternal rhythm in the external as well as internal nature æons ago. They named it as *ṛtam*. The word rhythm comes close to *ṛtam* both phonetically and etymologically. The Vedic seers used the word to mean truth in the higher level, namely, cosmic harmony. The word truth (*satyam*) is a relative term, and is limited within the bounds of relative existence. In that level, truth and falsehood are, like good and evil, the obverse and reverse of the same coin. The same fact, under a particular situation and condition, may be called truth and under another set of values it may be called falsehood. Further, the concepts of good and evil, truth and falsehood, and all such pairs of polarity are the antitheses of each other. Not so with *ṛtam*.

Though for all practical purposes of understanding the word *anṛtam* is used to denote untruth, it is actually a deviation from harmony, a phenomenon of 'losing the track,' and not withdrawing oneself from the journey. When Swami Vivekananda said that man travels not from falsehood to truth, but from lesser truth to higher truth, he had in his mind this Vedic idea of *ṛtam*. However sinful a person is, he need not be eternally damned. Instead, such exhortations will encourage him to shake off the delusions of his understanding that developed through wrong orientations toward life, to move ahead with all the more vigour and clearer understanding.

There is no mention of a hell or any such place of punishment in the Vedas. The greatest retribution is to come back to earth through transmigration and to start from where the journey finished last. In other words, one is given another chance to make amends, to come back closer to the central line leading to the goal.

The whole universe is in a state of flux. Every moment a fight is going on between the pairs of opposites. But in spite of all this, there is an established harmony in the whole universe. The goal of life is to catch up with this frequency called *ṛtam* by the Vedic seers, Tao by Lao Tzu, and Logos by the Greek philosophers. To live in resonance with this universal vibration is to live in harmony. To miss the rhythm implies moving away from the natural state.

Harmony and adjustment

Living in harmony means to live in peace, but we must also be aware of all the forces in action within and without. To get in touch with the ultimate truth we must be conscious of the presence of the great rhythm of God in all that we see. Great poets and artists sometimes chance upon such harmony when they are alone in the open or the countryside, with their heart bereft of all cares and worries of the world.

William Wordsworth, Lord Alfred Tennyson, and many other lesser-known people have had such rare experience in unguarded moments of life when they suddenly became aware of a larger existence, a greater harmony in nature. Poets give expression to their feelings in black and white in the form of immortal poetry. Hermann Hesse, in his much-acclaimed novel *Siddhartha*, has painted in idyllic style the realization of the natural harmony that came to Siddhartha at long last in his life of polarities.

Almost in a similar way, author and physicist Fritjof Capra came across a unique experience that led to his writing the celebrated book on science and religion: *The Tao of Physics*. His introductory lines are:

> I was sitting by the ocean one late summer afternoon, watching the waves rolling in and feeling the rhythm of my breathing, when I suddenly became aware of my whole environment as being engaged in a gigantic cosmic dance. Being a physicist, I knew that the sand, rocks, water, and air around me were made of vibrating molecules and atoms, and that these consisted of particles which interacted with one another by creating and destroying other particles... As I sat on that beach my former experiences came to life; I 'saw' cascades of energy coming down from outer space, in which particles were created and destroyed in rhythmic pulses; I 'saw' the atoms of the elements and those of my body participating in this cosmic dance of energy; I felt this rhythm and I 'heard' its sound, and at that moment I knew that this was the dance of Shiva, the Lord of Dancers worshipped by the Hindus.

Harmony on a collective or nationwide basis is often construed as adjustment with the whole group or indoctrination. Under the circumstances the individual is forced to repress his ego and surrender his aspirations to the herd or die. Having no choice left, people cannot but give in. The majority of the world's populace constitutes this group, which includes even many of the creative personalities. Even their creative urge is controlled by the anonymous authority called society. Such people give up their freedom to lead a happy life. The void created in their hearts as a result of such conformity has to be temporarily filled up with many distractions of modern times like idle gossip, media facilities, and movie entertainments. But such adjustment is earned only at the cost of freedom.

Harmony is a far cry for people under bondage. As a matter of fact, people are scared of their freedom. To be free means to take up all responsibility of one's past and present actions. With all the achievements of our vaunted civilization we miserably fail to do so. That is the reason why most people try to escape from freedom.

Śiva, the great dancer

Dance is a great art of representing the harmony of the universe through various symbolic stances and movements of the limbs. Hindu mythology demonstrates this art in the dance of the greatest dancer Śiva. Natarāja, the epithet of Lord Śiva, means the king of dancers. His dance posture traces its source to the harmony in the universe. Strikingly enough, the twentieth century scientists, after exploring the subatomic world of matters, have discovered a tremendous dynamic nature in the nuclear particles in the microcosm. To their astonishment, there goes on eternally a ceaseless flow of energy in the form of particle interactions, creating and destroying particles without end.

The whole process of interaction gives rise to stable, dynamic structures that move about in rhythmic movements. This continual activity involving creation, maintenance, and destruction of particles is known as the cosmic dance of energy. Different particles have different patterns of dance and, what is more, this dance is not limited within the subatomic particles but even the void also participates in this cosmic dance by creating and destroying energy.

Scientists have observed a marked similarity between this dynamic movement of particles in the subatomic universe and the macrocosmic dance of Naṭarāja, the king of dancers. This observation leads to the subsequent conclusion that Swami Vivekananda found in the depth of his meditation: 'The microcosm and the macrocosm are built in the same plan.' The *Kaṭhopaniṣad* also corroborates this concept of identity between the microcosm and the macrocosm in saying, 'Whatever exists here exists there too, and vice versa.'

'Shiva's dance is the clearest image of the activity of God which any art or religion can boast of,' said Ananda K Coomaraswamy in his book, *The Dance of Shiva*. As in the case of all other deities in the Hindu pantheon, Śiva represents the ultimate reality called Brahman. Nature remains inert when Śiva is in a state of meditation, and when he rises to dance, through his will nature also dances to his rhythm.

The word *Śiva* in Sanskrit means one who is benevolent. But in fact, as in the case of all other Hindu gods and goddesses, Śiva is neither good nor evil, but beyond both. It is a projection of the ultimate reality called Brahman from a certain angle that is named Śiva. The weak call Him 'good', 'compassionate', while the strong dare to face the Lord in His terrible form also.

The renowned Naṭarāja form of Śiva was first realized by the ascetics of yore in the depth of meditation and later thoughtfully cast by artists and sculptors of India, taking cue from those visions to symbolize the three aspects of creation, maintenance, and destruction of the Lord.

The Naṭarāja is a deity with four arms. One of the left hands carrying blazing fire indicates the destructive aspect;

the other left-hand pointing to the raised foot symbolizes the release from the spell of māyā or ignorance. One right hand is holding the drum called *ḍamaru*, which is the source of the ceaseless sound going on in the cosmos called *nāda-brahman* or *anāhata-śabda* (literally, unobstructed sound). The other right hand gives the symbol of blessing and fearlessness (*varābhaya mudrā*), assuring protection and maintenance. Naṭarāja stands with one foot trampling on a figurine representing the primal ignorance of the universe. Śiva's body is perfectly poised and the face is serene.

This shows his peaceful detachment amid the polarities of creation and destruction. The masculine aspect of the deity is represented by the right earring in the form of a snake. The left one is a discus indicating the feminine aspect. The matted lock contains the river Ganga, the sustainer of life; the crescent moon denotes the creative power. The skull on the forehead stands for the destructive aspect. The third eye symbolizes higher perception of knowledge. His besmeared forehead and body with ash points to the utter renunciation and detachment from all worldly concerns. The throat has become blue from the influence of the poison he drank to save the world from its bad effects. German Indologist and linguist Heinrich Zimmer in *Myths and Symbols in Indian Art and Civilization* has described this dancing form in his own style:

> His gestures wild and full of grace, precipitate the cosmic illusion; his flying arms and legs and the swaying of his torso produce—indeed, they are—the continuous creation-destruction of the universe, death exactly balancing birth, annihilation the end of every coming forth.

Bestower of knowledge

The dance of Śiva is not merely a cosmic dance. He can also impart through it profound knowledge to the aspirant who seeks it. Panini's monumental work of aphoristic Sanskrit grammar has proved to be very viable to computer language.

This great sage, with a view to giving a new shape to Sanskrit grammar, meditated on the Lord Śiva, bestower of knowledge. It is said that at the consummation of his *samādhi*, the Lord appeared before the sage and danced in his bewitching style. With his *ḍamaru*, the Lord made fourteen types of sound. Panini's mind, purified with austerity and spiritual practice, succeeded in deciphering them into arrays of symbolic letters named *Māheśwara-sūtras* or aphorisms of Śiva. These aphorisms are seminal in the formulation of the whole grammar of Panini. Students of the Paninian grammar are well-acquainted with the verse connoting this story.

The ultimate reality manifested itself first through the subtle aspect of sound, which found concrete expression through the pronunciation of letters. This is known as *śabda-brahma*. The *Book of John* in the *Bible* also gives an idea of this *śabda-brahma* of Hindu theology. 'In the beginning was the Word, and the Word was with God, and the Word was God.'

Sound is one of the main factors in the communication of ideas. Long before the *Bible*, the hymn of creation (*nāsadīya-sūktaṁ*) in the *Rg-Veda* (10:129:1) said that there was neither existence nor non-existence in the beginning; darkness was engulfed in darkness and time stood still. The time mentioned here is not the chronological time which is only a relative concept. In the depth of meditation, time stands still because there is no movement of the mind.

What insight do we derive from the cosmic dance of Śiva? It beckons us to participate in the eternal rhythm of the universe by attuning ourselves to it. It also bids us to remain perfectly calm in the midst of all the polarities of the world, to see inaction in actions and vice versa. This is expressed in the *Bhagavad Gītā*, Chapter 4, verse 18.

The word *Śiva-rātri* ordinarily means the night of vigil for the worship of the great God, Śiva. Night means darkness and darkness implies inertness. In this darkness, Śiva dances along with his two companions Nandī and Bhṛngī, who represent the full gamut of manifested universe. This world is said to be like a cremation ground haunted by ghosts and ghouls. Standing there, Śiva dances in perfect rhythm, absorbed in his own bliss 'that passeth all understanding.' His dance makes inert matter beam with life. He absorbs all life expressions into himself through his destructive aspect.

Communication through symbols

The dance of Śiva is nothing but a symbolic representation of some concept or knowledge. Communication through symbols is an alternative to language. The relationship between a mother and her child is accentuated through symbols rather than language. The mother's approval, disapproval, or appraisal can be understood by the child alone. The mother can also understand the child's urges from his gestures.

There are several modes of communication. The first of these is dance. Dance is simply a language communicated through various mudrās, gazes, gestures, and rhythms. To appreciate the idea behind a dance, one must be well-versed in the science of that art. The second means is ritual worship. At the time of worship one is not supposed to talk using sound. Worship is a way of establishing an intimate, heart-to-heart relationship with the Divine, and so one has to use the language of the gods and goddesses through signs or mudrās. Even dumb people and mute animals have their own signs for communication. Inferior animals have less sound symbols to communicate; hence they use different gestures to express different moods. A little close observation makes this fact clear. This, then, is the third category of communication.

The fourth is the communication through dreams. Dream is the language our mind uses to convey certain ideas to our gross, externalized self. One of the main tasks of psychologists is to analyse dreams correctly and find out the hidden urges and drives of the person. If rightly analysed, dreams reveal a lot of insight on human personality. Spiritual experiences form the fifth kind of symbols. They are in a way similar to dreams but the difference lies in the fact that dreams are unconscious experiences whereas spiritual visions are the experiences of the superconscious level. Besides, they leave their indelible stamp of conviction on the personality. Spiritual experiences do not need a psychoanalyst to analyse and interpret. They are rather self-explanatory. They do not have much significance to souls that are not pitched to the level of understanding of the seer. Hence spiritual experiences are not worth sharing with one and all except with the guru or spiritual preceptor.

The sixth type is expressed by an artist in abstract arts. To appreciate the quality of an art one has to view it through the eyes of the artist himself. The seventh type of symbol is certain characters used in Chinese, Japanese, or Korean languages. The permutations and combinations of those characters form words which may have a host of meanings.

One has to choose the right one from out of them to fit the context. For instance, the character 'wu', when combined with another character 'li', produces five meanings. They are:

1) Patterns of Organic Energy
2) My Way
3) Nonsense
4) I Clutch My Ideas
5) Enlightenment.

The last, yet most important, is nature's incessant communication to all creatures. Both internal and external nature does communicate to us all in its own language. When our body temperature rises above the normal, it indicates that some fighting is going on within the body due to the invasion of bacteria, virus, or alien bodies from outside. When we are hungry, thirsty, or emotional, our internal nature communicates it to us in a particular fashion.

When legendary poets and literati of Shakespearean fame find 'tongues in trees, books in the running brooks, and sermons in stones,' they do not merely express wild poetic imaginations. As a matter of fact, the brooks, the rocks, the wilderness, not to speak of the vault overhead with its patches of moving clouds—all these do communicate to us. 'He that hath ears to hear,' can hear it unerringly.

If we want to communicate to another person speaking a different language, we must first of all be conversant with his language. Likewise, to catch the language of the entities we must tune our souls to their level of vibration. This abstract idea has been given concrete form graphically in the unique novel *Siddhartha* by Hermann Hesse. The hero of it, an aspirant with sound spiritual background, possessed of the rare capacity to withdraw the mind at will and many other talents, found at long last in his chequered life the consummation of his wisdom from the mute eloquence of the river at the instance of another simple ferryman, Vasudeva.

It is this language of external nature that inspired the Vedic sages to live constantly in harmony with nature. From the *Chāndogya Upaniṣad* we come to learn the story of a simple Brahmin boy, Satyakāma, of unknown parentage. He was asked by his preceptor to tend the cattle of the hermitage in the wilderness and come back when they doubled in number. The disciple followed the order with all respect and at long last the story has it that the animals imparted to him the knowledge of Supreme Brahman. The story is not merely a figment of the brain of the Vedic sage but a truth valid for all time.

Koan is another type of language, started by the Zen Masters, in the form of a riddle that is apparently paradoxical. It needs a lot of intellectual exercise and intuition to crack the puzzle. The Indian counterpart of it can be found in the aphorisms of Paninian grammar or in the Nyāya philosophy. The hymn of creation (*nāsadīya-sūktaṁ*) in the *Ṛg-Veda* (10:129:1) said that there was neither existence nor non-existence in the beginning; darkness was engulfed in darkness and time stood still. This is a riddle that can be compared only to the koan of Zen Buddhism. The time mentioned here is not the chronological time which is only a relative concept.

Implication for life

The point that remains now to be explained is how the cosmic dance of Śiva can be brought to bear upon our daily life.

Hindu mythology brings in legendary gods and goddesses with all their prowess and exploits with a view to conveying even the highest truth in simple ways befitting a toddler. Every child is acquainted with dance and its rhythmic movements. First a novice is taught the various postures without attributing any meaning to them. As he masters the art, he gains knowledge about the meaning of each of them. In the course of learning the student gradually grasps more and more of the inherent meaning in the art and tries to integrate them into his own personality.

Before a high stage of maturity is reached, the significance of the cosmic rhythm cannot be realized. A strong jolt is needed to wean the soul away from its inordinate attachments to the world and to turn the face toward reality. Feeling the cosmic rhythm within and without is not an act of mere fantasy. It needs the rigorous and one-pointed effort of several births to integrate oneself with the vast ocean of rhythm surrounding us.

Scientists of a very high rank sometimes accidentally come upon such experiences, which may be called 'stumbling on truth.' They become speechless with wonder realizing the eternal relationship between science and religion.

The last question is, why should we try to attain harmony in life? The answer is, because that is our inherent nature. This harmony does not mean to keep pace with something that is alien. The whole universe, with its diverse activities and polarities, is in fact a single unit having tremendous potential of dynamism in it. Nothing is outside its periphery. Judging from the lower levels of body-mind complex with an infinite variation, we think the outside universe is different from us and thus isolate ourselves from it through selfishness. Living in harmony means to remove this barrier and remain one's own self in a larger dimension.

Who is said to have attained the state of Śiva? The answer is: one whose spiritual power has raised him to the level from which he can look upon all struggles for existence, all diversities, all polarities of the world with perfect equanimity; one who has succeeded in keeping himself static amid all dynamisms.

The Concept of Maturity

THE TERM 'maturity' is common and seemingly simple to understand. All possible achievements of human life seem to be associated with maturity. The bliss enjoyed by a mature person outweighs all other temporal happiness. But ironically enough, a small percentage of people are really mature. Indeed, it is one of the toughest concepts associated with human life.

Maturity is not a quality or a possession. It is an attitude towards life, involving the whole personality. In proportion to our physical, emotional, and intellectual growth, we become mature or immature. In the popular sense maturity is taken as 'coming of age' or stepping into adulthood. But that it is not so becomes clear when full-grown adults are seen to behave in a queer way that is far from the norms of maturity laid by society. From childhood to old age there are several stages of human development. Each of the stages has its own way of expression. When a person fails to respond in the way suited to his own stage of development, he is said to be immature.

Why does it so happen that grown-ups behave like

children in their day-to-day dealings? The answer can perhaps be found in Sigmund Freud, the father of psychoanalysis, who said that the problems of adulthood are chiefly caused by unresolved emotional conflicts of childhood. When a child experiences something and cannot meaningfully accommodate it to his own life; when because of some taboo imposed by the family he cannot discuss the matter openly with other members of the family, the experience creates conflicts in later years. If the child fails to resolve the conflict, similar courses of experience in later years will make him behave in an infantile, immature way. This proves that to expect mature behaviour from adults, we must pay due attention to the years of infancy and childhood.

It needs to be emphasized that each individual is not only divine but also unique. Each of us is unique in one aspect or the other. When one develops along a line incompatible with his unique feature, his energy cannot manifest in that direction and remains pent-up. As a result, the free growth of the person gets stunted and he seems immature.

Our present-day culture has given rise to inner conflicts in the individual. These conflicts, again, have created breaches in the personality resulting in an immature development. The causes are given below.

First, the adult member has to assume many roles in different circumstances, like father, son, husband, boss, colleague, manager, political leader, and many others. But he has not been taught to correlate each of these roles to his own self which is different from all these roles. More so, circumstances force him to become a prey to doubt, fear, tension, anxiety, worry, and boredom. These different roles quite often conflict with each other creating divisions in one's personality. At such points of crisis, man feels he can solve his problems by burrowing himself into infantile fantasy, dependence, and an irresponsible attitude. As a result, instead of growing into a mature individual, he remains immature.

Second, our market-oriented learning makes the child think he is a saleable commodity. The parents send the child to school to secure high rank and not knowledge, and tell the child that whatever his teachers teach is all meaningless, impractical prattle; that teachers are nobodies compared to movie stars, glamour queens, business magnates, and such like. This confuses the child's sense of values. Unable to decide the right path to follow, he transforms himself unconsciously into an immature individual in later life.

The third point is that the cheap philosophies of modern times fetch a larger following than those which demand a high level of discipline, purity, and austerity. People in general are not ready to pay a high price for achieving a higher end. They always look for a short cut. As a result, there develop a large number of mushroom-like organizations, best-seller books and sidewalk clinics that guarantee to fetch the desired ends to the people at a very short time and without strict discipline. All this is, however, eyewash to lead people astray. People start believing in a hypnotized way that they are satisfied and happy while in reality they are reduced to no better than children. This also makes room for immaturity.

To be mature in life is to realize one's power in full stature. Swami Vivekananda wanted people to become mature first. All his exhortations for 'educating' people aim at directing the people to a mature life. Mature men and women can change the history of nations for the better. That is why Vivekananda insisted on realizing the potential power inherent in us all.

The changing world gives us an opportunity to learn every moment. Sri Ramakrishna has said, 'as long as I live, so long do I learn.' One who thinks out of vanity that his store of knowledge is too full to allow any other fresh knowledge is only paving the way for immaturity.

World influences

What role does the environment or the world play in shaping our personality? There are broadly four major modes of influence. We have been interacting with them since our childhood. They are newspapers, radio, movies, and advertisements. Taken together, they are known by a common name, media. In modern times the media has become an indispensable part of our life. The media governs our life and economy in both overt and covert ways. They contribute as much to develop as to arrest our maturity.

The brighter side of the media is that it brings to us a lot of knowledge of the outside world, raising our awareness. The darker side is that it impedes concentration on a single matter and encourages hopping of an immature mind from one topic to another. Thus, each of the media functions in two diametrically opposite ways—in contributing to our growth and in keeping us from full psychological maturing.

Here three points need mention. One is that, though the media strategically casts a spell on the minds of the common people, it only takes advantage of the weakness of the human mind. The second point is that their chief aim being money-making, they like to keep the flame of our unfulfilled wants for worldly things awake forever. As a third point it can be said that there are ways to handle even immature, base information in a mature way.

Growth begins at home

Home is the most important place for a child's education through parents and relatives. This education depends on the moods of the adults in the household from time to time. Children learn to imitate those who are in close proximity and are heroic figures to them. In a psychologically tempered home, children grow up into confident, mature adults. Truly loving parents will always see to it that their child is not just pampered but develops a sense of responsibility and understanding for others.

On the other hand, when an individual is pushed into a state of helplessness either through over-indulgence, negligence, dominance, or a feeling of unwantedness in the family, he will grow up to be a person lacking in confidence, full of suspicion and self-hatred.

Parents cannot be held fully responsible, for society exerts an unseen, subtle influence over its members. The adults in the family are conditioned by the many institutions outside home like office, industry, business, education, government, communities, religion, and so on. Society exercises its remote control in shaping the character of children at home through the helpless parents.

The machine age has forced the father—and sometimes the mother too—out of touch with the family for the greater part of the day; joint families have been broken up into nuclear families; the stipulated number of children in a family has been whittled down to one or two; cutthroat competition has replaced cooperation with others. The problem becomes all the more troublesome when the adults in the family, unable to have a clear idea of the outside forces in action, refuse to accept any viable suggestion to change certain patterns in and out of the family. This is clearly a sign of immaturity.

Children must grow from ignorance to knowledge, from irresponsibility to responsibility, from isolation to communication, from egocentricity to feeling for others, and above all, from a narrow outlook to a new vista of wide horizons. But all these bold steps toward maturity must first of all be trailblazed by the adults of the family, whom youngsters will follow.

All the human values can be learnt at home first. The arts of cooperation, responsibility, philanthropy, living in harmony, and the like have to begin at home, especially at homes where adults are ready to accept their apparently invisible shortcomings instead of by-passing or winking at them, and are keen on transcending them whenever the occasion demands and the opportunity is open.

Maturing process at school

The school is an institution next to the home where the maturing process of children takes place. Next to parents and relatives, the school helps children in their journey towards maturity. Schools are the places for learning. The right type of training should be to encourage the student to develop an explorative and creative spirit. This calls for an enquiring, critical mind in the student. They are taught to accumulate data from innumerable sources without the technique to assimilate them in their own life. This is the shortcoming of money-oriented education. The students must learn to relate the facts they gather from the outside world to their own life. Instead of learning to 'fit themselves into the group,' they should learn to absorb their acquired knowledge fittingly into their own system.

In the general sense, education means just a process of 'data feeding' into the learner's memory. But first of all one has to build up the mind, the recipient of the knowledge, from childhood. To build a mind is to let it encounter problems and solve them after a thorough scrutiny. The mind should not accept anything uncritically or in a passive way. Every data should be weighed and checked before drawing a conclusion. Not only so, but even that conclusion should be tested on the anvil of life. In this way, education may successfully come out of its old sheath of learning by rote to get a new definition as 'living through novel situations,' which means to grow into mental, emotional, and social maturity.

Maturity in the spiritual context

Only a spiritually mature person can give love. As important as love is empathy. This trait gets a wider dimension—in fact it finds its consummation—in the spiritual context. As a matter of fact, the Advaita system of philosophy in Hinduism is based on this basic oneness of all that exists. The religious history of India records the story of a saint who was fatally stabbed by a Mohammedan mutineer at the time of the Sepoy Mutiny of 1857. When that person was held and brought before the dying saint by the Hindu mutineers seeking the saint's consent to kill the stabber, the saint looked up and said, 'thou art my beloved,' and breathed his last.

To attain spiritual maturity, one need not have to reach adulthood according to the biological time clock. Śrī Śankarācārya, the exponent of Advaita philosophy, Swami Vivekananda, Jesus Christ, and many others of great spiritual stature achieved this maturity at a very young age. Śankara clearly depicted this in the concluding stanzas of his famous

Dakshināmurti hymn: 'Behold! Under the banyan tree is seated the young master before the old disciples.' Swami Vivekananda in his early thirties conquered half the globe with his mature spiritual insight. He looked upon others—much older in age than he was—with a fatherly attitude born purely of spiritual maturity.

Apart from all these, spiritual maturity has another exclusive dimension. The spiritually mature person enters into an intimate relationship with the Divine. Then all cares of mundane existence fail to evoke any response from him. In that condition, 'the person does not grow a pair of horns,' as the Holy Mother Sri Sarada Devi said, 'but develops desirelessness for all worldly things.' That constant company with the Divine makes him forge a new relationship with the world outside.

Dialectics of maturity

The term 'maturity' is so closely knitted with responsibility that one cannot be precluded from the other. Responsibility is the tie that links the individual to the outside world. When an individual is strong enough to say, 'the buck stops here,' instead of eluding moral responsibility for all his actions, he is said to be mature. A mature person's responsibility means an active participation in life activities. This, again, presupposes his feeling of oneness with humanity—be it a society, group, or nation.

A person is mature to the degree that he relates himself affirmatively to his fellow men. To hate and to fear is to be psychologically immature. Hence a mature person is always ready to share his human experience with others. He will not try to be original, but neither will he be afraid of being different from other people.

Merely having a broad range of knowledge does not make one mature. It is the way one uses the acquired knowledge that decides maturity. A balance must be struck between one's knowledge and power of executing it. This means that both knowledge and action should be blended in a proportionate way.

Maturity is the ability to handle frustration, control anger, and settle differences without violence or destruction. From this point of view, Arjuna in the Mahābhārata, with all his prowess, war-skill, and dazzling past records, failed miserably in the test of maturity at the critical moment of the ensuing battle of Kurukṣetra. Only the company and long advice of a mature person like Sri Kṛṣṇa could restore him the mature resolve to fight.

The characteristic trait of a mature person is humility. He has the courage to say, 'I was wrong,' or 'I am sorry,' when occasion demands it. Such a person is dependable under all circumstances and the keynote of his success is his keeping his word.

The ability to take decisions, to act on it, and later, to accept the whole responsibility for the result, good or bad, is the sign of a mature person. His credibility and dependability ensue from this decisiveness and acceptance of the consequences with an optimistic attitude. And because a mature person has faith in himself, he knows how to trust others, notwithstanding their shortcomings. This trust is born not out of ignorance but from the faith that all are divine in essence. The history of the world is replete with examples where even criminals changed the course of their life to a better one, when pardoned and entrusted with some responsibility.

Finally, a mature person is one who calmly faces the evil consequences of being good. He takes in his stride all the unpleasantness and disappointments that are inevitable in life.

Conclusion

Throughout the history of the world there have been so many great souls who have delivered their sermons for the good of posterity. Each religion, each sect, each creed has given rise to many such noble souls who were spontaneously bent upon doing good to others. They have shown man the way to happiness and maturity. With such a huge treasure at our disposal, why are the majority of us not influenced or moulded by those teachings? During Sri Ramakrishna's stay at Dakshineswar, so many people came and listened to his ambrosial teachings. How many of them changed their life pattern after those sayings? Most of us want Sri Ramakrishna or any god-man to be born again and again to 'save' us. Supposing he grants our wish and assumes another human birth. Will we be able to recognize him? How many of us are mature enough for that? Why did the teachings of such incarnations not gain ground in the hearts of onc and all?

The reason is sixfold. Firstly, mature truths spoken to immature hearts are like seeds falling on hard rock. They will not bear any fruit in the worldly wise and spiritually callous listeners who will continue to be the same old fools. In the second place, the attendants lack vigour or interest to grasp and assimilate such profound truths strewn round them for want of rigorous spiritual discipline. Too much preoccupation with mundane things makes the recipients unfit to understand the truths, much less translate them into their own lives. As a third reason, the selfish nature of man is to be held responsible.

The fourth reason is that the great teachers of the world always insisted on the self-efforts of the disciples instead of transferring spiritual power through miracles. Precisely, they encouraged individuality. Paul Carus writes in *The Gospel of Buddha*, that the Buddha, while bidding final farewell to his disciples, said to them: 'Be ye lamps unto yourselves. Rely on yourselves, and do not rely on external help.'

Sri Ramakrishna had the power to transform the lives of his disciples with a mere wish, or at most, by a touch. But he generally did not do so, lest the disciples would not learn to 'earn' those spiritual treasures with their own efforts. Swami Vivekananda once said in clear terms to a disciple, 'individuality is my motto.'

There's an incident from Vivekananda's life captured by Swami Nikhilananda in his book, *Vivekananda: A Biography* that was published in 1953, which reveals his high regard for individuality beside his Catholicity. At one of the public meetings in New York, after addressing a tense audience for about fifteen minutes, he suddenly made a formal bow and retired. The meeting broke up and the people went away greatly disappointed. A friend asked him, when he was returning home, why he had cut short the lecture in that manner just when both he and his audience were warming up.

He answered that at the meeting he had felt that he had too much power. He had noticed that the members of the audience were becoming so absorbed in his ideas that they were losing their own individualities. He had felt that they had become like soft clay and that he could give them any shape he wanted. That, however, was contrary to his philosophy. He wished every man and woman to grow according to his or her own inner law. He did not wish to change or destroy anyone's individuality. That is why he had had to stop.

The fifth reason is that those who have not widened the horizon of their consciousness at least nearly as that of the speaker will never be able to grasp the depth of his sayings. When Jesus spoke to his disciples to 'bless them that curse you,' 'and to him that smiteth thee on one cheek offer also the other; and him that taketh away thy cloak forbid not to take the coat also,' the sayings would appear outlandish to those whose dimensions of life were not broad enough to conceive the affirmation of love to the fellow men.

True love is never possessive nor exclusive; it is affirmative and comprehensive. It gives freedom to the object of love, pleasure at other's happiness, gives the object of love full right to his unique manhood. True love and detachment go together. It is out of this love that the great teachers of the world allow full freedom to the disciples so that they may exercise their full inherent dormant power leading to maturity.

As a sixth reason it can be said that the mature words issuing forth from the lips of spiritual giants are too aphoristic for the general public to understand. Sri Ramakrishna used to say that when a big ship passes by, no effect is felt from the bank immediately. It is only after some time that big waves splash against the banks. This example has been given by 'M' who wrote *The Gospel of Sri Ramakrishna* quoting Ramakrishna's conversations in 1883.

Not even Arjuna could grasp the message of the *Bhagavad Gita* in full. He only evoked that great message by being an instrument. That is why it is said in the invocational lines of this great scripture that Partha assumed the role of a calf that butts at the udder to bring forth the nectar of Upanishadic essence, while the wise men of posterity were its enjoyers.

The epoch-making message of the great incarnations comes to fruition after years to those alone who can attune themselves to the frequency of that spiritual vibration.

The Courage to be Human

'MOM, WHAT is courage?' a five-year-old boy once asked his mother. But she could not find a satisfactory answer, immediately. That evening when mother and child were strolling in the countryside, they came across a place where a devastating fire had destroyed a large part of the forest the night before. There, amid the debris, they saw a beautiful, wild, red flower raising its head, as if to announce proudly its survival, challenging all notions of death. The mother's face lit up, as she pointed at the bravc, little flower, declaring: 'There, my son, that is what is called courage. A wild little flower standing bravely in the valley of death.'

The story reminds us of the unique definition of life given impromptu by Swami Vivekananda to the Maharaja of Khetri: 'Life is the unfoldment and development of a being under circumstances tending to press it down.'(Life of Swami Vivekananda, volume1, p.281)

Indeed, life is a saga of courage to grow amid all adversities. External nature challenges our existence every moment, but the soul forges ahead courageously amid the darkening gloom. Courage is life; fear is death. As long as we are afraid of the world, we are more dead than alive.

The famous neuro-biologist, Dr Kurt Goldstein, has defined courage as 'nothing but an affirmative answer to the shocks of existence, which must be borne for the actualization of one's own nature.' From these definitions it is clear that courage is closely linked to our being, or existence. The Sanskrit word for existence is *sattā*. The essential nature of the *ātman* is existence-knowledge-bliss *(sat-cit-ānanda)*. Hence, courage is the force needed to defend one's existence, which is an essence of the soul.

Courage finds expression in an infinite number of ways in our day-to-day life. Wherever there is lack of courage, life ceases to be worth the name. It is no better than mere vegetation. At present we are living in an era of conformity to the majority or group. When this conformity is related to an overt authority, we express our pent-up feelings against that authority through rebellion or violence.

But the case becomes tough when the authority demanding our conformity is a covert one, namely, society, market, public opinion, or economic necessities. One cannot crusade against an anonymous authority. In the present age man has made himself an automaton by trying desperately to conform to the group or society.

Courage is the only remedy for all existential problems like anxiety, loneliness, boredom and depression. That is why Swami Vivekananda was so intent on ingraining the spirit of courage into the masses. Without courage our very existence becomes meaningless. Courage may fittingly be termed as the saving challenge of life.

Two fields of expression

Courage being an existential challenge, there are innumerable fields of its manifestation. Wherever there is life, there is courage. Some call it a struggle of the conscious over the unconscious, while others call it a struggle between the soul and the matter; at other places, it is a struggle between good and evil, higher and lower values, and so on. Broadly speaking, there are two fields in which courage finds expression: the secular or the worldly level and the spiritual or mystic level.

Secular level

Courage at the secular level finds expression in several ways. One is momentary courage. This type of courage is called for during emergencies. For example, saving others from fire, an imminent accident or from the hands of hooligans. Swami Vivekananda in his teens once saved a boy from being run over by a horse carriage, risking his own life. The *Reader's Digest* records many such sagas of saving others from inevitable death by a hair's breadth. Sometimes, the rescuer loses his/her life in the attempt. Such heroic tales are written in golden letters on the pages of history.

Then there are various aerobatics and acrobatic displays of courage, of walking over hot charcoal, rope-walk, circus techniques, equestrian skills, ski dive, surf-ride, and scores of other sensational shows of courage and heroism. Though taken mostly as pastime, these need, beside intense concentration, persistence, perseverance, an indomitable courage to succeed and overcome fear.

Immense courage is needed in our day-to-day living. Every day we come across so many people and work with them. No two of people are of the same nature. The husband

and wife have to live and work together. Naturally, there arise differences of opinion, misunderstanding, intolerance, and fault finding.

To tolerate others with all their shortcomings, one needs courage. To forgive and forget the lapses of others, one needs heroic strength. Above all, man needs a stoic forbearance to live peacefully with others, which is another example of courage. When the Holy Mother Sri Sarada Devi said in her parting advice, 'If you want peace of mind, don't find faults with others; rather, find fault with yourself if you must,' she actually put before posterity a huge responsibility of practising courage in living happily, amid the unavoidable hardships of life.

Then there's that exemplary courage of a soldier during a war. He must be ready to go to the mouth of a cannon in the midst of a fusillade or jump into the fire whenever ordered to do so. Such acts call for a devil's daring. The soldiers leave behind no tale to tell. Except a handful of close mates, very few people come to know of the heroism displayed by a soldier who dies in the battlefront. They serve the country through their courage and die a martyr's death. Swami Vivekananda eulogized the courage of a soldier and wanted to ingrain that spirit into the lives of each and every monk of the Ramakrishna Order.

A rare kind of courage is seen in the lives of handicapped people. They do not just passively accept the disability or dysfunction of their organs but work hammer and tongs to make up for the loss they have suffered, perhaps by a decree of fate. And it is a strange phenomenon of nature that it compensates for the defect in one limb by raising the capacity in some other respect in that person. Blind people, for instance, are seen to develop some extrasensory nerves that an ordinary person lacks.

The legendary personality of Helen Keller speaks volumes about her resilience. As everyone knows, she was handicapped, not in one but in several respects. Still, her success in life was phenomenal. She knew every inch of the path of struggle ahead of her. The only capital she had was an indomitable courage, an unflagging zeal, and to top it all, an unwavering faith in God. Her words below, quoted in L E Watson's *Light from Many Lamps* are a great inspiration to rise above any handicap and live a courageous life of faith:

> When it seems that our sorrow is too great to be borne, let us think of the great family of the heavy-hearted into which our grief has given us entrance, and inevitably, we feel about us their arms, their sympathy, their understanding. Believe, when you are most unhappy, that there is something for you to do in the world. So long as you can sweeten another's pain, life is not in vain... Robbed of joy, of courage, of the very desire to live, the newly bereaved frequently avoids companionship, feeling himself so limp with misery and so empty of vitality that he is ill-suited for human contacts. And, yet no one is so bereaved, so miserable, that he cannot find someone else to succour, someone who needs friendship, understanding, and courage more than he...Often when the heart is torn with sorrow, spiritually we wander like a traveller lost in a deep wood. We grow frightened, lose all sense of direction, batter ourselves against trees and rocks in our attempt to find a path. All the while there is a path—a path of Faith—that leads straight out of this dense tangle of our difficulties into the open road we are seeking. I thank God

> for my handicaps, for, through them, I have found myself, my work, and my God.

Another kind of commendable courage lies in taking up responsibility for one's own deeds. The brave person is he who takes in his stride many a failure, frustration, and challenge of life and stays unmoved in his endeavour. A popular Sanskrit verse says in a lighter vein that people hanker for the result of their good actions but refrain from doing good; while they do not crave for the bad results; still they go on doing evil deeds willingly. [*puṇyasya phalam icchanti....*] This is nothing but a sign of cowardice, that is, passing on the buck to others. He who is really brave will say forever, 'The buck stops here,' with a spirit of acceptance of his capacities as well as limitations, with an air of equanimity in success and failure.

Taking responsibility is also one of the striking features of monastic life. The monk is supposed to renounce everything including his ego. The only exception is his taking this one vow, namely, of shouldering the responsibility for all his actions. As opposed to the general trend he never holds others responsible for his fate; rather he says, as Vivekananda has pointed out:

> Peace to all; from me no danger be
> To ought that lives. In those that dwell on high
> In those that lowly creep, I am the Self in all!'

The reader can find these lines in volume 4 of the *Complete Works*, on page 394.

Vivekananda has inculcated this profound idea in the hearts of posterity. In one of his lectures that are published in the *Complete Works*, volume 2, he exhorted:

> Therefore, blame none for your own faults, stand upon your

> own feet, and take the whole responsibility upon yourselves. Say, This misery that I am suffering is of my own doing, and *that* very thing proves that it will have to be undone by me alone. That which I created, I can demolish; that which is created by some one else I shall never be able to destroy. Therefore, stand up, be bold, be strong. Take the whole responsibility on your own shoulders, and know that you are the creator of your own destiny. All the strength and succour you want is within yourselves. Therefore, make your own future. Let the dead past bury its dead.'

Spiritual level

In the spiritual context also, courage manifests in a great number of ways. Spiritual life is one of freedom from compulsion, influence or bondage. It is a way of affirming our identity with the Divine. One can establish this identity in various ways—by negating or ignoring all back pulls of the world and the flesh, by being aware of oneself every moment of life, by rediscovering the static element amid all dynamism, or by seeing the eternal cosmic dance behind the apparently static condition of the universe. If secular life has tension, anxiety, frustration, and depression, spiritual life has discontent, inner struggle, forbearance, patience, at its crossroads, U-turns, and speed bumps. Strictly speaking, the paths of secular and spiritual life are not two different highways. They are not even parallels. They are two phases of one and the same path. The secular path ultimately merges into the spiritual. Depending on the mental state and attitude of the aspirant, the function of courage in spiritual context varies.

The first task of the spiritual person is the courage to seek the Divine. The external world is so attractive with its glitters that the senses naturally rush toward them. The *Kaṭhopaniṣad* (2:1:1) made a unique statement befitting the context:

> The Self-existent One (Divine) has made the senses outgoing, defective. Thus it is that people do not see the indwelling Spirit. However, there are some courageous people who dared to see the Self by shutting down their senses through will power and directing them inward. They sought immortality.

The whole world is crazy after achieving the petty ends of life. People run after ambition, name and fame, wealth, prosperity, and what not. However, all their mad pursuits are futile.

Seeking a Divine being whom we cannot see, and holding fast to that being through all the ordeals of life in the midst of the glamourous world is not an easy task. It needs superhuman courage and one-pointed will to live in tune with the Divine with unwavering enthusiasm for years, perhaps for births together. Faith and hope are the two weapons to win the battle. Of course, character is another weapon. How to judge the character of a man? Swami Vivekananda pointed it out in his lecture on 'Karma Yoga,' according to the *Complete Works*, volume 1:

> If you really want to judge the character of a man, look not at his great performances. Every fool may become a hero at one time or another. Watch a man do his most common actions; those are indeed the things which will tell you the real character of a great man. Great occasions rouse even the lowest of human beings to some kind of greatness, but he alone is the really great man whose character is great always, the same wherever he be.

This clearly means that the man of character can convert the most commonplace work into the worship of the Divine. For such a person the line of demarcation between the sacred and secular disappears.

The next brave characteristic is the courage to preserve inner freedom. The world we live in has a tendency to bind everyone to its bed of obligations, duties, social norms and mores, and even beliefs of the majority. Outwardly we cry hoarse on freedom of choice, civil rights, and many other such rights. But whenever any individual gathers up courage to maintain inner freedom, the majority is seen to antagonize him. It needs greater courage to preserve one's inner freedom than clamour for outer freedom.

The brave-hearted must possess the courage to develop self-awareness. One who desires to go within the recess of the heart must convert his life into a conscious flow of energy. We claim that we are aware of everything we do, while in truth we are being led helplessly by the impetuosity of work. Work controls us, not we it. This is the verdict of the *Bhagavad Gītā*. In the third chapter the Lord says, 'All are forced to work helplessly by qualitics born of nature.'[3:5]

In order to develop self-awareness, the first step is to do all work without any compulsion from external authority. Self-directed work leads to develop self-awareness in us. Swami Vivekananda also said in volume 1 of *Complete Works*: 'Everything that you do under compulsion goes to create a bondage for you.'

The primers on Vedantic texts prescribe four kinds of work, namely, obligatory (*nitya*), occasional (*naimittika*), desirable (*kāmya*), and forbidden (*niṣiddha*). Of these, the first type of work must be carried out regularly, even if in a casual way. For, refraining from it may give rise to adverse effects, just as the daily habits of eating, drinking, sleeping, must be carried out if we want to keep the doctor from our doors. Yet, even amid our busy schedule of daily chores, by doing all works with a spirit of worship, we can bring self-awareness even into the daily menial chores like sweeping, mopping, and cooking. No authority under the sun has the power to change the attitude of man toward the objective world unless he himself does it.

It takes great courage to pursue spiritual life. Many of us do lead spiritual lives. Hordes of people go to temples, churches, mosques and pilgrim centres. Then people make a lot of charities, engage in congregational services, and group devotional songs. Obviously these acts do not need any courage. Then where lies the courage to pursue spiritual life?

To get the answer, we have to be keen observers. It is a strange anomaly that religious people praise God for all their success only when things go well with them; but when the case is contrary, that is, when they fall in hard times, and more often than not, the faith of such people vanishes into thin air. This happens because, as Maharshi Ramaṇa has aptly pointed out, our idea of grace is success insured. We forget that God's grace also lies in our self-effort to brave all the adversities of life. God's grace is there when the honest person has to bear the evil consequences of his honesty. A truly spiritual person never cares to blame God for all his failures. He has deep, unshakeable faith in God's power to protect him under all circumstances. The lives of Brother Lawrence, St Francis of Assisi, Sri Ramakrishna, Meera Bai, and a host of saints from every clime and creed stand as beacon lights of such courage and faith in spiritual life.

The courage to face truth is very important, spiritually speaking.

Swami Vivekananda said, truth 'is like a corrosive substance of infinite power. It burns its way in wherever it falls—in soft substance at once, hard granite slowly, but it must.' (*Complete Works,* volume 5, page 71)

Truth cannot be kept hidden for a long time. It will make its appearance on the surface of our consciousness one day or the other. To bear its impact one needs a lot of self-awareness coupled with detachment of the will.

Spiritual aspirants sometimes feel a divine discontent in their hearts after years of spiritual practice. Life loses all meanings for them. This, of course, is a temporary setback. As a matter of fact, this discontent is a harbinger of the dawn of truth. It is a test of the capacity of the aspirant to hold on to truth at all costs. Such crisis came to Swami Vivekananda also.

During his itinerant days once he became disgusted with himself and decided to give up his body in exclusive meditation. So, he entered a trackless forest and spent the whole day walking without food. He became exhausted at sundown and lay down under a tree. There he saw a tiger approaching him. He resolved to offer his body as a sacrifice to the hungry beast, and quietly waited for the tiger to pounce upon him. But for reasons unknown, the tiger retreated and disappeared into the darkness. Vivekananda waited the whole night, but the tiger never came back. This is called courage to face the baldest truth of life, namely death, with a calm bearing.

Courage to be human

The human species has several distinctions above all other

species. Human beings experience much more mental suffering than the physical suffering of animals. This mental suffering is called the pain of being human. In the words of Father Eugene C Kennedy in *The Pain of Being Human*:

> Man cannot run away from this pain without running away from himself...He can narcotize himself in a hundred ways against it but at the high price of numbing himself to the very deepest meaning of life. Man can only face and deal with it honestly. Indeed, his manner of responding to its challenge becomes the best measure of his maturity.

This response to challenges is called the courage to be human. Generally, our response to any threat is bestial. Whenever our ego is threatened, we try to counter it by reviling or backbiting. When we are humiliated, we stick to the maxim of retaliation. In other words, we tend to switch over to animal nature. Very rarely do we find people who possess the courage to assert humanness in exchange for all the crookedness and bestiality from the world. Swami Vivekananda was an exception, and he lived mainly to demonstrate indomitable courage to assert his humanness through thick and thin. Despite so much defection, disloyalty, antagonism from others, he went on doing good to them. Towards the end of his life he proclaimed, 'The older I grow, the more everything seems to me to lie in manliness. This is my new gospel.' (*Life of Swami Vivekananda*, volume 2, page 465)

Once Gautama Buddha went to a king's court where some sacrificial rites were being observed. A little lamb was made ready for sacrifice. But suddenly he entered the spot, and hearing the bleat of the lamb he rushed to the site, took it in his arms and asked the king quietly the purpose of sacrificing the lamb. The king replied that it was arranged to incur the merits for his subjects. Buddha then said: 'O king, I am ready to sacrifice my body, which has earned a lot of merit, in lieu of the lamb's. This body has committed no sin. You will incur more merit by sacrificing me.' The king hung his head in shame and the upshot was that from that day forth, all animal sacrifices were abolished from that kingdom. Swami Vivekananda, inspired by the life of Buddha, wrote in one of his letters, 'They alone live who live for others; the rest are more dead than alive.' (*Complete Works*, volume 4 page 363)

Another channel through which the inspiration for courage to be human descends is love. True, unselfish, detached love makes the impossible possible. The most touching illustration of this transforming power of love has been depicted in Victor Hugo's immortal epic, *Les Miserables*. The hero of the story, Jean Valjean, was released from gaol after a long period of rigorous imprisonment, with a passport that did not enable him even to buy a frugal meal in France. All the doors were slammed in his face. Overcome with hunger, thirst, and frustration, the man at last forced his way into the house of a reverend bishop.

The bishop welcomed the stranger and, ignoring his fierce appearance and the opposition from family members, made the best arrangements due for a venerable guest. At night, when the guest was resting in the cosy bed provided for him, the old bogey of evil tendency raised its ugly head, and the man once again stole the gold and silver utensils arranged for his dinner.

Next morning he was caught red-handed by the vigilant cop sergeant and brought before Bishop Myriel for identification. But, to the consternation of the sergeant, the noble bishop said that he had gifted those vessels to the man. Not only so, but he handed over the remaining silver candle-stands to the man in front of the dumbfounded inspector Javert who left the place disappointed. Through that small, momentary act of love the bishop ushered in an unprecedented change in the life of the convict. What could not be brought about through years of incarceration was done in a few moments.

The reaction was revolutionary and phenomenal. Gradually the man became transformed into a great Mayor who saved the life of a poor cartman stuck up under the wheel of his own loaded cart. Jean Valjean had gained the courage to exercise his humanness even though the law was breathing heavily down his neck. Was he not initiated from bestiality to humanness by Bishop Myriel?

Again, he went to save the life of a poor woman assaulted by the mob. The woman could not survive the shock, but died peacefully after handing over the charge of her only little daughter to the mayor. The daughter was in the custody of a hotelier. But long before reaching her, Jean Valjean was once again sent behind the bars. This time he fled, and released the child from the clutches of the hotelier for a huge ransom. Keeping himself carefully away from public gaze, he brought up the child, and after she came of age, married her to a suitable young man.

But the most dramatic part of the story still remained to be told. Inspector Javert was caught by a group of young rebels during a civil war. Jean Valjean happened to be present on the spot. The group unanimously gave the verdict of capital punishment for Javert. When no one came forward to murder the unarmed captive, Jean Valjean appeared at the scene and took the onus of killing the man on himself.

After everyone left, he untied his sworn enemy and set him free, and fired the bullet in the air. The inspector could not believe his eyes. How could he know what revolution had transformed a criminal into a man! How could he know that divinity was peeping incessantly through the personality of Jean Valjean whom he had been looking upon as a veritable beast! Torn between his conscience and duty, Inspector Javert at last chose suicide as the only solution.

To many, this may be just a novel. But let us ask ourselves: 'Do we not encounter in our real life such cruelty and tough situations as has been depicted in this realistic, life-oriented novel?' Every moment our dignity of humanness is challenged, and we have to stand the acid test boldly. Epics like *Rāmāyaṇa* and *Mahābhārata* inspire us only because we find striking parallels in real life even in this modern age. This fact should never be lost sight of.

One who has once tasted the bliss of pure, unselfish love will not even care for any opposition from the world. He gives love freely in an unbroken stream. He will patiently and stoically bear all the pathos of being human. This is what we call the courage to be human.

Conclusion

Swami Vivekananda in an enthralling poem expressed the idea that one who is mature enough to give love will give only sweetness in return for harshness and cruelty. Such characters are not just found in novels. Even in this relentless world such noble souls move about incognito. Their role is like that of the unseen, unheard dewdrop that falls in the night behind the common gaze and brings into blossom the fairest of roses. Those who come into the proximity of such people get completely transformed into real human beings. Here are the lines from the small poem by Vivekananda entitled *To An Early Violet*:

What though thy bed be frozen earth
Thy cloak the chilling blast?
What though no mate to cheer thy path
Thy sky with gloom o'ercast?

What though if love itself doth fail
Thy fragrance strewed in vain,
What though if bad o'er good prevail
And vice o'er virtue reign?

Change not thy nature, gentle bloom,
Thou violet, sweet and pure,
But e'er pour thy sweet perfume,
Unasked, unstinted, sure.

The Pros and Cons of Obedience

RIGHT FROM our very childhood we are more than familiar with the word 'obedience.' There is hardly a child who has not heard his parents hurling this word at him on several occasions. Our elders want us to be obedient to them, to the teacher, to society and what not. To be a 'nice kid' amounts to being an obedient child. Yet, for good or evil, the word has led to no less controversy. In other words, the word 'obedience' has come to stand as one of the misunderstood and misrepresented concepts in the world. But what is obedience really?

Obedience and authority

The very word 'obedience' raises a question: obedience to what? 'To an authority,' comes the prompt answer. The authority may be our parents, teachers, elders, society, government, king, powerful persons, and so on. To complete the list, there is the authority of our conscience which functions in a covert way, guiding, disciplining, and shaping our character from within through the ordeals of life. The external, overt authority fixes for us the types of obedience and sets certain arbitrary norms in the continuance of a good society. These norms are called 'values' of life. Our conscience is also built up after the pattern of values set by the group of people we live with. All of us are bound to follow one or the other authority if we are to live with others.

When we come up to others' expectations we are praised; otherwise, we are admonished. So obedience, in a sense, is a sort of a covenant, a contract with an authority. Conformity or submission to the authority is extolled as obedience, and its reverse is deplored as disobedience. Authority is not a kind of possession; it is an interpersonal relationship and, depending on mental attitudes of individuals, it has two aspects: rational authority and inhibiting authority. Both are exercised in different types of interpersonal relationships.

Parent-child relationship

This is chiefly a biological bond, starting from the umbilical cord itself. The first object outside the child's body is the parent. His relationship with the world is also established through them. Since the child comes out of the parent's body, the expectations of the parents from the child are more. The parents can foster the child either through love or through strict discipline. Within a reasonable limit both the ways may imply a rational authority and obedience, which under such cases also comes unsolicited in the normal course. But too much pampering or strictures may even lead to a breach in the relationship.

Nowadays most parents verbally say that they wish their children to be free to fulfil their potential. However, in practice they only want their children to achieve their potential by remaining under their control. The anxiety which the parents develop at the idea of the child becoming free, clearly indicates their tendency to continue their domination. This only makes the child all the more dependent and cripples him in facing the world all by himself.

Says American psychotherapist, Dr Rollo May, 'Being merely obedient undermines the development of an individual's ethical awareness and inner strength. By being obedient to external requirements over a long period of time, the child loses his real powers of ethical, responsible choice. Strange as it sounds, then, the powers of these people to achieve goodness and the joy which goes with it are diminished.'[1]

Teacher-student relationship

This relationship begins when the child starts going to school, and is the first training outside the loving care of the parents. Once the student feels at home with the teachers, he or she become receptive to them. Then obedience comes naturally. The teacher's authority helps the child to develop intellectually and psychologically. The teacher feels elated at the success of the student, and his or her failure upsets the teacher.

Employer-employee relationship

This relationship is like a contract of obedience in the form of faithfulness of the servant to the superior. If either party caters to the well-being of the other and evinces genuine human interest in the concerns of the other, this relationship may prove to be an ethical one. Problems arise when the subordinate is ordered by the superior to do what offends his moral values. Then the employee is left with two choices:

either to give up his service or to leave the responsibility to his superior. Of course, in many instances, this type of problem can be solved by a free discussion between the two.

Conjugal relationship

This is mainly based on love and understanding between each other. Through many a love-hate relationship leading to bitter experiences, couples are realizing that to establish a strong bond through marriage and to perpetuate a lineage of happy and healthy progeny, love should be tempered with some detachment.

Obedience in the armed forces

Nowhere else is obedience so much demanded as in the armed forces. Unquestioning obedience is the be-all and end-all of life in the army, navy or air force. Each soldier is trained to follow what the superiors command, no questions asked. The fate of the whole lot depends solely on the discretion of the commander and any question from the subordinate can be met with dismissal. The fateful picture of unquestioning obedience has been graphically depicted by Lord Alfred Tennyson (1809-92) in his immortal poem *The Charge of the Light Brigade.*

Forward, the Light Brigade!
Was there a man dismayed?
Not though the soldier knew
Some one had blundered:
Their's not to make reply,
Their's not to reason why,
Their's but to do and die:
Into the valley of Death
Rode the six hundred.

King-subject relationship

The ideal of kingship is represented by Rāma in the *Rāmāyaṇa*. The sole duty of a king is to look after the well-being of his subjects as if they are his own children. Even punishment can be cracked down on the outlaw for the good of the many. Moreover, the authority being conspicuous, the subjects have a voice in the court even against the king himself. In a normal relationship of this kind, both authority and obedience work in such harmony that they are hardly noticed. According to Swami Vivekananda:

> The subjects should, in every respect, look up to the king and stick to their king with unreserved obedience, and the king should rule them with impartial justice and look to their welfare and bear the same affection towards them as he would towards his own children.[2]

Anonymous authority

There are many relationships which demonstrate rational and inhibiting authority. They fall under a common denominator, 'external authority.' If it is favourably inclined to your well-being, you naturally feel an obligation to obey such an external authority; if it is not, you may even raise your protest or withdraw yourself from this overt type of authority. However, there is another type of authority against which man has no power, and he is helplessly led by such queer authority. This is called by various names like anonymous, covert, invisible, or alienated authority. In this case, nobody makes any demand on you openly, yet you feel propelled by it. The main factors worth mentioning under this category are public opinion, the market, economic necessities, common sense, and so on.

Anonymous authority casts its spell on its subject in the

form of conformity or adjustment to the common trend, which is only another name for obedience. It implies a helpless merging of one's self into the group just for survival. Man groans under its tyranny because such conformity only strangulates his creative urges and his genius.

On the opposite pole stands the internal authority of conscience, sense of values, power of judgement, strength of character, or the individual creative urge. The only antidote is to obey the internal authority, that is, to listen to the 'still small voice' of one's conscience.

Religious obedience

In the religious sphere, obedience has more dimensions than in the worldly level. Religious obedience implies a voluntary submission to a specific religious authority—be it a principle, law, a divine being, or God. Unconditional obedience to an ancient custom, priestly enactment, or the ordinances of some sacred books is emphasized in almost all world religions. This obedience may originate from fear, religious convention, hope of reward, belief in the real excellence of the law, or trust in authority. The important point to note here is that obedience in the religious context always implies that the person in question is either spiritually dependent or immature. A person is free to obey or disobey a particular principle or deity; but he cannot question its authority which is taken for granted.

In Hinduism, the word obedience is replaced by *śraddhā*, which is explained as a deep faith in both the words of the scriptures and the guru. Besides, obedience or adherence to set rules applies only for the novitiate and not for spiritually advanced souls. Obedience in the Hindu context may act as a means of spiritual discipline.

In the Judeo-Christian tradition, the importance of obedience is demonstrated by condemning Adam and Eve for disobeying the commandments of God in the *Genesis*. The very fact that disobedience is sin points to the covenant of God imposed on humanity. In recent times, a part of the Christian world consisting of eminent psychologists, sociologists, among others, has started asserting that the very fact of original disobedience need not be called sin.

On the contrary, disobedience is the condition for man's self-awareness, for his capacity to choose for himself instead of helplessly depending on another being called God. The fall of Adam and Eve from Eden did not corrupt man in the least; rather, it paved the way for man's progress towards freedom. Some scholars go to the extent of saying that it was only because man was expelled from Eden that he was able to make his own history, to develop his human powers, and to attain a new harmony.[3]

By obedience, the *New Testament* means to follow in the footsteps of Jesus Christ, and to submit to those who represent Him here on earth. Obedience finds expression in letters of the apostle St Paul to the Romans and Corinthians, but nowhere in the teachings of Jesus Christ himself—the preacher of love. The Nazarene, with his mature sense of life, preached: 'Blessed are the meek,' 'Blessed are the peace-makers,' 'Do unto others as ye would that others do unto you,' 'The kingdom of heaven is within you.' These sermons do not, in the least, remind man of his first ancestor's disobedience, much less the helplessness of modern man. On the contrary these words point to the fact that man can save himself only by growing into the fullness of his powers and knowledge.

In Buddhism, obedience means the observance of the corporate rules of the *Sangha* (monastic organization). Here the master-disciple relation has been less emphasized; but each of the new recruit is put under the care and tutelage of an elder monk. As a reason to the establishment of the *Sangha*, the Buddha pointed out: 'A man that stands alone, having decided to obey the truth, may be weak and slip back into his old ways. Therefore, stand ye together, assist one another, and strengthen one another's efforts.'[4]

Buddha also insisted on the obedience to the laws of righteousness.[5] At the same time, he bade his disciples in his farewell address to be lamps unto themselves; to rely on themselves and not on external help.[6]

The Islamic dictum requires unquestioning obedience to the *Quran*; but simultaneously it leaves enough room for the exercise of reasoning, known as *ijtihād*, which means exerting oneself. Here also, provision is kept for obedience to one's spiritual mentor called *pīr*.

Confucianism makes filial relationship a paradigm for obedience of all kinds. Obedience is considered important as the master-disciple relationship is akin to spiritual parentage. The disciple is supposed to undergo a period of religious tutelage and this requires the unquestioning obedience of a child.

Monastic obedience

The very words 'monastic organization' point to a spiritual abbey of renunciates who work for the same ideal. As already shown, in various religious contexts obedience forms the very foundation of all religious communities, lay or monastic alike. But whereas in some religious contexts unquestioning obedience is demanded, some of the religions also advocate the coexistence of obedience and freedom.

Obedience and slavery or bondage are not synonymous terms. One can be as free within his own world, while being obedient to his superiors or certain laws, injunctions, values, or authority. A monastic organization is established with the aim of standing as a bulwark for its members to attain a spiritual goal, enlightenment, or freedom. The disciplines of obedience and chastity imposed on its members are means for that goal. No member can claim himself an exception to those impositions which are rather self-disciplinary.

Conflicts come only when the seniors in power assert themselves in exploiting others by using various chicaneries in the name of religion. Such attempts are chiefly aimed at making robots of the juniors and subordinates. In such attempts, the superiors reduce themselves to the level of company bosses who like to have slaves rather than employees. To use a fitting simile of a renowned satiric-humourist poet of Bengal, those seniors want 'a couple of snakes without fangs, claws, eyes, horns, with simple food habits (no extravagance) and no trouble.' As a matter of fact, far from struggling for the welfare of the organization, such people run after the petty aims of their individual life like name, fame, power, money, and so on.

Another point is that in a spiritual organization obedience is imposed on those who are young and still undergoing training. There need not be any restriction for the advanced soul, or precisely, the spiritually mature soul. In an organization where the elders or the persons wielding authority live up to their sermons themselves, obedience for the juniors becomes as smooth as the flow of the southern wind.

Disobedience raises its ugly head due to several

reasons. For one, it happens when the confidence of the youngsters on the elders wanes due to their laxity on being disciplined themselves. For another thing, purposeful disobedience is indicative of a strong protest on the part of the juniors against authority due to some shortcoming in the management or policy.

For yet another thing, disobedience is caused by a deep sense of guilt within one's being due to a conflict between an ideal and conscience. A fitting example of it, though not related to monastic organizations, is Claude Eatherly, the person who gave the signal to drop the bomb at Hiroshima. He was not told beforehand what the bomb would do. But after witnessing the whole episode, he was cut to the quick with contrition. As an atonement for this sinful act, he started committing all sorts of civil disobedience with a view to drawing attention of the authority and to be sent behind the bar.[7]

The monastic members, after realizing their inability to hold on to a high ideal which they chose in the flower of youth in a fit of inchoate inspiration, start disobeying the authorities on various pretexts. Also, when they observe their respected superior preaching high ideals in public while committing the most wretched, unmonastic, heinous crimes in private, the sense of values ingrained in the juniors gets shattered and they start deliberately disobeying.

The problem of conformity to the majority is much relevant in this context. Those who are too weak to follow the voice of their conscience generally give up the struggle sooner and continue with their 'unconditional obedience' to the commands of the authority, however whimsical it may appear. This is known as conformity to the group or majority.

Such people choose their personal comfort and ambition in preference to a life of rigorous self-discipline. Their idea of freedom is the ability to enjoy as they like.

But in such cases they remain obedient to authority at the cost of their real freedom. Real freedom is the ability to choose between the opposite poles like the better and the worse, between the preferable (*śreyaḥ*) and the pleasurable (*preyaḥ*), between independence and dependence, at the critical moment of need. This ability, again, comes from an awareness of what constitutes good or evil, of the unconscious desires, of the consequences of the choice.

One who wants freedom while continuing in an organization must be careful to keep himself aloof from the opinion of the majority and tread the thorny path of conscientious judgement. Only then can one remain as free as the sky, while being as faithful as a dog. In this context, Swami Turiyananda, a disciple of Sri Ramakrishna, made a significant comment: 'In matters of opinion, float with the current; in matters of principle, stand as firm as a rock.'

Holy Mother on obedience

Once two American ladies approached the Holy Mother, Sri Sarada Devi, with the question that when the spiritual teacher belongs to the opposite sex how far one should obey him in all matters. Now, as a matter of fact, the spiritual teacher of the Holy Mother was none else than her own husband, Sri Ramakrishna. Hence, she was never assailed by such a problem in her life. Yet she gave a bold answer: 'In spiritual matters alone you should follow your teacher's instructions unconditionally, but not in worldly matters.' This was an epochal answer that set at naught all chances of exploitation or manipulation in the name of spiritual ministration.

Sri Ramakrishna on obedience

Besides many other sterling qualities of the head and the heart, Sri Ramakrishna was a spiritual teacher nonpareil. He was capable of moulding the lives of his disciples at will. He could easily demand unquestioning obedience from his disciples. The disciples also placed their full trust and confidence in him, and there never was any hitch in the master-disciple relationship. Yet Sri Ramakrishna always put spirituality head and shoulders above obedience. In this context he gave his view citing from the pages of our hoary legends.

He said: 'There is no harm in disobeying your elders for the sake of God. For Rāma's sake Bharat did not obey his mother Kaikeyī. The *gopis* did not obey their husbands when they were forbidden to visit Krishna. Prahlāda disobeyed his father for God. Vali disregarded the words of Sukrāchārya, his teacher, in order to please God. Bibhishana went against the wishes of Rāvana, his elder brother, to please Rāma. But you must obey your elders in all other things.'[8]

Swami Vivekananda on obedience

Vivekananda was passionate about the idea of organization. This was because his study of India revealed the only way to her regeneration was an organized way of doing work. Quoting a popular Sanskrit saying, Vivekananda used to say, when blades of grass are twined into a rope, the latter is strong enough to hold back even a wild elephant.[9]

During his first visit to America, Vivekananda once disclosed to his host Mrs Lyon that he had had the greatest temptation of his life in America. On being queried by Mrs Lyon, Vivekananda said it was the organizing acumen of America that fascinated him. So he wrote to his brother disciple Swami Shivananda after his return from America: 'The work cannot succeed unless there is perfect obedience to the authority of the Order and sacrifice of individual views for the sake of the Order.'[10]

He said, 'In India the one thing we lack is the power of combination, organization, the first secret of which is obedience.'[11]

He also emphasized the necessity of loyalty to the work undertaken, to the leader, and to the organization. 'But,' at the same time he also warned, 'the leader must command respect and obedience by his character.'[12]

In this regard he said in an unequivocal tone: 'Obedience and respect cannot be enforced by word of command; neither can they be exacted. It depends upon the man, upon his loving nature and exalted character. None can resist true love and greatness.'[13]

All this discussion opens our eyes to the truth inherent in the idea of obedience. It also enjoins on us to harmonize the apparently conflicting ideas, namely, freedom and obedience. One can be outwardly obedient while maintaining an inward freedom and poise.

Moreover, man's freedom has to be realized not by breaking away from an established order but rather by exercising his inherent right. Should there be antagonism between the convictions of an individual and the course of action demanded of him, he must be at liberty to state his views publicly. Similarly, the authority claiming his obedience must be prepared to set forth the other side, and must not fall back upon any arbitrary dictum or ancient convention.

In conclusion, let us repeatedly remind ourselves of the alarm raised by Vivekananda: 'I disagree with the idea that freedom is obedience to the laws of nature. According to the history of human progress, it is disobedience to nature that has constituted that progress. This life is a tremendous assertion of freedom; and this obedience to law, carried far enough, would make us simply matter—either in society, or in politics, or in religion.'[14]

End Notes

1. Rollo May, *Man's Search for Himself*, The New American Library, Inc, NY, 1st print, August 1967, p.170
2. *Complete Works,* volume 4:461
3. Vide Erich Fromm, *The Heart of Man*, Harper & Row Publishers, Inc, 1st Perennial Library edition, 1971, pp.10-11
4. Paul Carus, *The Gospel of Buddha,* National Book Trust, India, New Delhi, 3rd Indian edition, October 1971, p.51
5. Ibid. p.136
6. Ibid. p.211
7. Bertrand Russell, *Has Man A Future?* Penguin Books Ltd, Middlesex, 1st edition 1961, p.41
8. 'M', *The Gospel of Sri Ramakrishna*, Red Letter edition, 2000, pp.722-23.
9. *Complete Works*, volume 9, page 99

10. *Complete Works*, volume 9, page 99

11. *Complete Works*, volume 5, page 107

12. Swami Nikhilananda, *Vivekananda: A Biography*, p.165

13. His Eastern and Western Disciples, *The Life of Swami Vivekananda*, Vol.2, p.569

14. *Complete Works*, volume 5, page 286

The Lure of Power

THE *RĀMĀYAṆA* narrates a highly educative story in its last canto. Once a dog came to Rāma's palace seeking justice. The dog was severely injured by a blow on the head. The dog said that a brahmin of high birth had hit him in an angry mood. The brahmin was summoned, and he confessed his sin. An ideal king that Rāma was, he sought the plaintiff's suggestion on the type of punishment.

The dog humbly implored that the Brahmin be made the chief administrator of a certain abbey named Kalanjar. The dog revealed that he himself adorned that post in his last birth. He was an honest person, pious, and possessed of many qualities of the head and heart. Yet unfortunately, he fell prey to delusion and went the wrong way. As an atonement of his bad deeds, he had fallen to the present condition of dog birth. Such being the case with him, what would be the plight of the irksome, envious, vain Brahmin when put in a similar post! The vanity of power and position would throw him all the more into delusion.

Power-mongering is not merely an individual problem.

It has its long roots extended deep into every nook of the world. Swami Vivekananda said in the *Complete Works:*

> Each word of power had to be followed by the groans of millions, by the wails of orphans, by the tears of widows… There was a time when at the sound of the march of big Greek battalions the earth trembled. Vanished from off the face of the earth, with not even a tale left behind to tell, gone is that ancient land of the Greeks. There was a time when everywhere Rome's power was felt and pressed on the head of humanity; the earth trembled at the name of Rome. But the Capitoline hill is a mass of ruins, the spider weaves its web where the Cæsars ruled. There have been other nations equally glorious that have come and gone, living a few hours of exultant and exuberant dominance and of a wicked national life, and then vanishing like ripples on the face of the waters. Thus have these nations made their mark on the face of humanity.[1]

Dimensions of power

The difference between nations is recognized by the difference in their powers. Human status is controlled by power. There is none on earth who is stripped of any power. Power is the force which keeps up one's vitality. Indeed, without power no work, no dynamism would have been possible.

Vedanta philosophy holds power as one of the essential natures of the soul. Just as ego and egotism are not the same, power should not be confused with its ramifications. One cannot do away with the ego, which is an existential reality. When it is said that the ego must be crushed if we want spiritual progress, it actually means to harness the ego, to keep it from wrong orientations, to whittle down the harmful parts of it.

The same idea holds true for power. Power, again, is rooted in the will. Pure, untainted, unbiased will is what is called *ātman* in Vedanta. The same will, when focused on worldly objects or ends, becomes attached and scattered in its power. Then it finds expression in domination over others, and may even wreak havoc. This is the view held by Indian philosophers.

The western psychologists ascribe two dimensions to power. According to them, the first meaning of power is capacity. The other is domination. They represent these two dimensions as 'power of' and 'power over.' The German social psychologist, Erich Fromm has portrayed the subtle distinction between the two concepts. Said he:

> The ability of man to make productive use of his power is his potency; the inability is his impotence. Where potency is lacking, man's relatedness to the world is perverted into a desire to dominate, to exert power over others as though they were things. Domination is coupled with death, potency with life. Domination springs from impotence and in turn reinforces it, for if an individual can force somebody else to serve him, his own need to be productive is increasingly paralyzed.[2]

Thus far we gather that power has both benign and malignant effects depending on the direction of the will. If the will turns to worldly gains, power manifests in domination over others, exploiting the innocence of others. But when the same will is focused on its creative aspect, the result is a manifestation of the inherent dormant potentialities. Such manifestation can never be harmful to others.

It is a common experience that most people change

radically toward the worse when invested with a power of authority. They ignore all their previous relations with others. The behaviour that they extend toward others is far from human. The only aim of most of the modern managers seems to force other people to their own line of thinking by hook or by crook.

People in general try to change the world by coercion. But then things get more complicated. An office boss, to take revenge on his subordinate, sacks him through crooked means and gets a replacement. But more often than not the successor is found to be a worse person than the one before. It is an inscrutable adjustment of nature that a crooked person finds himself surrounded by a group of crooks only. Nature pays him back in his own coin.

As a corollary to Patañjali, man's environment, birth, and lineage are determined by his own actions and man cannot change the world outside except through a change in his attitude to work and attitude towards himself. When these are taken care of, the environment automatically changes favourably for him. But this seldom happens. On the contrary, man thinks he is very clever and none can surpass him in his cunning. This is a mistake.

Man cannot deceive nature. He cannot elude his destiny which is his own creation 'of faults and passions ages long ago/in the deep years of yesterday,' in the poetic language of Swami Vivekananda.[3]

He cannot elude his destiny which is his own creation. Sri Ramakrishna used to say sarcastically, 'The crow, too, thinks he is a clever bird; but the first thing he does when he wakes up in the early morning is to fill his stomach with nothing but others' filth.'[4]

The question that naturally arises in this context is: what prompts people to behave in such queer, inhuman ways after ascending to a high post. To get the answer it will not be enough to float on the surface level. One must dive deep into the human personality to find cogent answers.

Reasons for exploitation

The first cause is ignorance of our real nature and potentiality. It is a mystery of human nature that even though the soul is possessed of an immense and inexhaustible source of power like a dynamo, yet man forgets all about it. The Vedanta philosophers account for this anomaly by positing an entity called māyā. The word means that which *(yā)* is not *(mā)*. They went on to demonstrate a twofold function of this strange entity: covering the real nature of things (*āvaraṇa*) and making things appear as something else (*vikṣepa*).

Everything in the universe, both gross and subtle, come under the purview of *māyā*. Under its spell, man's real identity shrinks and he projects his infinite power into the worldly perspective. It is through *māyā* that man forgets his nature and starts wallowing in the mire of the world through various 'dances of death' expressed in competition, jealousy, and power-mongering. The source of all power is within him, but man seeks it outside in the world and tries to dominate over others in his desperate bid to crave for more and more. At last, man dies in his futile attempt, with hopes blighted.

The second reason follows from the first one. It is fear from other contestants in the battle. If the covering aspect of *māyā* bars one from seeing the truth, the scattering aspect produces fear of being overtaken by others. There is no creature that is completely free from fear. Traumatic previous experiences are stored in the memory and under similar circumstances they warn man of the impending danger. There is nothing in this universe that is not fraught with fear.

According to the *Bṛhadāraṇyaka Upanishad* all fears spring forth from the idea of duality. What is the way out of fear, then? Detachment is the only force that drives away this fear. Detachment naturally follows from a clear understanding of the transient, impermanent world.

Fear also creeps into our mind from a sense of otherness. 'Where there is the sense of oneness, there can be no delusion, grief, or any such feeling.' (*Isha Upanishad*, 6,7).

When one becomes free from fear, a confidence comes up on the surface of one's personality. This confidence is not of the nature of elbowing out others or going ahead of others. It is a confidence in the power and efficiency of human nature.

The third cause of exploitation can be traced to an existential vacuum within oneself. This means that due to some unknown reason we get disconnected from the true source of our being. Spiritual people call this source divinity. When this void is created, man becomes frustrated in life, which finds expression through a compensatory device known as 'the will to power...' This is followed close at the heels by the desire to accumulate riches. When the will to power is dominant, man stops listening to others' views, however correct or cogent. He only values his own whimsical, emotional, and momentary views.

We now come to the fourth cause for power-mongering. Judging by the nature of man, psychologists have divided humanity into two broad classes: lovers of life and lovers of death. People with death instinct are responsible for all the destructive propensities found in man. Necrophilia, the technical word for death instinct, manifests itself in a wide variety of character traits. Literally it means an unusual attraction toward corpses.

But its root goes deeper into the human psyche. Hitler and Stalin were ideal examples of necrophilia. Hitler was fascinated by destruction and felt a bestial joy at the smell of death. The necrophilous person fosters in his bosom the wounds of insult, and ill-treatment. They are very fond of forcing others because force means the power to kill and destroy.

Murder being illegal and criminal, the alternative of it is to deprive others of their legitimate right to freedom. The other expressions of this trait are humiliating others, and taking away others' possessions. When a necrophilous person wields power, his tendency is to convert all people working under him into lifeless, mechanical beings. Such people claim unconditional obedience from their subordinates.

Those necrophiles who do not get an opportunity to kill others find out a number of alternative devices to subdue others so that no court of justice can accuse them of any offence. These are: to deny hope to others, to refuse to recognize talents in others, backbiting, assassinating the character of the victim, being insensitive to the feeling of others, and so on.

As a fifth cause, various types of violence can be traced. Violence may be of several types. One is reactive violence. It comes as a result of a reaction to the ill-treatment from others. Clearly this violence is in defence of life, freedom, and dignity. But unlike death instinct, this violence chiefly aims at preservation, and not destruction. Reactive violence is sometimes caused by frustration. Animals, children, and even adults sometimes behave in a violent way when they feel frustrated. Frustration leads to envy, jealousy, and backbiting.

The next form of violence is revengeful violence. It is an attempt to pay back in the same coin after a damage has already been done. But such tendency is of a destructive nature. On the other hand, one who lives a productive life can easily forget injuries, and insults that are inflicted on him. The very process of productive living makes him change his mentality for the better.

Sometimes the long-standing faith of a person on another shatters due to adverse treatment. If it happens to a child, he can go on shifting his faith from one person to another for experimentation. But at a mature age this is not possible. As a result, the person either becomes sceptical or starts hating life. The believer and lover of life, when disappointed, turns into a hardcore cynic with destructive tendencies. When such people come to power by a decree of fate, they only become a source of trouble to their associates and subordinates.

Violence finds expression in yet another form widely known as sadism. It is not merely the desire to inflict torture on others, but its chief purpose is to exercise complete mastery over others, to make others helpless objects of one's mercy. Humiliating or enslaving others are just different strokes of sadism.

It is unfortunate that with the source of all powers within him, man becomes perverted after ascending to power and position. Our wrong way of training in the family since childhood is chiefly responsible for such aberrations. Is there no remedy for such deep-seated problems?

Some remedies

No problem is called a problem unless it has a solution. For each of the causes cited there is a specific remedy. But for the sake of brevity all the remedies can be strung into a single factor. If every individual can be trained to live a productive life by switching on to the inexhaustible source of *ātman*, all the sinister effects of power-mongering can be easily abolished from the face of the earth.

To live productively means, in the first place, to live in close proximity with people who are beaming with life energy, who love life. Such people teach by their own example. They teach the principles conducive to inner harmony and strength; they can give ample guidance in the art of living. Above all, their company helps one establish one's own freedom—not merely freedom from the shackles of social norms and bindings, but freedom to express the inner urge of his soul to create and construct, to learn from nature with a spirit unbiased by the thought of others.

Security, justice, and freedom—these three are the means to come in touch with one's life force.

When man lives an active life, he may realize the higher values of human life through creative work or by enjoying the world through beauty, art, and nature. But there are periods in life when one is barred from all the enjoyment and bliss of creation. Under such circumstances the way in which man accepts his inevitable fate and the subsequent suffering, determines his success in finding out meaning in life. Suffering is an ineradicable part of life. Man can maintain his high human dignity even under straitened circumstances. What one chooses under such circumstances decides his success or failure in life.

In the *Kathopanishad*, the little boy, Nachiketas faced this crisis and brilliantly came out successful with one telling blow of right judgement. In contrast, in the *Bhagavad Gītā,* Arjuna also faced this sudden crisis on the battlefield and failed to make the right choice between fight and flight. So Krsna had to come forward to convey the right choice of path. But after preaching the whole sermon of the *Gītā,* Krsna said, 'I have imparted to you the most secret knowledge. Imbibe this and do whatever you feel.' It means the Lord left the choice of path to Arjuna. What one chooses under such circumstances decides his success or failure in life.

Pros and cons

Power by itself is not always harmful. It is the attitude that matters. Sri Kṛṣṇa vanquished many demons and devilish people by extremely cruel means. The motive was to establish the supremacy of virtue over vice, truth over falsehood. 'Truth alone triumphs, not falsehood,' says the Upanishads.

Man's attitude toward the world depends on how he looks upon himself. This truth was laid down by Sri Ramanuja.[6] To put it explicitly, one who hates oneself will arouse hatred in others through his behaviour, while one whose self-image is good will treat others lovingly. This principle can be used as a hallmark for judging powerful people.

Another way to judge resourceful people has been beautifully hinted at by Bhartṛhari, the king-turned-sage, in his celebrated work *Hundred Verses on Morality*. There he divides humankind into four classes. The first comprises those who do good to others even at the cost of their own interest. They are termed as 'noble' people (*satpuruṣāḥ*). Though rare in count, there are people who are ever ready to sacrifice their own life for the sake of others, do good for the sake of good only.

The second class consists of those who are ready to do good to others so long as their selfish interest is not tampered with. They are marked as the 'common run' of people. The major part of the world's populace comes under this category.

The third class, sardonically expressed as 'human devils,' includes those who smash others' hopes to keep their own hopes alive.

Yet this is not all. As if to fill the cup of human misery, there rises on the surface of humanity the ugly head of another class of people. Bhartṛhari humbly regrets his inability to define this fourth class of people who go on doing harm to others without any apparent motive for themselves. These people, in contrast to the first class, do evil for evil's sake alone. *(Neetisatakam)*

Swami Vivekananda went to the extent of saying that the craze for power and fame is a deadlier enemy than even lust. Every citizen of the world is aware of the truth, 'As you sow, so you reap.' Besides, the wheel of karma makes every creature reel under its sway. It moves incessantly making man a slave of his unconscious drives. The inexorable law of Karma does not relieve anyone from the king to the pauper, the high and the low, the scholar and the illiterate. If one can keep in mind this truth forever, he will never feel infatuated when placed in power and position. Vivekananda has described this terrible machinery of work in his own style in the *Complete Works*:

> This world's wheel within wheel is a terrible mechanism; if we put our hands in it, as soon as we are caught, we are gone. We all think that when we have done a certain duty, we shall be at rest; but before we have done a part of that duty, another is already in waiting. We are all being dragged along by this mighty, complex world-machine.[7]

Sage Patañjali in his *Yoga Sutras* (2:13) has clearly stated in his yoga aphorism that man's birth, longevity, enjoyment, and suffering, are decided by his work.[8] This aphorism, while holding each individual responsible for his own actions, stands as a warning to those who do not hesitate to stoop low in order to control and subjugate others.

Man cannot do away with work. It is work that connects him to the world. Again, it is work through which he comes to grief. Then what is the way out. Said Vivekananda:

> There are only two ways out of it; one is to give up all concerns with the machine, to let it go and stand aside, to give up our desires. That is very easy to say, but is almost impossible to do…The other way is to plunge into the world and learn the secret of work, and that is the way of Karma-Yoga. Do not fly away from the wheels of the world-machine, but stand inside it and learn the secret of work. Through proper work done inside, it is also possible to come out. Through this machinery itself is the way out.[9]

The *secret of work* is unselfish, self-directed work. When man does every bit of work with this spirit, he is never tempted by the desire to dominate over others. Everybody wants to rule over others, to lead others. But very few are indeed fit to take that responsible role. Only he is fit to lord over others who is ever ready to sacrifice everything for others. Vivekananda warned his disciple Alasinga against this desire. He wrote:

> Do not try to lead your brethren, but serve them. The brutal mania for leading has sunk many a great ship in the waters of life. Take care especially of that, that is, be unselfish even unto death, and work.[10]

Sri Ramakrishna, in speaking of power, always stressed on a commission from God. In his opinion, the people will obey the orders of him who is officially entrusted with a particular duty. In his words,

> ...a worthless man may talk his head off preaching, and yet he will produce no effect. But people will listen to him if he is armed with a badge of authority from God. One cannot teach others without the commission from God. A teacher of men must have great power.[11]

Sri Ramakrishna gives another beautiful and more substantial example:

> Some people used to befoul the bank of the Haldarpukur at Kamarpukur every morning. The villagers would notice it and abuse the offenders. But that didn't stop it. At last the villagers filed a petition with the Government. An officer visited the place and put up a sign: 'Commit no nuisance. Offenders will be punished.' That stopped it completely. Afterwards there was no more trouble. It was a government order, and everyone had to obey it.[12]

Conclusion

Sometimes, rarely though, this commandment may come from the highest of all authorities, that is, from the Divine. The individual on whom this divine dispensation descends is the fittest person to exercise power. In such a case the power he wields is not his but belongs to the divine. The *Ṛg-Veda* records an unparalleled statement in the form of a mantra, which is popularly known as *Devī-sūktam*. It says that the person whom the Divine Mother chooses is made mighty, powerful, wise. This knowledge can stop once for all the desperate rat race for power and fame.

We will bring our long discussion on power to an end with a story of subtle humour. Adhar Sen, a lay disciple of Sri Ramakrishna, held a high post of deputy magistrate. He used to come to Dakshineswar after a day's work in the evening, and slept in Sri Ramakrishna's room for quite some time before leaving for home. This practice lasted for a long time. One day, Adhar challenged Sri Ramakrishna with a snobbish air, 'People call you God; what supernatural power do you possess?' To this Sri Ramakrishna's prompt repartee was, 'Why, I can put the deputy magistrates to sleep in my room!'

End Notes

1. *Complete Works*, volume 3, page 106
2. E.Fromm, *Man for Himself*, London, Routledge & Kegan Paul Ltd., Reprint 1975, pp.87-88.
3. The Cup.
4. 'M', *The Gospel of Sri Ramakrishna*, Ramakrishna Math, Chennai, Red Letter edn, Feb.2000, pp.669-70.
5. *Vedārtha-Saṅgrahaḥ*, §245.
6. *Neetiśatakam,* 75.
7. *Complete Works*, volume 1, page 115.
8. P.Y.2:13.
9. *Complete Works*, volume 1, page 115.
10. *Complete Works*, volume 5, page 36.
11. 'M', *Gospel of Sri Ramakrishna*, p.446.
12. op.cit. p.668.

The Inscrutable Dynamics of Karma

ONCE TWO friends were walking on the street, when they came upon a place where some people were listening to a recital of the *Bhāgavatam*. One of them was drawn towards the recital, while the other preferred to go to a house of ill fame. Moments later each of them felt ashamed of his decision and reflected wistfully on the enjoyment of the other. When both of them died, the messenger of death took the soul of the Bhāgavatam listener, while the messengers of God fetched the soul of the other.

Sri Ramakrishna, who told the story to his devotees, commented: 'As is a man's feeling of love, so is his gain. Verily, the Lord looks into a man's heart and does not judge him by what he does or where he lives.'[1]

It is extremely difficult, indeed, to delve into the mystery of karma. Swami Vivekananda has called karma 'a terrible mechanism of wheels within wheels.'[2] Lord Krishna said, 'inscrutable is the movement of karma.'[3] He said, 'the wise people get deluded as to decide what an action is and what an inaction is.'[4]

A search into the secrets of karma, often proves futile. Human beings with good intentions, enthusiastically and honestly do their work, expecting good returns, hoping that it would be a positive score in their karmic account. But at long last, man only discovers that he has not gained a whit, nor has he made any progress by dint of such karma. Spent and confused, he starts blaming the whole world and an imaginary cruel, partial God for all his failures at the fag-end of life.

But there is hope. The mysteries of karma can be unravelled by two simple but concrete steps. 1) Acquire knowledge of the workings of karma and 2) relate this knowledge to our day-to-day life.

Concept of karma: All works are not karma

Life in this planet bristles with activities. Everything—static and kinetic alike—is in motion. In fact, the Sanskrit name, *jagat*, for the universe implies that which is on the move. Sri Krishna also says in the *Bhagavad Gītā* that none in this universe can exist a moment without doing work.[5] Still all types of activity cannot be called karma, the Sanskrit word, which is not exactly synonymous with action or work.

There are innumerable types of work: flowing of a stream, raining, displacement of an object, flowering of plants, breathing, heart-beat, car-driving, swimming, yachting, and so on. Though each of these is an action involving the use of energy, some of these actions do not come under the category of karma. According to the *Bhagavad Gītā,* five factors are responsible for every karma to be worth the name. These are: the body (seat of the doer); the doer (agent); the instruments of work; various techniques or skills of work and the Divine

Dispensation. By 'instruments of work' is meant, in yogic parlance, the work done by the five organs of knowledge (*jñānendriyas*), the five organs of work (*Karmendriyas*), the five vital forces (*prāṇa*, *udāna*, *vyāna*, *apāna*, *samāna*), and the modifications of the mind.

From this it becomes clear that for every action to be worthy of the name 'Karma,' there must be a doer or agent to appropriate the work for itself by thinking, 'I am the doer as also the enjoyer.' Where there is no life force, no connection with the doer, the action is not worth the name karma even though it is called work.

Thus, karma is a conscious effort to bring about some change in nature—external as well as internal. As a logical corollary to this involvement of the doer in all karmas it can be said that the will comes into force in the performance of every karma. And so long as the will power is not purified, it will wreak havoc on nature with its wanton ways, thus inviting unwanted trouble for man.

Ramifications of karma

Depending on the direction of the will, karma comes into play in two ways: through *puruṣakāra* or self-effort, and through *prārabdha* or earned karma. Of these, the first one is like going upstream against the current. Conscious will is to be applied if one wants to get rid of the bondage of karma. The second one occurs as a result of unconscious ways of doing work. Some results are good, while others are bad. Accordingly, the doer enjoys or suffers. It is like going down the stream effortlessly.

In his comments on a Yoga aphorism of Patañjali, Vyāsa has presented this idea graphically: 'The stream of will, indeed, flows both ways—toward good as well as evil. Between these two, that which forces its way through discrimination up to the attainment of unity carries with it all goodness; and that which, through indiscrimination, becomes burdened with worldliness, leads to evil consequences.'[6]

This bifurcation of karma into individual will and earned results makes the performer of karma responsible for all his actions, good and bad. With this knowledge, man will not try to hoodwink others by bringing in an entity called God as a scapegoat for all his wrongdoings.

When a stone is dropped on the still water of a lake, it produces two types of motion in the water: Transverse, that is, perpendicular to the water level, and longitudinal, that is, along the surface. The first reaction is the bobbing up and down of waves vertically due to buoyancy. The other reaction comes in the form of ripples making circles that move toward the bank, only to come back with the same force.

In a similar way, all karmas produce two results: A repetitive tendency for the same action in the doer, and a subtle vibration which travels toward the cosmic mind and comes back to the doer. Of these two, the first result is in the control of the doer, for he can repeat the action or stop repetition by the force of his will. Here *puruṣakāra* comes into function. But he has no control over the second type of result which is stamped as 'fate' by the majority, and is known as *prārabdha* in yogic terms.

Karma-samskāra

When someone experiences happiness by doing a particular work he develops, like the 'transverse' type of waves, a liking to repeat the same work just for the sake of pleasure. This creates an impression in the mind named *samskāra*. It is this force of *samskāra* that gives rise to the desire to repeat an action defying all restraints. The process goes like this: First a picture appears in the mind. It is called *smṛti* or *vāsanā*. Then the will of the seer wants to own it and reacts whether to run after it as if it were a golden deer or feel a repulsion against it. This love-hate process goes on ad infinitum, and, according to Patañjali, the sum total of all such good and bad *samskāras* decide the type of birth (*jāti*), longevity (*āyus*), and good and bad experiences (*bhoga*) of the person.

The surroundings in which we find ourselves in any birth are actually directed by the work done by us in the past. The sum total of all the samskāras of an individual is known as *karmāśaya (*reservoir of karma). It consists of all the good and bad habits of an individual. If the good *samskāras* outweigh the bad ones, the person will get good company, conducive environment, and in the reverse case, contrary will be the result. The yoga philosophy says that when the intensity of the resultant action is too much in an individual, it comes to fruition in this very birth.

Such work is called *dṛṣṭa-janma-vedanīya* karma. On the other hand, if the *samskāras* are not ripe enough to bear fruit in this birth, they are accumulated in the mindset like a reservoir of karma (*Karmāśaya*). Such actions which do not yield any result in the present birth are kept in waiting for fruition and are known as *adṛṣṭa-janma-vedanīya karma*.[7]

All these *samskāras* and their subsequent enjoyments or sufferings come under the periphery of *prārabdha* karma. These workings go on in our psyche almost in an unconscious stream, shaping our character. We feel out of ignorance and vanity that we are doing as we like, while we are, in fact, helplessly driven by our hidden impressions of past karmas.

This discussion shows that we can change ourselves but not our environment. The meaningless, knee-jerk repetition of an action can be stopped—or at least controlled—by conscious, wilful withdrawal. Side by side, one has also to engage oneself in good actions that interest one and are also helpful to others. This is called *puruṣakāra*, self-effort, the positive aspect of all actions. The other aspect, *prārabdha*, is the 'coming back' of the previous actions with all their intensity to the doer.

Not only so; they direct our birth and environment. Man has no control over them. Sankaracharya has unequivocally expressed it in his masterpiece, *Vivekacūḍāmaṇi*: '*Prārabdha* is indeed very strong for the wise, and can be exhausted only through suffering.'[8] If anybody goes to counter it by reacting or reviling, that itself becomes the source of another misery.

This is why all the spiritual teachers have taught us the art of changing ourselves instead of changing the world.

The idea of duty

The concept of duty is intrinsically connected with work or more precisely, self-effort. The Sanskrit word for duty is *kārya*, which also means the effect of a cause. So, the composite meaning of the word takes us to the understanding that duty is the work that has befallen us as an effect of our past actions. As a matter of fact, the idea of duty is too complicated to understand. Swami Vivekananda said, 'This idea of duty is the midday summer sun which scorches the innermost soul of mankind.'[9]

'We should do our obligatory duties with detachment of mind,' we are counselled. But suppose the duty is disagreeable, or abominable, or will incur demerit to the doer. What will be our attitude to it in such a case? This is an age-old confusion that assails the minds of even great men. Arjuna, for one, was beset with the same question about his duty at an hour of crisis. In answer to this conundrum, Sri Krishna gave him a long sermon on his immediate duty, and, exhorted Arjuna to abandon all ideas of duty and take shelter in Him.[10]

Our scriptures clearly define duty as: That which is unselfish and conducive to the welfare of others is virtue, and that which is selfish and harmful to others is vice. In our day-to-day life we cannot help doing some harm to other creatures, careful though we are. Even in breathing, we kill a large number of microbes every moment. But that is an accidental killing; the main purpose, perhaps, is different.

Judging by the Yoga-aphorisms of Patannñjali, even our present duty is decided by our past actions. Swami Vivekananda also said in a similar tone: 'Our duties are determined by our deserts to a much larger extent than we are willing to grant.'[11]

Hence, instead of complaining of a thankless duty, we should continue to perform with care the duty given to us by Providence. Our purpose is to become free from all entanglements. All our duties are fraught with an element of evil in some way or the other. However wary we are, we cannot avoid the stigma of sin by doing work. 'All undertakings are tainted with faults like fire covered by smoke,' says Sri Krishna in the *Bhagavad Gītā*.[12]

The human body is said to be the seat of sufferings and no one is free of that. Even highly evolved spiritual souls are seen to suffer untold misery. The duty of all is to do our duty voluntarily, while keeping the door of awareness wide open.

The cause-effect network

The maxim, 'As you sow, so you reap,' is the bedrock on which ethics and morality stand. The Hindu scriptures say that souls take up bodies in accordance with their work and in conformity with their knowledge.[13] So possessing the right knowledge is also a factor in the network of karma. But this like-work-like-effect principle has led to a lot of misunderstanding. For example, if a person is harmed in any way in this life, that does not necessarily imply that he did exactly the same harm to others before. A fisherman, a butcher, has to do his duty of cruelty to other animals just for the upkeep of the society as well as himself. He does not engage in that work for pleasure or cruelty. Society has assigned that job for him through the division of labour. His 'sin' of killing animals may not come back to him in the form of being killed by others.

The hawk kills the pigeon as its prey; that does not mean that the pigeon had done any similar sin before. It is the weakness on the part of the pigeon that causes the tragedy. If someone is waylaid by brigands, that does not mean the looted person was a brigand in his last birth.

We find that the bad and cruel people enjoy life while the good and honest suffer immensely.[14] Why is it so? We must get the cogent answer to this pertinent question of all ages if we want people to have faith in higher values of life.

Virtue *(dharma)* is a trait comprising knowledge, power and detachment. Its opposite is vice, which comprises ignorance, adversity, and attachment. To be virtuous, one must be able to apply these three aspects of dharma in day-to-day life. Dharma also implies twelve sterling qualities such as harmlessness, truthfulness and so on. A man is called virtuous when he possesses all these qualities; and the person having the opposites is known as wicked. If you are worldly wise you will get the company of worldly people only. This is the plain truth. If the bad person's power and confidence in himself outbids the good person's power and confidence in goodness, the former wins.

Another point is that all our sufferings may not be the results of our past actions as is generally thought. They may also be reminders for us to shield ourselves against any probable adversity, or a warning to strengthen our inner bastion against further attacks. The enemy attacks at our weak, unguarded nooks, and not on the strong side of us. Moreover, the saying, 'to dine with the devil you must have a long spoon' is very much applicable when we cannot avoid moving about and working with shrewd, worldly-savvy people.

Sri Ramakrishna said that one must exercise a lot of discrimination while dealing with the shrewd people hell-bent upon harming others; they are of the nature of a snake. That is to say, whenever Sri Ramakrishna's keen eyes espied a weakness in any of his beloved disciples, he would be out to train him to dispel that weakness.

Mahābhārata motto was, 'Where there's virtue, there is victory' *(yato dharmastato jayaḥ).* But many brows are raised when we go through the whole epic. The truthful Yudhiṣṭhira had to lie on the battlefield that led to the unlawful murder of Droṇa; Bhīma had to defeat his archrival Duryodhana with a forbidden stroke, and so on. Though sinful, these acts were aimed at recovering their legitimate right for the lost kingdom. Both sides committed sins, but the Pāṇḍavas had a greater proportion of goodness and higher values of life.

When we say, 'Virtue triumphs,' it not only implies victory

of virtue over vice or ignorance; it also implies the victory of conscience and morality. But from another angle, the virtuous person, for lack of desire to lord over others, sometimes gets defeated by his undeclared and unpredicted enemies. The Pāṇḍavas, under the leadership of Yudhiṣṭhira, vanquished the Kauravas in a ghastly, gory battle and established the supremacy of virtue over vice once again. But, as individuals, each of the Pāṇḍava brothers, along with their wife Draupadī, had to suffer the consequences of their individual sins.

At times, guided by our vanity, we feel that our sinful acts will go unpunished if we can act cleverly enough taking care of each of our steps. In other words, we try to direct the course of our actions. That this is a wrong notion is demonstrated in the tragic end of the legendary demon Hiraṇyakaśipu. Sunk deep in his arrogance, he engaged himself in hard penance, just for winning a boon of invincibility over all, including gods. But although his desire was fulfilled, he could not escape the cause-effect network and was overpowered in the fullness of time. He could not be killed by man, god, or animal; so he was killed by a chimerical being. He could not be killed in day or night; so he was killed during twilight. He would not die from any weapon; so the claws of a lion were used. His death would not come in land, in water, or midway; so he was laid on the lap for 'capital punishment.' Thus, every part of his boon was countered. In a similar way, clever and shrewd people come under the sway of more clever and dishonest people to outwit or vanquish them.

Practical aspects

Man's attitude towards work depends on his attitude towards the world and towards himself. Under all circumstances man should maintain a balanced outlook on his habits and he should neither overestimate nor underestimate himself.

The soul, mind, and body can be compared to the three vertices of a triangle. They are inseparably connected to each other. There is mutual communication eternally going on among these three. The body communicates through physical reactions, sickness, and so on; the mind speaks through various psychic phenomena; and the soul conveys its message through spiritual visions. Perfect balance is that state when the triangle is equilateral. In that state the body, mind, and soul work in harmony.

This points to the fact that one who wants to attain perfection in life must strike a balance between all his endeavours and inner urges. He should be able to read the different languages of his body, mind and soul to respond rightly to their communications.

Now, on our way to perfection, one of the stumbling blocks is our inability to choose the right course of action when we are given freedom to do so. However queer this statement may appear, the truth is that we are not free to choose. We can choose our future course of action only on the basis of our previous *samskāras.*

When we have pleasurable previous experience, we become lax, easy-going, and egoistic in our bearings and with painful memory of experiences we become revengeful. But little do we realize that such reactionary attitude leads only to an equal and opposite reaction as per Newton's third law of motion, causing successive birth digressions from the reality. To put it graphically, the soul keeps moving in a zigzag motion around a straight line—the shortest route to perfection—wending its way through many births. The soul is like one endpoint of a straight line, the other extremity being the Super soul or *Paramātman*. Due to various deeds the soul moves away from the straight line by the centrifugal force of some aspects of karma. As a result of that wrong action, the soul suffers from another deviation and travels to the other side of the line in an equal and opposite reaction, either in this very life time or in the next.

With repentance and right understanding, the soul tends to make amends, comes back to the central line and moves forward again to his goal. But again, desire raises its ugly head and forces the soul away. This to and fro motion goes on perpetually until the soul becomes fully aware of its spiritual destiny. This is the story of man's struggle for liberation.

Epilogue

Now comes the main question: how are we to escape suffering and rid ourselves of the pains of human life? What is the way out? The toughest question of human life is that of human suffering. Sri Ramakrishna was asked this question for the umpteenth time by his young devotees. Even the globe-trotting Swami Vivekananda, the large-hearted Buddha, and all the spiritual stalwarts of the world had to face the question from all quarters. This age-old problem of human life is the basis of existential philosophy.

The answer is that as long as we continue to be arrogant, vain, lazy, irresponsible, malicious, intolerant, domineering, hypocritical beings, any attempt to assuage our misery will prove futile, however much money and manpower we may possess. Until we succeed in perfecting the world within us, vain is our attempt to perfect the world outside. The outside world is conditioned after the pattern of the inner world. So, in brief, the way out of our misery lies in the way in, that is, within our being, where the root cause of our misery lies.

But just the knowledge of the cause is not enough. We must learn to act according to the guidelines of that knowledge. One notable psychologist, Edgar Cayce, made a remarkable statement in this connection: 'Not what one was, but what one does about what one knows—that is what is important...Knowledge not lived is sin!'[15]

Knowledge of something, coupled with self-effort, comes to stand as a powerful weapon for the soul to forge ahead through all ordeals. Once knowledge is gained, man can continue to do the same work as before, with a change in his attitude and understanding. He will accept the world as it is. He will then stop sneering at others for wallowing in the mire of the world. Instead, he will kneel down by the side of the suffering person and pray like that great saint who said, 'But for Thy grace, O Lord, there go I.'

Once someone asked St Francis what he would do if the world would end forthwith. St Francis was hoeing his garden. He quietly replied, 'I would continue to hoe my garden.' This is a significant idea that guides us to the quiet acceptance of all polarities in the world without twitching a nerve. This idea of acceptance of oneself in a constructive and not pessimistic way and the subsequent self-effort is expressed in crystal-clear style in the following inspiring message of Swami Vivekananda:

> Therefore, blame none for your own faults, stand upon your own feet, and take the whole responsibility upon yourselves. Say, "This misery that I am suffering is of my own doing, and that very thing proves that it will have to be undone by me alone." Take the whole responsibility on

> your own shoulders, and know that you are the creator of your own destiny. All the strength and succour you want is within yourselves.
>
> Therefore, make your own future. "Let the dead past bury its dead." The infinite future is before you, and you must always remember that each word, thought, and deed, lays up a store for you and that as the bad thoughts and bad works are ready to spring upon you like tigers, so also there is the inspiring hope that the good thoughts and good deeds are ready with the power of a hundred thousand angels to defend you always and for ever.[16]

The same context reminds us of another telling poem from Vivekananda entitled *The Cup*. It seems to reveal in a nutshell, more than anything else, the whole gamut of struggle encompassing his own life. The poem runs as follows:

> *This is your cup—the cup assigned to you from the beginning.*
> *Nay, My child, I know how much of that dark drink is your own brew*
> *Of fault and passion, ages long ago,*
> *In the deep years of yesterday, I know.*
> *This is your road—a painful road and drear.*
> *I made the stones that never give you rest.*
> *I set your friend in pleasant ways and clear,*
> *And he shall come like you, unto My breast.*
> *But you, My child, must travel here.*
> *This is your task. It has no joy nor grace,*
> *But it is not meant for any other hand,*
> *And in My universe hath measured place,*
> *Take it. I do not bid you understand.*
> *I bid you close your eyes to see My face.*[17]

End Notes

1. M, *The Gospel of Sri Ramakrishna*, Red-letter edn, 2000, p.204 (conversation of 8-4-1883)
2. CW1:115.
3. *gahanā karmaṇo gatiḥ*, *Bhagavad Gītā* 4:17
4. *Bhagavad Gītā*, 4:16
5. *Bhagavad Gītā*, 3:5
6. *PatanjaliYoga Sutras*, 1:12
7. Cf. Vyāsa's commentary on *PatanjaliYoga Sutras,* 2:12.
8. Sankaracharya, *Vivekacūḍāmaṇi*, Verse 453.
9. *Complete Works,* volume 1, page 103; Cf. A.S.18:3
10. *Bhagavad Gītā*,18:66
11. *Complete Works*, volume 1, page 71
12. *Bhagavad Gītā*,18:48
13. *Kaṭha Upanishad*, 2:2:7
14. Op.cit. 18/10-11
15. G. Cerminara, *The World Within*, A.R.E. Press, Virginia Beach, Va, 2nd printing, October 1988, p.202.
16. *Complete Works,* volume 2, page 225
17. *Complete Works,* volume 6, page 177

Understanding the Significance of Tantra

CONTRARY TO age-old misconceptions about the purity and importance of Tantras, some of the greatest souls of yesteryears had respect, even adoration for this important branch of study. Bāmākhyāpa and Rāmprasad are the two singular names that pop up first in the minds of those who think of the Tantric way of spiritual discipline in Bengal. They were two outstanding souls who reached perfection in the path, and are adored by people all over India.

Tantric practices made a firm footing on the soil of West Bengal (erstwhile Gauḍa), as well as Kashmir and South India. But this esoteric yogic tradition suffered a setback in the course of time because of aspersions cast on some of its methodology.

Sri Ramakrishna dispelled this misunderstanding. Right from assuming the post of assistant priest in Dakshineswar Kālī temple, his mind was possessed with the idea of realizing Divine Mother Kālī whose form was not bound within a life-size stone image, but pervaded everything. The divinity which was named *mahāmāyā* because of her bewitching and inscrutable power, was adored by Sri Ramakrishna as Kālī. And for the first time he embarked upon a search for that power in a scripturally sanctioned path under the guidance of a Brahmin lady well-versed in all the sixty-four Tantric disciplines.

Sri Ramakrishna's guru in Advaitic discipline, Totāpurī, came only after Sri Ramakrishna had attained perfection in all those Tantric paths. What is more, Sri Ramakrishna duly sought permission of his beloved 'Mother in the temple' for undergoing the non-dual path of knowledge, though he did not pay any heed to his erstwhile Tantric guru Bhairavī Brāhmaṇī's non-approval in the matter.

This shows that the ultimate realization of Advaita is not possible without the grace of *Śakti* (the power of Brahman). When the situation demanded the removal of all forms from his mind, in the course of meditation on the non-dual plane, he mentally wielded a sword of 'knowledge' and cut the image of Kālī recurrently occurring in his mind due to past habits, into two—*nāma* and *rūpa*, name and form—and merged Her into the endless ocean of Existence-consciousness-bliss.

In that plane of deepest samādhi he became one with Brahman. And as soon as he came down from that state, he identified himself with that very *mahāmāyā* consisting of all names and forms that constitute the phenomenal universe in a relationship of mother and son.

The same *māyā*, which is looked upon as insignificant by Advaitic proponents, and indefinable by the aspirants,[1] is the summum bonum of all Tantric followers. She is identified with Śiva, and is held as the dynamic projection of that Supreme Reality. Creation, sustenance and dissolution are, according to Tantra, the functions of that *Śakti* called *mahāmāyā*. Since the word *śakti* is in the feminine gender, this inscrutable power is painted as the female goddess Kālī.

The consummation of all Tantric disciplines is in realizing Śiva or Śakti in every being. Curiously enough, the goal of Advaita philosophy is also this realization of oneness or non-duality in all beings. It is only after attaining that supreme state that Sri Ramakrishna gave out his message of service of God in living beings as the motto of all spiritual aspirants. Even the Advaita exponent Ācārya Śaṅkara took to the worship of *Tripurasundarī* and arranged to install the Śrī-yantra in all the monasteries founded by him. Buddhism also abounds in Tantras. This shows the wide and all-pervading influence of Tantras.

Etymology and origin

The word tantra has been derived from the root *tan* meaning, to spread. In a special sense it means the scripture by which the knowledge is spread.[2] This does not, however, mean that Tantra means any branch of knowledge, though, in a general way, the word signifies text of a particular system.

Tantra is concerned with the application of *tattva* and *mantra*, the science of cosmic principles and that of the mystic word, respectively. In the *Kamikagama* tantra, a standard tantric text, the word tantra has been defined as that subject which disseminates *tattva*, and mantra, and also that which shows the way to emancipation.[3]

India's primary scripture, the Vedas, have shown two paths in life. They are, *bhoga*, enjoyment, and *apavarga*, emancipation. Those who desire the former path are required to perform certain rituals called *yajña*. The major portion of the Vedas is covered by various types of such rituals. They have a twofold effect. In the first place, those rituals purify the minds of the performer, and in the second, they give back by way of a cosmic effect certain results fulfilling the desire of the performer.

Such rituals aim at propitiating certain presiding deities like Indra, Mitra, Varuna, and Kubera. Since the *yajñas* are associated with certain types of karma or work, the ritualistic part of the Vedas is called *karma-kāṇḍa*. There is, however, another philosophical part known as *jñāna-kāṇḍa* in the Vedas, covering a very small portion, the conclusive part.

That is meant for a very few eligible and advanced persons who do not care for enjoyments in this life or hereafter. For them has been prescribed the royal path of renunciation. This part is called Vedanta, the conclusive or end part of the Vedas.

The Tantric tradition, being synthetic as against the analytic Vedanta tradition, is acceptable to people of all types. In other words, it is inclusive rather than exclusive. It prescribes different types of practices for aspirants of different dispositions. This division of fitness also prevails in some way in the Vedantic tradition in which priority is given to the eligibility of the aspirant.

The Tantras fall under five heads: *Śaiva*, *Śākta*, *Vaiṣṇava*, *Saura*, and *Gāṇapatya*. These five classes of worshippers are collectively called *pañcopāsaka*. Each of these classes of worshippers has its own Tantra or mode of practice.

The Yāmalas

The *Yāmalas* constitute a class of Tantric literature. They indicate a great development in the Tantric *sādhana*. The principal *Yāmalas* are eight in number and are said to be communicated by the eight *Bhairavas*. They are: Rudra,

Kanda (or Skanda), Brahmā, Viṣṇu, Yama, Vāyu, Kubera, and Indra. Whereas the Śiva Tantras represent the Rudra or Sadāśiva tradition, the *Yāmalas* represent the *Bhairava* tradition. These *Bhairavas* seem to have been human teachers who had attained complete spiritual emancipation, and had almost become Śiva.

Practice

The word Tantra also means 'that which rules or governs.' It is the science of living a way of life that leads to the desired goal. So, it is characterized by practice combined with esoteric knowledge. The Tantras lay down different forms of practice for the attainment of the highest aim of human existence by one living the ordinary life of a householder. In this respect, they correspond to the worship portion of the Vedas.

The proponents of Tantra say that when the Vedic rituals became outmoded, Śiva replaced them with Tantric rites. The Tantric system besides synthesising the two distinct paths of enjoyment and renunciation, acts as a conduit between the rituals and philosophy of the Vedas.

Each act in the process of worship in the Tantric system has to be performed with some sort of meditation symbolising the unity of individual soul with God. Thus Tantra, being both a modification and synthesis of Vedic literature, owes its origin to the Vedas. According to some it is said that at the beginning of creation, the supreme Lord Śiva revealed from his five faces pure knowledge in five streams for the enjoyment as well as liberation of all living beings. These are *laukika*, empirical; *vaidika*, scriptural; *ādhyātmika*, spiritual; *atimārga*, transcendental; and *mantra*, aphoristic. According to some other schools, *āgama* is the advice of Śiva to Pārvatī, his divine consort, on this subject.

The three letters forming the word *'āgama'*—*ā*, *ga*, and *ma*—signify that the Tantric literature (*āgata*) came from Śiva, and (*gata*) went to Pārvatī. In the *nigama*, Pārvatī is the speaker and Śiva the listener. But this distinction between the two terms is not adhered to everywhere in the context of tantric literature. A scholar writes:

> 'One of the oldest Tantras available in manuscript, *Nilvasatattva Samhitti*, holds that the Tantra is the culmination of the esoteric science of the Vedanta and the *Samkhya*.'[4]

If the Vedanta path is called analytic, the Tantric path is said to be synthetic. Sri Ramakrishna's whole life of *sādhanā* was replete with this attitude, the positive way of approach. He used to say: 'Suppose you have *separated* the shell, flesh, and seeds of a Bel fruit, and someone asks you the weight of the fruit. Will you leave aside the shell and the seeds, and weigh only the flesh? Not at all. To know the real weight of the fruit, you must weigh the whole of it—the shell, the flesh, and the seeds. Only then can you tell its real weight.'[5]

The religious attitude in Tantric rituals is twofold: the exoteric ritual of the Vedic type, which aims at the acquisition of control over the forces of nature, and the esoteric ritual, its aim being the union of the two prime principles—Śiva and Śakti. Even this ritual traces its origin in the Vedic Brāhmaṇa and Upaniṣhad passages like 'The head is the chariot of *Soma*; the mouth, the *āhavanīya* fire; the crown of the head, the sacrificial post; the belly, the cart-shed; the feet, the two fires; the sacrificial items, the limbs.'[6]

Similarly, in the *Brihadaranyaka Upanishad,* the limbs

of the horse meant for the *Ashvamedha* sacrifice have been equated with certain subtle elements: 'The head of the sacrificial horse is the dawn, its eye the sun, its vital force the air, its open mouth the fire called *Vaishvanara*, and the body of the sacrificial horse is the year. Its back is heaven.'[7]

Tantras emerged out of the Vedic religion, and were then developed into a type of esoteric knowledge. But they can be called a development rather than grafting from the Vedic religion.

The practice of Tantra dominates in three zones in India: Bengal, Kashmir, and Kerala. Kashmir is dominated by the philosophical aspect, Bengal the practical aspect, while in Kerala there is some philosophical thinking, dualistic in nature, in contrast with the non-dualistic thinking in Kashmir. From ancient times, Bengal is predominantly a Tantric zone where we find very little of Vedic culture and influence. The Tantric pattern of Bengal was unique and distinct from those of Kerala and Kashmir. The tradition of Tantric Kālī worship in Bengal is known as *Kaula-dhārā*, which has its seat at the Kāmarūpa Kāmākhyā temple in Assam. In Kerala, Lakṣmī or Tripurā is worshipped, and in Kashmir both the forms of worship are found to exist.

In the Tantras, *bhava* or disposition is an important factor in spiritual practice. Humankind is classified under three heads—*divya-bhāva*, one with a divine disposition, *vīra-bhāva*, one with a heroic disposition, and *paśu-bhāva*, one with an animal disposition.

One with an animal disposition can hardly be expected to see beyond the gross aspect of things. So such a person is guided along the path of strictest control of desires and passions. The one with an heroic attitude is fighting with the six passions to reach the plane beyond matter. And the one possessed of divine disposition is by nature endowed with qualities of controlling his lower propensities.

According to *Kāmākhyā Tantra*, such a person is quiet, steady, sagacious, truthful, attentive, and endearing to all. Depending on the prevalent disposition of an individual, the Tantra texts have prescribed seven *ācāras* or codes of conduct in Tantric practice. These are given in the *Kulārṇava Tantra* as *veda*, *vaiṣṇava*, *śaiva*, *dakṣiṇa*, *vāma*, *siddhānta*, and *kaula*. They represent seven stages of development in the aspirant.

One aspect of Tantric discipline is the practice with the five m's, namely, *madya*, wine; *māṁsa*, meat; *matsya*, *fish*; mudra, signs, cereal fries, or closure of evil company; and *maithuna*, ritual sexual union. These five articles have different significance for different classes of aspirants.

The goal of all Tantras is to realize oneself as *paśupati*, the Lord of all animals, another name of Śiva, by gaining control over the basic passions. Sri Ramakrishna meticulously underwent all the methods of *sādhanā* prescribed in the sixty-four Tantras, but his mind was tuned to such a high pitch of purity that when wine sanctified by offering to the Divine Mother was brought before him for drinking, he merely touched it with his fingertip and made a mark of it on his forehead as a sign of respect, and just this action sent him into deep absorption into the primal cause of this world.[8]

When he was brought to witness the Tantric discipline of ritual sexual union, just the vision of extreme joy of the couple indulging in such an act reminded him of the infinitely blissful Divine Mother assuming those human forms, and he lost himself into deep meditation of Her supremely blissful aspect expressed even through sexual union.

Mantra and dikṣā

In the Tantric system, mantra plays an important role. The word mantra in Sanskrit means that which releases the soul by repeated remembrance.[9] The word *'diksha'* literally means a process by which the guru transmits the mantra and attenuates or destroys the sins of the disciple.[10]

A mantra is composed of a *bīja*, seed, *iṣṭa*, name of the chosen ideal, and a word of salutation. In sharp contrast with the Vedic mantras in the Brāhmaṇa portion, Tantric mantras are extremely brief, each letter bearing a mystic significance. Besides, they are not to be taken for mere words.

The guru or the preceptor adds his own vital strength into the mantra with intense aspiration by repeating it ardently and meditating on its meaning. In this way, the spiritual power of the mantra is transmitted from the guru to the disciple down the generations. This process of transmission is technically called *dīkṣā*. Along with the transfer of such power, the guru becomes the spiritual preceptor of the disciple, and such an occasion is marked as a new birth for the disciple.

According to the Tantras, the real Guru is none else but the Supreme Lord Śiva, who is not only the creator, sustainer, and destroyer of the universe but also holds the twin power of *anugraha*, grace, and *nigraha*, punishment. Individual effort without God's grace can never lead to spiritual success. The power of the mantra is thus transmitted from the supreme God and handed down from generation to generation by a traditional line of competent preceptors and disciples.

Dīkṣā or initiation is a must for the performance of any Tantric worship. Dīkṣā has been classified by the teachers of Tantra into three types—*śāmbhavī*, *śāktī*, *māntrī* or *āṇavī*—depending on the spiritual status of the disciple. The first of these is done with a mere meet, touch, or conversation with the disciple, as happened in the life of Narendranath on his second meeting with Sri Ramakrishna.

In the *śakti* type of initiation, the guru forces into the disciple his own spiritual power with his divine wisdom, thus awakening the spiritual dimension of the disciple. In this process, the *bīja-mantra* is written by the guru on the tongue of the disciple, and he at once merges into a vision of his chosen ideal (*iṣṭa-devatā*). And in the *māntrī* or *āṇavī* type, the Guru whispers the mantra into the disciple's ear.

Constant repetition and meditation on its meaning by the disciple bursts out the hard outer crust of the mantra. This phenomenon is known as *mantra-caitanya*. It is the awakening of *nāda*, the eternal sound. At this stage, words or letters of the mantra melt in the moving stream of an unbroken vibration called *akhaṇḍa-nāda*. This vibration of sound leads to illumination, and the aspirant becomes blessed with the vision of one's chosen ideal.

Varṇamālā, śabda, and speech

A mantra is composed of some letters of the Sanskrit alphabet, *varṇamālā*, which constitute *śabda*. These letters are not mere letters, but each of them is endowed with the powers of various aspects of the Divine Mother. The Divine Mother is present in the words of benediction as also in vulgar words of abuse. The demonstration of this power of letters is witnessed in Tantric worship. During all such ceremonial worships, a rite called *nyāsa* (reinforcement) is performed by the worshipper.

According to the Tantras, *Śakti*, the primal energy, came out from the supreme Self, and from this *Śakti* originated the basic vibration or sound, *nāda,* which later compressed itself into a *bindu*, a nucleus of power. The *bindu*, again, burst into *nāda* to create complete focal points termed *bījas*. The process by which these *bījas* are transmitted by the guru is known as *dīkṣā* or initiation into the spiritual path. Tantric literature makes it imperative for the aspirant desirous of conducting worship of any deity to be initiated by some guru.

The external union of Śakti with Śiva is indicated by the letter 'i' in 'Śiva.' Take it away from the word, and it changes into *śava*, lifeless corpse. This unique philosophy demonstrates that the order of the Sanskrit alphabet like a, i, u has a definite link with the process of creation. This is why, when the great Lord Śiva appeared in his dancing Naṭarāja form before Pāṇini, who wanted to explore the secret of grammar, the first sound that came out of Śiva's *ḍamaru* (small drum played by one hand) gave the seeds of the entire creation.[11]

The first three letters in Sanskrit, a, i, and u, are said to be the three vertices of the basic triangle of the universe. Of these, the letter 'a' represents the ultimate reality beyond which nothing exists. But, left to itself, this letter is not capable of creating anything unless desire arises in it. This desire is indicated by the second Sanskrit letter 'i.' These two letters, when combined, sprout the first sign of creation given by the third vowel 'u.' Now, the first vowel 'a,' in order to have the desire for creation, has to split itself into two, which gives the letter '*ā*,' meaning *ānanda*, the symbol of delight. Thus, the first of the fourteen *Māheśvara-sūtras* expresses the delight of self-expression in creation. Again, as per grammar rules, the Sanskrit letter 'a,' joined with 'i' yields the letter 'e,' which is the root of all existence. Hence the letter 'e' is looked upon in the Tantras as the root letter procreating the phenomenal world.

Another notable feature in the *Māheśvara-sūtra* is that the starting letter 'a' in the first sutra and that in the fourteenth sutra 'ha' together constitute the entire gamut of our existence, as it begins with the first vowel 'a' in the alphabet and ends in the last consonant of the alphabet 'ha'; and these two poles, when joined by the point represented by 'm', makes it *aham*, 'I.'

In the Tantric context, the word *aham* represents the whole world of living beings. Like the cardinal sentence in Vedanta—'*ahaṁ brahmāsmi*, I am Brahman'—the two words *aham* and *idam* in the Tantric context represent the eternal relationship between the individual soul and Śiva. It also means the elimination of the difference between the knower and the known, the enjoyer and the enjoyed. Śaṅkara also said in the introduction to his commentary on the *Brahma-sūtra* that the physical world consists of the infinite variety of relationship between the two words *aham* and *idam*, 'I' and 'this': 'A natural human behaviour based on self-identification in the form of 'I am this' and 'This is mine.'[12]

The science of words is closely associated with speech. In Tantric literature all words we express through speech are only at the gross level. The words undergo four levels to express themselves in articulate speech.

First, they remain in a causal, undifferentiated, balanced, dormant, and subtlest state. In Hindu scriptural parlance it is called *parā*, and is situated in the spinal cord at the level of the navel, *maṇipūra*. The next stage is arrived at the middle of the seven *cakras* called *anāhata cakra*. This is the subtler stage called *paśyantī*, seeing. It lies in the spinal cord behind the heart region.

The next level in the spine is behind the throat at the *viśuddha-cakra* called *madhyamā*. In that stage the words come to the subtle state, more defining than the earlier one, and are ready to become manifest. At the next stage the words come up to the mouth, become fully manifest with articulation and audibility. This stage is called *vaikharī*.

Significance of Śrī-yantra

Like all other dualistic systems of worship, the Tantric system also makes use of a special type of symbol called *Śrī-cakra* or *Śrī-yantra*.

The word '*yantra*' occurs frequently in all Tantric contexts of worship. All dualistic forms of worship need an image or a symbol. Since the ordinary aspirants need an object of adoration or worship, a gross form is made after the desired pattern of the worshipper thinking about the form of the worshipped. Thus, there may be an innumerable variety of symbols depending on the mental make-up of individuals. *Śālagrāma* and *Śivaliṅga* are some such symbols.

The *Śrī-cakra* or *Śrī-yantra* symbol is a beautiful piece of geometric figure representing Divine Mother in her individual and universal forms. It consists of several fields or planes of existence, two sets of triangles, and two groups of lotus petals. The *Śrī-cakra* is of immense significance in the Tantric method of worship.

As a whole, it represents the universe—the macrocosm and the microcosm—and its divine cause. At the centre of the *cakra*, there is a point, which represents the co-existence of *Lalitā* and *Kāmeśvara* in an undifferentiated union. An inverted triangle encloses this point. This triangle represents the triple dimensions of Śakti known as knowledge, will power, and action (*jñāna-bala-kriyā*), and also the three qualities of *sattva*, *rajas*, and *tamas*, and their presiding deities.

Circumscribing this small triangle there is a group of eight triangles, and circumscribing even this group of eight there are two sets of triangles, each containing ten triangles, one surrounding the other. Still outside these two sets of ten triangles, there exists a set of fourteen triangles circumscribing them.

Next, circumscribing this set of fourteen triangles stands a circle of eight lotus petals, another concentric circle of sixteen petals. Still outside that region are three concentric circles and three concentric squares outside the three circles. Thus, reversely from outside inward, the nine *cakras* are: *Vṛttatraya* or *Bhūpura*, *ṣoḍaśa-dala*, circle with sixteen petals; *aṣṭa-dala*, circle with eight petals; *manvaśra*, circular area with fourteen triangles; *daśāra-yugma*, two circular areas with two sets of ten triangles each; *aṣṭakoṇa*, circular area with eight triangles; inverted triangle; and *bindu*, point.

The order of these nine *cakras* starting from the *bindu* outwards is called *sṛṣṭikrama*, the order of the creation, while the reverse order—starting from the *bhūpura* inwards—is known as *laya-krama*, the order of dissolution.

The central point *bindu* represents *Kāmeśvara* and *Kāmeśvarī* in eternal union. That is contained within the yoni—represented by the triangle with vertex down—the source, cause, or womb of the universe. The triangles and petals in every *cakra* represent various cosmic principles, each having its distinct presiding deity. The ultimate object of worship in the *Śrī-cakra* is, as the *Bhāvanopaniṣad* says, 'the realization of the unity of the knower, known, and knowledge.'[13]

Epilogue

The Tantric view is that wherever there is Śiva, Śakti is identified with it. Because Śiva is wisdom, and wisdom implies power. So, the one cannot exist without the other. Many people erroneously identify Śakti with a woman or female principle, and Śiva with the male principle. However, they are neither male, nor female, nor neuter. The aspirant who worships this wisdom aspect of reality is called a *Śaiva*, and one who worships the power aspect of the same reality is called a *Śākta*.

The worshipper of the knowledge aspect will be spontaneously endowed with power. But if one wants to attain perfection in the acquisition of power, one has to stop the wastage of energy by all means. The aspirant has to identify his inner Self with the source of power, keep the channel of descent of that power clean by purifying himself through an ardent invocation, worship, and self-surrender with a yearning heart. It is in this way alone that the great power becomes propitiated and gives a boon to the worshipper.

Endowed with that boon, the aspirant comes to realize the manifestation of the same Divine Mother in all women, and the living presence of Śiva, the source of knowledge, in all beings. It is then that the aspirant truly feels the meaning of the maxim, '*yatra jīvastatra śivaḥ,*' meaning, wherever there is *jīva*, there is Śiva, and proceeds with all conviction to serve God in all beings because, according to Tantric injunction, no individual can attain liberation until all others reach that state.

The main idea of Tantras is the deification of the object of the senses, which lure a person and bind one in the endless chain of birth and death, thus preventing one from realizing God. The Tantras show the way to the struggling soul to look upon all sense-objects as visible representations of God, so that one's inordinate attachment to those may be curbed.

In this way, the aspirant gradually becomes transformed from the bound state of the *jīva* to the liberated state of Śiva. The shackles that one created in the course of innumerable births fall off and one becomes God. Sri Ramakrishna put this fact in a poetic way: 'When bound by ties, one is *jīva,* and when free from ties, one is Śiva.'[14]

The Tantras are unique in their preaching the idea of the motherhood of God, and simultaneously, the glorification of the woman. The *Saṁhitā* portion of the Vedas gives only rutdiments of this idea. There the husband is instructed to look upon the body of his wife as sacred, and to worship the gods there, so that she may be the mother of a worthy child. The Tantras sublimate this idea and develop it on new lines with conspicuous results, suited to certain temperaments of the age when Tantras came into vogue.

End Notes

1. See Vidyaranya Muni, *Panchadashi*, 6.130: 'Maya is insignificant according to the scriptures, indefinable according to the rationalists, and real according to the materialists.'
2. *Tanoti vistaryatejnanam anena iti tantram.*
3. See *Kamikagama, Purvabhaga, Tantravatarapatalah*, 2.9: *'Tanoti vipulan arthan tattva-mantra-samashritan. Tranam cha kurute yasmat tantramityabhidhiyate.'*
4. P C Bagchi, *'Evolution of the Tantras' in Studies on the Tantras* (Calcutta: Ramakrishna Mission Institute of Culture, I989), no. s.

5. M., *The Gospel of Sri Ramakrishna*, trans. Swami Nikhilananda (Chennai: Ramakrishna Math, :z.oo:z.), 32.8.
6. *Shatapatha Brahmana*, 1,3,2.-3,
7. *Brihadaranyaka Upanishad*, I.I.r.
8. Wine is called *karana* in Sanskrit, which also means 'the cause.'
9. *Mananat trayate iti mantrab.*
10. *Diyate mantram kshiyate papam iti diksha.*
11. Fourteen types of sound were created by Nataraja with his *damaru.* Together these codes are known as *Maheshvara-sutra.*
12. *Ahamidam, mamedam iti naisargiko'yam lokavyaharah; Brahma-Sutra Bhalya* of Sankacaracarya, trans. Swami Gambhirananda (Calcutta: Advaita Ashrama, 1983), I.
13. *Bhavanopanishad*, 10.
14. *Gospel,* 315.

Healthy and Wise with Patanjali's Yoga

INDIA IS the birthplace of philosophy. Since the dawn of civilization, the best brains in India have been engaged in finding solutions to the intricate problems of life. The ancient seers down the ages have been giving birth to an innumerable number of theories, isms, systems, and philosophies. Even materialist philosophy has found a berth in the list of accepted systems. Whether they are theists, gnostics, agnostics, Buddhists, Jainas, monists, or pluralists—all the systems of philosophy have found a place in the list of philosophies.

The book *Sarva-darśana-saṁgrahaḥ* compiled by Mādhavācārya has mentioned a few of them. There arose debates among many of the champions of these philosophies from time to time, to prove the supremacy of their own faith, and not to kill or destroy the upholders of other faiths. This is a distinctive feature of India's great thinkers.

All these philosophies have been classified into six systems of philosophy—*Nyāya*, *Vaiśeṣika*, *Sāṁkhya*, *Yoga*, *Pūrva-mīmāṁsā*, and *Uttara-mīmāṁsā* or Vedanta. Barring the first two philosophical systems, or rather, the science of logic, the Yoga philosophy may be said to be the common denominator of all the other systems. Besides, judging by its methodology, it seems that the Yoga system of philosophy forms the main support for all the other systems.

For aspirants on the path of knowledge, devotion, or work, the mainstream of their struggle is to be established in Yoga. That is why Sri Krishna said in the *Bhagavad Gita*, 'Therefore, O Arjuna! Be poised in Yoga at all times in your life.'[1] Here this word is used in the most comprehensive sense. The demonstration of yogic results is found in the life-stories of almost all spiritual stalwarts. Buddha, Christ, Shankara, Ramanuja, Sri Ramakrishna, Swami Vivekananda, and many others had recourse to yogic supernatural power for the good of mankind.

In the literary sense, the word seemingly means a union between the aspirant and God. But Sri Krishna puts a wider sense to this word Yoga in the *Bhagavad Gītā,* chapter 6, verse 23 by defining it typically as 'severance from union with pain.' Indeed, a little reflection reveals the fact that union with God or the supreme Truth implies disunion from all physical, mental, or intellectual 'pains' (*kleśa*). This is one of the salient features we must keep in mind before taking a holy dip into the Yoga system of philosophy.

Distinct features

The Yoga system of philosophy existed long before the Advaita system, and even before the Buddhist systems of philosophy. It was later systematized through aphorisms by Patañjali. The Yoga system has become popular over time because of the cogent, viable, practical, and scientific approach in its methodology. No other system has such widely acceptable features which can be adopted in a graded course of discipline based on experimental realization in the soul's journey to its goal. Since this system starts from the very basics, no other prior disciplines for eligibility are required to follow its course.

A distinct feature of this philosophy is that it can be approached by anyone professing any religion, caste, creed, or sect. For example, from Swami Vivekananda's letters we come to know that Pavhari Baba, the great Yogi of his time, was originally a Vaishnavite monk. Swami Vivekananda, Sri Aurobindo, and almost all the monastic disciples of Sri Ramakrishna reached extraordinary degrees of concentration in their own paths of *sadhana*, despite the diverse individual bents of their nature. Hence, they may also be called Yogins.

This system has no dogma or presupposition of its own, and hence it can easily be blended into any philosophical or theological system. Another distinct dimension of the philosophy is that even though it is a theistic one, God is not given much importance in the Yoga system.

Meditation on God only forms one of the many methods of concentration.[2] The goal of Yoga is not realization of God but attainment of one's original Self (in the *kaivalya* state) through higher concentration (*samādhi*). This system declares the worship of God as just one of the means—not indispensable—to the realization of its goal.

Many call it an offshoot of Kapila's *Sāṁkhya* system; but strictly speaking, it may be called as theistic *Sāṁkhya* system. Unlike *Sāṁkhya*, this system has a place for God in it, though its aim is not the attainment of Godhood but samādhi, or the 'complete control over the movements of the mind under all circumstances.' (*Yogaścitta-vṛtti-nirodhaḥ).*[3] Patañjali has taken up the concepts of bondage and liberation from the *Sāṁkhya* system, and defined bondage as the identification with mental waves that rise incessantly in the mind. Liberation is the attainment of complete freedom from them.

Another special deviation of the Yoga system from the *Sāṁkhya* lies in the method of attainment of its goal. Whereas *Sāṁkhya* recommends reasoning to reach discrimination, the Yoga system prescribes different methods for aspirants with various inclinations.

Yet another salient feature of distinction of the Yoga system is that whereas systems like *Sāṁkhya* and others try to control the gross from the subtlest level, this system conversely prescribes the control of the subtle by starting from the grossest level. This peculiar method has made the Yoga system so popular. Whatever is within the grasp, one can handle it.

As a concrete demonstration of this, we find that by *prāṇāyāma* the vital forces inside an individual's body are brought under control; and this in turn controls the pranic forces working outside of him too, because intrinsically the internal and external pranic forces are parts of an integrated whole force system known as Energy. Even the scientific minds of today find this amazing.

To explain this method of going from the gross to the subtle, our ancient sages used to present a beautiful metaphor of a minister incurring the wrath of his master, the whimsical king, and captivated in a high castle. Seeing his wife weeping at the foot of the castle, the minister jotted down on a piece of paper the following instruction to her: 'Bring a honey-bee, a little honey, a very thin thread, then a stronger thread, and another very thick rope. Smear the bee's head with the honey, tie the thin thread in its hind part, make the insect face upwards, and let it go up.'

This was done. When the minister got the insect in his hand, he let it go and caught hold of the thin thread hanging behind it. Then he asked his wife to tie a thicker string to it and next a very thick rope was tied to that string. This being done, the minister got hold of the thickest rope, and with its help got down from the castle and ran away from the kingdom with his wife.

Discussion on aphorisms

Patañjali has aphoristically classified his Yoga system in four parts or quartets *(pādas): 1) Samādhi pāda; 2) Sādhana-pāda; 3) Vibhūti-pāda*; and *4) Kaivalya-pāda*. When an aspirant launches into study and practice of the Yoga system, he must have at least a rough idea about the end, which is *samādhi.* Without this he will not feel the urge to go ahead, and will be confused about the goal.

So the first part acquaints the aspirant with several definitions that follow one another, starting from the definition of the term yoga. They have been aphoristically put in succession so as to leave no questions unanswered. In the second part, the various practices have been shown. But it is not that the methods (*sādhanā*) have been exclusively provided in the second chapter alone (named *sādhana-pāda*). Rather the first chapter itself has shown some methods of attaining some lower goals.

Thus, the second chapter starts with some practices called *kriyā-yogāḥ*. The third chapter gives the acquisition of various powers as a result of attainment of perfection in each of the practices. As a side effect of the persistent practice of certain acts, some extraordinary powers (*vibhūti*) happen to come to the aspirant. Most of the aspirants who have the hidden desires of worldly attainment are seduced by these powers and thus miss the mark.

The fourth chapter is on the final goal, named *kaivalya* state in yogic parlance. It is not the attainment of Oneness because it is beyond one, two, or many. Only the pure witness Self remains. It cannot be described in words. This justifies the name *kaivalya* ascribed to it.

Patañjali starts his aphorisms with this sentence: 'Herewith start the teachings on the yoga.' Then he proceeds to explain the technical term yoga defining it as, 'Yoga is the state of complete control over the *vṛttis*,' waves of thought in the lake of the mind. What happens when one is in this state? Here comes the answer, 'At that time the witness self stands identified with its real state.' A question may crop up here as to what happens until that state is arrived? So the sage explains, 'At other times the practitioner finds himself identified with the *vṛttis*.'

The mind-stuff has been compared here to a huge lake on which waves or ripples arise incessantly due to visible or invisible *samskaras*. When an aspirant tries to withdraw his mind from all thoughts, he recognizes these waves arising in the mind due to earlier memories or associations. They may be pain-bearing or without pain, yet they are some or other kinds of waves. The goal of the aspirant is to gain full control on these waves and their subsequent reactions.

Patañjali classifies the vṛttis into five categories, namely, *pramāṇa* or right cognition, *viparyaya* or wrong perception, *vikalpa* or cognition about a thing that does not exist, *nidrā*, sleep, a mental modification produced by inertia; and *smṛti* or memory of the past. Now, all these five types of cognition are either painful or happy for one aspiring perfection.

How to get rid of these *vṛttis*? The terse reply comes in the twelfth aphorism of the first chapter: 'By practice and detachment they can be stopped.' The natural tendency of the mind is like a river in tide and ebb—it flows in both good and evil directions. This mind can be trained by persistent practice (*abhyāsa*) for the path of discrimination by seeing the right and wrong values in all worldly things; and the flow of the mind towards sense-objects can be reduced by renunciation (*vairāgya*) alone—giving up a lower thing for the pursuit of a higher goal.

Concentration with strong mental, moral, and physical discipline is the aim of such practice, which should always be steadfast. Remember, practising evil results in misery, while the practice of good leads to happiness.

By making the practice and renunciation more intense, one can move towards perfection at a faster pace. But does everything rest on one's individual efforts alone? No. There are already perfected souls endowed with superhuman qualities resting on higher planes. When one strives to stick to higher thought planes, one's good thoughts become resonant with their similar thoughts and boost the aspirant's thought pattern.

By taking refuge in them also, one can brave through the difficulties. Another substitute method has been presented in the 23rd aphorism as, '*īśvara-praṇidhānād vā*,' or taking refuge in *īśvara*. By this, sage Patañjali means that a superhuman person is unaffected by bondage, affliction, deed, result of action or the latent impression, and is omniscient, most sublime, having unsurpassable excellence. This is contained in the 24th and 25th aphorisms.

As he has no limitations, he is the teacher of all the former teachers. Such an *īśvara* is symbolized verbally by the mystic syllable Aum. By repeating this *praṇava* mantra and dwelling on its true meaning, one can also reach Him. It is, as Sri Ramakrishna had said, like reaching a boat holding its anchor chain links. The *Mundaka Upanishad* has also depicted beautifully the way to do this: '*Praṇava* is the bow, the self is the arrow; Brahman is the target of that arrow. Becoming one with the target like the arrow, the aspirant should pierce it without flickering his mind.'[4] From such repetition comes the awareness of the individual self and the obstacles on the path are removed thereby.

What are these obstacles? They are listed in Patanjali's *Yoga Sutras* (PSY 1.30) and are mostly self-created ones and nine in number, such as disease, incompetence, doubt, delusion, sloth, non-abstention, erroneous conception, non-attainment of the yogic state, and inability to stay long in the yogic state after attaining it. These nine are the impediments in each step causing distraction of the mind. To get rid of these impediments, the mind should be focused on a single goal (PSY 1.32). But that can only be done when the mind is calm, pure, and content under all circumstances. How can that be brought about?

Yoga offers a healthy suggestion in the matter, advising the aspirant to apply antidotes to each type of obstructive idea that arises while dealing with others. Seeing others happy, one should be friendly. Even others' happiness may attract one's mind towards that. Similarly, the aspirant's attitude towards those who are in distress should be one of compassion. To those who tread the path of virtue, the attitude of goodwill should be maintained. Likewise, towards those following the dark path of vice, indifference, instead of anger, should be the attitude. This way the aspirant's mind becomes purified from worldly stains.

Another alternative way is through the control of the pranic force working inside the body. By exhaling and restraining the breath outside, the body can be made calm and the mind pure. The mind being on a higher level than the pranic forces, it is more powerful and subtler than the gross. Then Patañjali proceeds to suggest a number of alternatives aimed at keeping the mind on higher spheres. These alternatives are applicable from time to time as per the mental stability of the individual aspirant.

The second chapter of Patanjali's Yoga Sutras is devoted chiefly to practice *(sādhanā)*. It begins with the acts to be taken up for this, which are three in number: *tapas* (austerity), *svādhyāya* (study of the sacred literature), and *īśvara-praṇidhāna* (surrender to God).

Together, these three are named *kriyā-yoga* or the union through various acts. Why are these to be taken up? There is a twofold purpose: It minimises afflictions unavoidable in daily life (*kleśa-tanūkaraṇa*), and goads the aspirant ahead towards higher meditation called *samādhi*. In the context of *vṛtti* spoken about earlier, we have come across the words, *kliṣṭa* and *akliṣṭa vṛttis*. Here their root term, *kleṣa* is further explained. They are the miseries of five types created by man himself: (1) *Avidyā* or misapprehension of one's real nature or the world; (2) *Asmitā* or egoism, (3) *Rāga* or attachment; (4) *Dveṣa* or aversion or malice, and (5) *Abhiniveśa* or fear of death.

Of these five, the first, that is, *avidyā* is the root of all the other four.[5] Avidyā is an abstract term and it can only be recognized by its effects. For instance, some people see permanence in impermanent things, purity in impure things, happiness in miserable things, and *ātman* in that which is not *ātman*. This last type of delusion needs further clarification. Those who look upon animate and inanimate objects as part of their own self and rejoice at their prosperity or bemoan their decay are all victims of such delusion termed *avidyā*.

Asmitā means confusing the *buddhi* or intellect with pure consciousness. *Rāga* or attachment for someone or something rises in the mind following the memory of pleasure associated with it. Its reverse is *dveṣa*, exemplified by anger or propensity to hurt objects inimical to attain, causing misery experienced earlier. Lastly, *abhiniveśa*, which is found not only in ignorant people but also in the learned, is the inordinate clinging to life and avoiding death. Psychologically, it may be termed as the 'fear of annihilation.'

We now come to a very unique proposition of the Yoga system which can solve a lot of day-to-day problems of man. Squeezed under adverse circumstances, man loses faith in himself when, in the poetic words of Swami Vivekananda, 'fate its hundred horrors send/And clotted darkness block the way.' Man starts blaming someone or other for his failures.

Vivekananda expresses man's plight in his inimitable words: 'We human beings are very slow to recognize our own weakness, our own faults, so long as we can lay the blame upon somebody else. Men in general lay all the blame of life upon their fellow-men, or, failing that, on God, or they conjure up a ghost, and say it is fate.'[6] So they rush frantically to priests and soothsayers, who concoct all imaginary hobgoblins making their subjects weaker in mind and subservient to their evil plans. It is here that the Yoga system comes forward and boldly declares, 'Man is the maker of his destiny.' Your own past karmas have given rise to this situation. Henceforth, do virtuous deeds more and more to bring good results.

Says Vivekananda, 'Therefore, stand up, be bold, be strong. Take the whole responsibility on your own shoulders. All the strength and succour you want is within yourselves. Therefore, make your own future. You must always remember that each word, thought, and deed, lays up a store for you and that as the bad thoughts and bad works are ready to spring upon you like tigers, so also there is the inspiring hope that the good thoughts and good deeds are ready with the power of a hundred thousand angels to defend you always and for ever.'[7]

Sage Patañjali says, 'Man's future birth, span of life, and the experiences therein are controlled and decided by his deeds done so far.' Again, 'These birth, span, and experience produce pleasurable or painful results because of virtue and vice' (PYS 2:13-14).

The Yoga system of philosophy teaches us to take the whole responsibility of our deeds on ourselves and bids to stand on one's own without passing on the buck to others. Spiritual life starts with the words, 'The buck stops here,' meaning, henceforth 'I will be responsible for all my good or bad deeds and none else.'

Practice and applications in life

A path becomes acceptable to the masses to the extent it has its utility in their lives. In recent times, scores of people are taking to yogic courses to gain good health, build a tension-free mind, and manage auto-immune disorders. One can even lead a blissful life amidst the din and bustle of the workaday world by practising Yoga, which improves not only physical health but also endows one with a strong mind, and sublimates thought patterns.

The eight limbs of yoga

What is recommended is *aṣṭāṅga-yoga* or eight-limbed Yoga. The eight limbs (*aṣṭāvaṅgāni*) are *yama-niyama-āsana-prāṇāyāma-pratyāhāra-dhāraṇā-dhyāna-samādhayaḥ* (PYS 2:29). Translated, the eight limbs (*aṣṭāvaṅgāni*) stand for restraint, observance, posture, regulation of breath, withholding the sense organs, fixing the mind, meditation, and perfect concentration.

Yama

Yama means the ought-nots and *niyama* means the oughts. Yama has five aspects, namely, *ahiṁsā*, *satya*, *asteya*, *brahmacarya*, and *aparigraha* (PYS 2:30). *Ahiṁsā* means to abstain from doing harm or injury to others in word, mind, and deed, plus to develop an attitude of amity towards all creatures. Many people take to a vegetarian diet to refrain from killing inferior animals, but if they bear malice, jealousy, or revenge, towards their fellow beings, they cannot be said to be observing the *ahiṁsā* aspect of *yama*.

Satya means to be truthful under all circumstances. It is the effort to make the mind and speech correspond to what has been correctly understood in the practice of truth, that is, saying or thinking of what has been seen, heard, or inferred. Words uttered for the purpose of communicating one's thoughts to others are true provided they do not appear deceitful, delusive, and meaningless to listeners. The words should be uttered for the benefit of people, and not for inflicting harm on them. Truth which is painful or hurting to others should not be spoken.

The law-giver Manu explains the concept well, with his famous words: 'Truth which is benevolent should be spoken, not an unfair or harmful truth; again, that which is acceptable but actually a falsehood should not be spoken.'[8]

In worldly life, sometimes, people cannot help fibbing under certain situations. One should keep in mind that if a 'lie' is spoken not with selfish interest but for a higher, noble purpose, that is not wrong. That untrue statement which helps serve one's selfish interest is sinful and must be shunned at all costs.

Asteya is abstention from taking things that belong to others unlawfully. Brahmacarya or continence is the control of the sense-organs in the physical, pranic, and mental levels. It means restraining all sense-organs like eyes from such activities as might cause sexual urge.

Our sagacious ancestors said that even to think of sexual things (*smaraṇam*), to talk about those (*kīrtanam*), to flirt (*keli*), to look intently at the physical form of the opposite sex (*prekṣaṇam*), to converse in secret with the opposite sex (*guhyabhāṣaṇam*), to make a resolve of intercourse (*saṁkalpa*), to get ready for such acts (*adhyavasāya*), and to be engaged in intercourse (*kriyānirvṛtti*)—all these eight come under the purview of sexuality.[9]

Seekers of salvation should practise the opposites of all these. In order to achieve this end, the aspirant should try to transcend gradually the physical, pranic, and mental levels and develop a deep love for things higher than those levels. But merely high intellectual achievement, subtlety of intellect, or dwelling in that plane cannot keep one from these things. The intellect has also to be purified. This has been instructed in the *Kathopanishad* in a mantra. There it is said that this *ātman* can be realized by a *buddhi* which is subtle as well as very sharp like the head of a pin.

A *brahmacārin* should maintain a diet of frugal, easily digestible meals and moderate sleep. *Aparigraha* is not to seek or covet, much less cast a glance at things beyond one's minimal needs. Through discrimination the aspirant realizes that in keeping things that give us pleasure and enjoyment, he invites trouble in the form of anxiety to preserve them and feels worried or miserable on losing them. Only things needed to maintain the body should be accepted, and not a bit more.

Niyama

Niyama is of five kinds: *Śaucaḥ* (purity or cleanliness), *santoṣaḥ* (contentment), *tapas* (mental and physical austerity), *svādhyāyaḥ* (study of scriptures), and *īśvara-praṇdhāna* (devotion to God). This is outlined in PYS, 2:32. *Śauca* means internal and external purification of the body. The body can be purified by washing, ablution, with water and other ingredients, and by consuming pure food. This external cleanliness helps the aspirant maintain continence. The mind can be purified by cleansing it of arrogance, conceit, and malice.

Santoṣah is the contentment that comes from whatever one gets for one's mere subsistence. People go on craving for more and more objects of enjoyments which in the long run, fetch only misery. King Yayāti realized this truth at the fag end of his life and gave out the famous statement, 'Desire for objects can never be appeased by enjoying them endlessly. It only goes on hopping from one object to another and adding in intensity like fire when clarified butter is added to it.'

Tapas or austerity is the attempt to desist from actions which might bring momentary pleasures. Practice of austerity for getting only a desired worldly object, is far from Yogic austerity. Those who get upset by small sufferings cannot aspire to practise Yoga. That is why endurance has to be practised through the observance of austerities. If one is able to endure hunger and thirst, one is not easily disturbed during meditation. When the body develops the power to endure hardship and when the mind does not get easily upset by lack of physical comfort, one is qualified for practising Yoga.

Svādhyāya is to gain deep knowledge of one's adopted spiritual path by the study of scriptures and holy books and uttering the holy mantra *Aum*. It is only through in-depth study that the practice of *śravaṇa* (listening carefully), *manana* (pondering on the meanings), and *nididhyāsana* (practising them through meditation) come to help the aspirant. *Svādhyāya* also means keenly studying one's inner tendencies.

Īśvara-praṇidhāna is total surrender to God of all actions the yogin undertakes by thinking that all endeavours become successful only through His grace.

The aspirant practising these five kinds of restraint called *yama* has to encounter the inhibitions of perverse thoughts like injuring others by mind, word, or deed, speaking untruths, or stealing. In yogic parlance, these are called *vitarka*. What should a person do under such constraints? The yoga scripture comes forward like a benevolent mother to her child in distress. PYS, 2:33 says, 'Whenever inhibiting thoughts appear, they are to be countered by opposite thoughts.'

It is quite possible that the aspiring one often strays away from his uniform struggle. It all happens due to the natural inertia of the mind. Thus, at the arousal of hatred or passion towards worldly things, he should remind himself of the noble vow he has taken for the well-being of the world.

Repetition of the earlier bad tendencies in life should not be allowed if one wants to go upward. If one is confident of the positive, benevolent effects of practising qualities of *ahiṁsā* and the like, one will automatically get rid of the inhibitions. It has been said that when one is established in *ahiṁsā*, even cruel animals will lose their cruelty when they come in his proximity. When one gets established in truthfulness, whatever he says happens invariably (PYS, 2:36). When one gets rooted in the practice of non-stealing even mentally, all the jewels present themselves to man (PSY, 2:37).

When established in Brahmacarya, one acquires unobstructed knowledge, action, and special powers like minimising or maximising the body and others. Such powers are called together as *vīrya* (PYS, 2:38). When one attains perfection in non-acceptance of more than the bare necessity, the memory and knowledge of the past and the future births arise in him. He comes to know clearly what he was in past births, and also what glorious future awaits him (PYS, 2:39). These are the positive measures that will goad all aspirants ahead to their practices or *sādhanā*.

From the practice of purity (*śauca*) arises the aversion towards one's own body and a distaste for contact with others' bodies (PYS, 2:40). Purification boosts up the potential divinity of the soul, pleasantness of feeling, one-pointedness, subjugation of the senses, and the ability for self-realization (PYS, 2:41). From contentment, unsurpassed happiness is gained (PYS, 2:42). Practice of austerity brings about perfection of the body and the organs (PYS, 2:43).

From study and repetition of scriptures, communion with the chosen ideal is established (PYS, 2:44). From total surrender to God, one gradually becomes established in the state of samādhi (PYS, 2:45).

Asana

For yogic practice one has to learn the technique for staying in the same posture for sustained periods without any movement of any part of the body. There are innumerable postures to be mastered, but to serve the purpose of meditation, suffice it to say that those postures which are conducive to making the aspirant forget even the existence of his own body and help him sit at ease and without movement are known as *āsanas* (PYS, 2:46). When a posture is perfect, one spontaneously loses all consciousness about the body. It is then that the thought of God comes in him effortlessly.

These *āsanas* are to be practised slowly and under the guidance of an expert master. As a by-product of perfection in *āsana*, the aspirant ceases to get affected by the pairs of opposites like heat and cold, or other afflictions like hunger or thirst.

Prāṇāyāma

Prāṇāyāma should be practised only after mastering the seating posture. *Prāṇāyāma* is the regulation in the movements of the vital forces working inside the human body through inhalation and exhalation. It constitutes suspension of breath following either inhalation or exhalation. *Prāṇāyāma* as mentioned in this Yoga is not identical with what is mentioned in the context of Haṭha-yoga, even though some commentators have tried to make the two correspond.

Prāṇāyāma practised with a restless mind cannot be regarded as a part of yoga.

Breathing and quietening the mind are to be synchronized together. The technical words *recaka* (expulsion of air), *pūraka* (drawing in of air), and *kumbhaka* (suspension of air) were not used in ancient times in the sense they are understood now. They were coined later. Sage Vyasa in his commentary on the yogic aphorisms has described *bāhya-vṛtti* (external operation) as stopping the pranic force outside after exhalation. This is not the same as *recaka*.

Similarly *ābhyantara-vṛtti* (internal operation) also is a combination of inhalation and suspension of breath. Then there is another operation known as *stambha-vṛtti* (suppression). It is a form of internal effort which causes internal contraction of all the limbs of the body. After practising this, suspension of breath can be maintained for a long time. In Haṭha-yoga, this is enforced through various *bandhas* (contractions) and *mudrās*. But such enforced operation succeeds only in stopping the pranic functions in the body temporarily. It does not stop the activities of the mind.

Pratyāhāra

Pratyāhāra is the withdrawal of all the internal and external sense-organs that have a natural tendency to rush towards their objects outside. In this process, the sense-organs are withdrawn from their corresponding objects outside, either by concentration on some higher aspects like the detached mind, or by *prāṇāyāma*, or by surrender to God. Thus, having been separated from their corresponding objects, the senses follow the nature of the mind. This is *pratyāhāra*. But the mind has already recoiled from its function with the world. Hence the senses also cannot but follow suit. Yogic *pratyāhāra* is entirely self-regulated. When a Yogi does not want to know a thing existing outside or inside, his power of perception for the object stops immediately.

Dhāraṇā, dhyāna, samādhayaḥ

Dhāraṇā, fixing the mind or concentration is achieved after withdrawing the mind and the senses from all external distractions. It has to be fixed on a particular space like the nerve-centre at the navel, heart-centre, tip of the nose or tongue, space between the brows (third eye), and so on.

When after long practice, the mind gets fixed on certain internal centres, it flows continuously towards that holy object. This uninterrupted flow of the mental modifications is called *dhyāna* in yogic parlance. When this practice of unbroken flow becomes firm, gradually the mind (*dhyātā*), the objects (*dhyeyaḥ*), and the process of meditation *(dhyānam)* lose their difference, and the three become merged into one; that is called *samādhi* (total absorption).

Conclusion

Millions of people from all walks of life are deriving palpable effects from the regular practice of Yoga. Many forms of meditation are being taken up by various groups. All these attempts aim at getting peace in these troubled times. But one should not get carried away. It's a long way up the yogic path. Sitting postures, regulated inhalation and exhalation, and other techniques may give us a healthy body immune to all diseases, but more important for an aspirant is adherence to basic values of ethics and morality.

In the good old days when Buddhist missionary monks from India went to Far East countries, they took recourse to some defence arts apprehending violent opposition from the native people. Doesn't it sound strange? How can monks who have taken the vow of non-injury to others adopt martial arts for self-preservation? Still it is true.

Over time, the Buddhist missionaries got a large number of followers in China, Japan, and other countries of the Far East. Their followers found that the newly imported religion fitted very well into the warp and weft of their old religion like Confucianism and others.

Today, we find that innumerable kinds of martial arts are spreading like wildfire all over the world. Strictly speaking, those arts are actually extensions and practical applications of Yoga. With the passage of time, they underwent various modifications in the countries of their origin.

It is so strange to hear that although the arts have been popularized by the name, martial arts, in the strictest sense they are the most practical demonstration of keeping the mind calm amid the busiest place in life, like a duel, or in the battle-field. Karate, Kung Fu, Tae Kwon do, Tai chi, and many other such martial arts have developed of late.

What is to wonder at is that the masters in all these martial arts and even in archery and other sciences teach the disciples that the first thing is to keep the mind completely calm, collected, and unruffled by any disturbance or movement. Anger or the idea of revenge should not be nurtured under any circumstance, for such attitudes take away all attention of the mind by force. There should be a blend of lightning speed with fixed aim at target.

In archery, the stages of taking the arrow from the quiver,

setting it to the bow-string, fixing the mind on the target, and shooting at the bull's eye—all these details are to be practised with so much alacrity and steadfastness over a long period that finally all these acts taken together become casual and take place in a wink. In the duel and group fights (with or without weapons) also, one has to pay attention to every movement of oneself as well as of the opponent.

These are undoubtedly the greatest applications of Yoga that can challenge the modern world. Even though about ninety-nine per cent people are using these techniques all over the world, very less number among them attain perfection and mastery over the art. Many terms have been coined by those masters in association with similar practices like Vipassana, Mindfulness, Awareness, Walking meditation, Sitting meditation, Tea ceremony, and so on.

The end and aim of all these modes is nothing but Yoga. The demonstration of the *Bhagavad Gita* by Sri Krishna to Arjuna is nothing but the apt application of yoga amidst the din and bustle of the world. In ancient India, every phase of life used to be looked upon as expressions of yoga. Thus, from the very Vedic period, life itself came to be treated as yoga, that is, a keen attempt to be united with one's real nature, which is Divinity.

End Notes

1. *Bhagavad Gītā*, 8:27
2. *īśvara-praṇidhānād vā*, *Patanjali's Yoga Sutras* 1:23
3. *Yogaścitta-vṛtti-nirodhaḥ*, *Patanjali's Yoga Sutras* 1:2
4. *Mundaka Upanishad,* 2:2:4
5. *Patanjali's Yoga Sutras,* 2:4
6. *Complete Works*, volume 2, page 221
7. *Complete Works*, volume 2, page 225
8. *Manu-smṛti,* 4/138
9. *Dakṣa-saṁhitā*, Ch.7

Visions of Advaita Vedanta

'ONCE A MAN entered a wood and saw a small animal on a tree. He came back and told another man that he had seen a creature of a beautiful red colour on a certain tree. The second man replied: 'When I went into the wood, I also saw that animal. But why do you call it red? It is green.' Another man who was present contradicted them both and insisted that it was yellow. Presently others arrived and contended that it was grey, violet, blue, and so forth and so on. Soon, they started quarrelling among themselves. To settle the dispute they all went to the tree.

They saw a man sitting under it. On being asked, he replied: 'Yes, I live under this tree and I know the animal very well. All your descriptions are true. Sometimes it appears red, sometimes yellow, and at other times blue, violet, grey, and so forth. It is a chameleon. And sometimes, it has no colour at all. Now it has a colour, and now it has none.'[1]

This is a well-known illustration cited very often by Vedanta teachers to explain the inexplicable nature of God. Each person describes God after his own conception. In this story, the person living below the tree is the Vedantin, who clearly knows that the visions of all the contenders are partially true. In fact, the 'thing' all of them saw would at times assume no hue at all, that is, exist beyond all truths also.

A great riddle

To all ordinary levels of intellect or reasoning, Advaita Vedanta is the most complicated philosophy among all the six systems in Indian philosophy. Not only from the standpoint of reasoning, but also in points of conclusion, the Advaita system excels all other philosophies. To a beginner, the final verdict of Advaita reasoning seems really weird and outlandish. Readers of Swami Vivekananda's life are well acquainted with the fact how, in his younger days when he came to meet Sri Ramakrishna and heard the great sage saying, 'God pervades all,' he burst into laughter.

He was also a keen seeker of God, albeit a beginner. And although a simple 'divine touch' of the master metamorphosed the whole world before his eyes instantaneously into an undivided single existence, Swami Vivekananda's body and mind were not mature enough at that time to hold that ineffable realization. That being the case with a spiritual stalwart like Swami Vivekananda whom Sri Ramakrishna addressed at the first sight as *nara-ṛṣi* reborn, one can imagine how enigmatic it would be to all other intellectual minds.

But the scenario radically changed in later years. Swami Vivekananda realized the truth of Advaita Vedanta to its very depth. The realization made him all the more spontaneous, so much so that in every dealing with his close friends, even when he was in a lighter mood, he continued to give out that truth. In a poetic way, once he jotted down some stanzas depicting the song of the free to Mary Hale, one of the daughters in the Hale family. The last stanza ran thus:

From dreams awake, from bonds be free,
Be not afraid, this mystery,
My shadow cannot frighten me,
Know once for all that I am He.

Mary could not catch the deep significance of it. So she replied in another poem:

...For you have made them clearly see
The one main truth that 'all is He'.

In reply Swamiji proceeded to convey the truth:

So Mary Hale,
Allow me tell,
You mar my doctrines wronging, baulking.
I never taught
Such queer thought
That all was God—unmeaning talking!
But this I say,
Remember pray,
That God is true, all else is nothing,
This world's a dream
Though true it seem,
And only truth is He the living!
The real me is none but He,
And never, never matter changing!

This is exactly the conclusion of Advaita Vedanta: God is true, all else is nothing, and not that 'all is God.' But this difference between the two phrases is so subtle as to be lost to the ordinary intellect. When one says that only God is true, none else exists, it emphasizes that God only exists—not the visible universe; but when it is said that 'all is God', emphasis goes to 'all'—and not to God. That is why to the realized soul this phrase becomes 'unmeaning talking.'

Cracking a riddle

A novice in the Vedanta studies will first find himself surrounded from all sides by the mist of such riddles. Vedanta may be called a diary of spiritual realizations of various wise men in ancient India. It was impossible for them to narrate every phase of realization verbatim, because narration is possible only within the range of the sense world, while Vedantic realization takes an aspirant beyond sense-organs, and mind.[2]

Those realized sages honestly confessed their inability to describe that with all exactitude. No worldly illustration would suffice to indicate precisely that reality. Can one see one's eyes without a mirror or some other medium? Still, as far as their organ of speech went, they tried to give a verbal sketch of their visions in the form of worldly similes. As for example, one of the Upanishads says, 'It moves, yet It moves not; It is near, yet far; It exists in the innermost core of all, as also It covers everything outside.'[3]

Statements like this are rife throughout Vedantic literature. A novice cannot but find in these apparently contradictory truths a source of fun or at most a riddle. But to the expert eye it all is nothing but truth. Vedanta is full of visions that can bring us great bliss in life. When one succeeds in cracking an age-old riddle, one becomes immensely full of bliss. To put it differently, as soon as one cracks a riddle, one discovers a vision of Vedanta.

As a matter of fact, Vedanta is a subject full of visions made by the sages of yore. They help humankind solve all problems in this worldly life that cause misery.

Vision 1: Scientific outlook of Vedanta

A special trait of Vedanta is its scientific approach in all walks of life. It stands on the firm foundation of reason plus realization in addition to scriptural support. Let us take an example from life. We all hear such moral advice from elders and well-wishers, 'Do not steal others' possessions, do not harm others,' and so on. All religions corroborate this teaching of being moral. But the moment anyone raises the question 'why' against such advice, no other religion but Vedanta can withstand the shock with the answer, 'Because others are none but your own self, your own reflection; by harming others one harms oneself.'

Here it is noteworthy that no incurring of sin is mentioned, no threat of hellfire that weakens one's mind. Isn't it a scientific approach? In this context, the word 'scientific' means a firm basis of logic or reason. Whereas the other religions are based on unconditional faith, obedience, belief in scriptures, and teachers, Vedanta straightaway points to the truth. Swami Vivekananda advised the parents and guardians of children, 'Do not teach fearful things to others through fear of society and public opinion. What is there to be taught more in religion than the oneness of the universe and faith in one's self?'[4] In fact, it is scientific reasoning with its positive approach that dispels all fears.

Besides, Vedantic teaching allows an aspirant to experiment in a laboratory when it is called for. To illustrate this, the *Chāndogya-Upaniṣad* presents many such examples.

In one of them the master asks the disciple to bring a glass of water, add a spoon of salt to it, and stir it. After the disciple does so, he is asked to taste the glass-water from the top, middle, and the bottom portion successively. The disciple obeys and reports the nature of the taste as equally saline everywhere. But in the brine water being saturated there was no trace of salt seen anywhere.

From this phenomenon the preceptor concludes that Brahman is in the same way 'saturated' everywhere in the universe. In fact, there was nothing else than Brahman. Brahman is both immanent and transcendent. This means Brahman is beyond nature as well as present intrinsically in it like the thread all over the cloth. A cloth cannot be imagined without thread. Similarly, in order to demonstrate how the physical body (*annamaya*) affects the pranic body (*prāṇamaya*) as well as the mental body (*manomaya*), one master bids the disciple to gradually reduce his food intake in fifteen instalments until on the last day he has to go without food, and on each day of such reduction he asks the disciple to repeat whatever Vedic text he had learnt earlier.

The disciple felt the gradual reduction of his memory power until on the last day he could not remember anything at all. Then, day by day for fifteen days he is allowed to take one morsel more than the previous day until on the last day he eats to his fill; and the disciple was again able to reproduce as before all the Vedic texts he learnt. What experiment can be more logical and reasonable than the ones cited here? Are these in any way inferior to laboratory experiments? Thus, it is established that Vedantic outlook is scientific.

What is the practical utility one gets from this vision? It is that religion as explained through Vedanta is actually a combination of religion and science, and carries science to limits which science cannot reach alone. People will discover that science and religion are compatible with each other and that religion does not consist in doctrines or dogmas or blind belief, or mere faith in holy books, or on persons with supernatural power.

Vision 2: Triumph of truth alone

Vedanta boldly declares that truth is the beginning and end, the alpha and omega of spiritual life. It is one of the prime requisites through which one can ascend the mansion of spirituality. The *Muṇḍaka Upaniṣhad* boldly proclaims this very fact: 'Truth alone triumphs, not falsehood. The path to divinity lies through the path of truth alone.'[5]

To uphold this lofty principle, Vedanta posits innumerable stories from life demonstrating how far an aspirant should sacrifice everything for the sake of truth. We come across the anecdote of the truthful Jābāla of uncertain parentage in the *Chāndogya Upaniṣad*. At the age of five the boy went to the hermitage of a sage to live there as a student. As the preceptor enquired of his lineage the boy spoke out the unshielded truth even risking humiliation from his fellow friends. But the master felicitated him saying that only a Brahmin boy can speak out such a bald truth that is damaging to himself. Later he was entrusted the task of tending five hundred cows of the hermitage in the wilderness and not to return until their number swelled to double.

The boy was left alone in the company of the cows, served them with unflinching devotion and love, and at long last an unearthly voice spoke through a bull addressing the boy, thereby imparting him a part of the supreme knowledge. In succession a bird and other animals also imparted the rest of the knowledge to the boy. Actually, it was his purified heart that took the role of various creatures in the outside world who taught him the truth. At last, when the boy returned to the master, he exclaimed at one glance, 'My son, your face shines like a realized soul!'[6]

This anecdote highlights the fact that a Brahmin's greatest possession is truthfulness under all circumstances. Empowered by truth the aspirant can reach the goal.

The *Kaṭhopaniṣad* also cites the story of a fearless boy of eight years who dared to go to meet the king of death, Yama, to know the truth. With its characteristic boldness, the Vedanta launches the age-old, eternal, existential question of humanity in the form of a dialogue between the little prudent boy Nachiketā and the king of death. The boy asked: 'Some people say that the soul endures even after death, while some say not. Can you teach me the secret of this?' This is a timeless question that assails every human being from the very dawn of civilization. No other question has ever been asked a greater number of times; no other question is so inseparably connected with our existence. Whenever we see our near and dear ones die, this existential question springs up from within our hearts, 'Where do the departed go?'

But the next moment our minds are swept away in pursuit of other cares of life and we forget that important question. Thus, the greatest truth of life remains unanswered to the common folk. But Nachiketā was made of a distinct nature. The king of death felt that Nachiketā had asked the greatest question in the world. The answer was with the king of death, but was the student ready to grasp it? Was the question a genuine one or just a trick of the fleeting mind?

Was he ready to renounce all desires of the world for that One Truth?

So, it was time for Yama to test the grit of the student, and he started tempting the student with a number of wants one can covet in this life—name, fame, power, long life, enjoyment, and so on. But Nachiketā was quite introspective and wisely rejected all those offers just for the sake of that ultimate knowledge after which he was hankering. Here we get a very developed idea of renunciation and Vedic morality that until one has conquered the desire for enjoyment, Truth will not shine upon one.

So long as the vain desires of our senses are clamouring inside and dragging us outwards every moment, the Truth will not come to our hearts. Vedanta is uncompromising in this respect. Thus, truth is both the end and the means in the visions of Vedanta.

The second vision will convince people to embrace truth so as to solve one's existential problem, an unavoidable necessity to live this life, stick to a new undertaking with steadfastness, and boldly approach new ventures in life in the face of all obstructions and threats.

Vision 3: Fearlessness

Vedanta is that sort of a religion which, in the language of Swami Vivekananda, 'does not depend upon books or teachers or prophets or saviours, which does not make us dependent in this or in any other lives upon others.'[7]

That is why he further reiterates, 'There is no question of believing. Believe nothing and disbelieve everything—that is the first step. Dare to be a rationalist. Dare to follow reason wherever it leads you.'[8]

In other words, the Vedantic message exhorts everybody to become fearless. The moment one believes everything without question, fear sneaks into his personality.

The great *Bṛhadāraṇyaka Upaniṣad* narrates one such story in which the aspirant, even after renouncing everything for the sake of delving into the greatest truth of life, evinces fear at one point of a dialogue between a couple—Yājñavalkya and his wife Maitreyī. Fear does not leave one easily, it being an existential problem to all living beings. When Yājñavalkya confided to his wife of his desire to renounce the world after equally distributing all his wealth between her and another wife Kātyāyanī, Maitreyī said, 'What shall I do with that which cannot give me immortality?' Yājñavalkya became immensely pleased with his wife and proceeded to impart her the ultimate knowledge about the Truth. He proceeded step by step towards that end. At the last stage of advice as Yājñavalkya said that the individual consciousness loses its separateness from the Supreme consciousness and merges in the latter, Maitreyī said she felt confused by the statement since she was scared to lose her individuality which means extinction.

In reply, Yājñavalkya said it is her misconception. One does not become extinct after merging in Pure Consciousness. One rather attains immortality thereby. A rain-drop falls in the ocean; seeing the vastness of the ocean it cries out, 'Oh no, I am dying.' Does it actually die, or gets merged in the whole? This knowledge of oneness with the whole makes one fearless, bold, and immortal.

The phenomenon of death is always an intriguing question to us all. What attitude does Vedanta have towards this event of death? According to Vedanta, death means the dissolution of the body; the body will go back to its original state of matter called the five elements. But the sum total of the actions remain undestroyed in its subtle form. Each work we do, each thought we think produces an impression, called in Sanskrit *saṁskāra,* upon the mind; and the sum total of all these impressions becomes a tremendous force called character.

Thus, the character of every person is the resultant force of all actions one has committed. Accordingly, one takes birth again in places or surroundings suitable for one's progress towards freedom. In the language of Vedanta, this human birth is another chance to use up all the effects of karma to become liberated from this unending and painful cycle of birth and death. Man creates his own destiny. A good karma yields good result, while a bad karma creates bad result. But one cannot say with all certainty that a good karma yields only good effect.

The fact is that there are always mixed results involved in all types of work. This has been declared by Sri Krishna in the *Bhagavad Gītā,* chapter 18, verse 48 as 'All endeavours, good or bad, are covered with sins like fire covered by smoke.' Then what is the way out? The way out is the way in, that is, to dwell on the inner self and do everything for its sake.

This technique to convert all works into a way to freedom has been specially named by Sri Krishna as Buddhi-yoga. It is a modified form of Karma-yoga. It needs only a threefold change in our attitude: towards our own selves, towards the world, and towards the work in hand. All work can be divinized through such attitude. What good result will such an attitude fetch? It encourages one to think confidently in the lines laid down beautifully by Swami Vivekananda: 'You must always remember that each word, thought, and deed, lays up a store for you and that as the bad thoughts and bad works are ready to spring upon you like tigers, so also there is the inspiring hope that the good thoughts and good deeds are ready with the power of a hundred thousand angels to defend you always and for ever."[9]

So vision 3 gives one the impetus to give up age-old superstitions in the name of religion forever. It is seen that when people meet with success they feel delighted and claim all credit to themselves. But when faced with repeated failure and threatened with nature's frown, they become pessimistic and accept it all as the result of past sins. This attitude in its turn brings in utter disappointment and depression. But the moment one learns that this world is a grand gymnasium in which millions of souls must come and get exercises, and make themselves strong and perfect,[10] all deluded concepts of fate and destiny will vanish. The aspirant will then muster up all courage to brave through all obstacles, showing the courage to be human.

Vision 4: Potential divinity of soul

The one great idea that comes out through masses of superstition in every country and in every religion is the momentous conclusion that man is divine; that divinity is our real nature. Whatever else comes to us is, in the language of the Vedanta, is mere superimposition. This inherent divinity has to be called out, and it will work itself out. We have just to seek, and it will manifest itself. All schools of Vedanta are unanimous in this one matter. They believe that there is an ultimate spiritual reality called Brahman, which forms the substratum of the universe and of all individual souls.

However, the schools differ in matters of the nature of Brahman and its relationship with the individual souls. They agree in the point that every soul is a part or reflection of Brahman. The knowledge of this identity either remains covered by ignorance or 'contracted.' The evil or bad element in every individual is not his soul or *ātman*, but his impure mind. This is the central idea of all schools of Vedanta.

This doctrine of Vedanta has also immense practical value in human life. Firstly, it gives a new definition of religion. The word 'religion' is very difficult to define. Semitic religions mean by it the despotic rule of the world by a supernatural being called God. The Sanskrit word for religion is dharma. This word gives a wide range of meanings. Kaṇāda, the founder of the Vaiśeṣika school, defines the word religion as 'that through which *abhyudaya* and *niḥśreyasa* are attained'.

According to the Greek philosopher Aristotle, religion implies well-being, meaning the activity of the soul's powers in accordance with reason. It can be achieved by the balanced use of the intellectual, moral, and aesthetic powers of man. This is exactly what the word *abhyudaya* conveys in the Indian context. And *niḥśreyas* means total freedom from all bondage including not only gross sensual desires but also the subtle desires for name, fame, and so on.

Swami Vivekananda defined religion as the 'manifestation of the divinity already in man.' Here by the word 'divinity' he meant Brahman which is inseparable from the individual self or *ātman*.

This Potential Divinity of the soul gives a new existential philosophy of life. The Vedanta does not believe in the concept of sin. Rather it is a standing libel on human nature. Vivekananda went one step further and cried out: 'Blessed are my sins. Through sin I have learned virtue. It is my sins, as much as my virtues, that have made me what I am today.

And now I am the preacher of virtue. Why do you dwell on the weak side of man's nature? Don't you know that the greatest blackguard often has some virtue that is wanting in the saint?'[11]

What an invigorating exhortation!

So this idea of potential divinity of the soul gives man the strength to overcome all his weaknesses. Life is not a prison but a battlefield, and every man has within him enough strength to come out of it victorious. Vedanta makes use of the psychological phenomenon 'what we think we become.' The remedy for weakness is not brooding over it but thinking of strength. This will help man solve his existential problems in life. Vedanta says that the only prayer we should have is, 'I am not under the sway of any superstition; I am Existence-Knowledge-Bliss Absolute; I am the Blissful One.'

This is the only way to reach the goal, to tell ourselves as well as to everyone else that we all are divine. As we go on repeating this, strength will come. Gradually this truth will take possession of our hearts and course through our veins. Then all delusion will vanish, loads of ignorance will vanish, all goodness will come to such a soul when it wakes up to that consciousness.

This idea of potential divinity also gives a New Philosophy of Work. In spite of Sri Krishna's masterly exposition in the *Gītā*, Hinduism had never developed a comprehensive philosophy of work even as a means, much less as a goal. Work was considered at most a dispensable first step in the spiritual path. The Mīmāṁsaka philosophers had their work philosophy just on the basis of Vedic rituals which they meant by the word karma.

Swami Vivekananda took hints from the teachings of the

Gītā and included even the secular activities of man in the concept of Karma-yoga. He made no distinction between the sacred and the secular. In Vivekananda's view, to labour is to pray, to conquer is to renounce. To have and to hold is as stern a trust as to quit and to avoid. To him, the workshop, the study, the farmyard, and the field are as true and fit scenes for the meeting of God with man as the cell of the monk or the door of the temple.

In fine, this doctrine of intrinsic divinity of the Self saves all souls from self-alienation, feeling of uncreative, listless life, and meaninglessness. When one discovers one's real source of existence, it becomes a channel for the expression of glory and power of the *Ātman*. Then life will also appear meaningful and worth living to him. The *Ātman* is full of glory, power, and purity. If everyone believes that all power is within him, he can do anything and everything. People of the West have gained much by developing confidence in their inherent power. Not only so, but man will also elevate in moral and ethical standard by this doctrine.

But how can this idea of potential divinity enter all strata of society in general? Vivekananda himself gave out the answer: 'These conceptions of the Vedanta must come out, must remain not only in the forest, not only in the cave, but they must come out to work at the bar and the bench, in the pulpit, and in the cottage of the poor man, with the fishermen that are catching fish, and with the students that are studying. They call to every man, woman, and child, whatever be their occupation, wherever they may be. The way has been shown. If the fisherman thinks that he is the Spirit, he will be a better fisherman; if the student thinks that he is the Spirit, he will be a better student; if the lawyer thinks that he is the Spirit, he will be a better lawyer, and so on. This is the utility of vision 4.

Vision 5: Principle of harmony of religions

Another salient feature in Vedantic vision is its principle of harmony. The Vedanta gives this unique sanction that we must allow the infinite variation in religious thought and not try to bring everybody to the same opinion. The goal of life according to Vedanta is direct spiritual experience, *aparokṣa anubhūti*. This concept of the common goal of life tends to foster the spirit of harmony, because the proof of one religion depends upon the proof of all the others.

Vedanta accepts three degrees of reality: *Vyāvahārika* (empirical), *Prātibhāsika* (apparent), and *Pāramārthika* (absolute). This view of reality had formed the backdrop of all creative activities in ancient India. Śaṅkara gave this doctrine a philosophical basis with his theory of non-dual nature of consciousness. In modern times, the practical significance of this approach in the field of religion was Sri Ramakrishna's discovery. By practising the spiritual disciplines in various religious paths, he came to the conclusion that they all lead to super sensuous experiences of bliss and fulfilment. Hence each is equally true. This idea can set at rest all controversies among the various sects in Hinduism, thus bringing about the Integration of Hindu religion. Most importantly, it will bring harmony among the religions of the world, too.

Along with the Principle of Harmony of Religions, Vedanta also envisions another principle called the Principle of Harmony between Science and Religion. We have already discussed this point in brief in the beginning. Yet some more points are necessary to mention here for clarity of understanding. The term 'science' is used in two senses. (a) It means the scientific method which consists of accurate collection of facts, their classification, and the discovery of their inter-relationship based on unbiased judgement and experiment. (b) It is used to denote the corpus of systematic knowledge, including hypothesis, theories, and laws, concerning the physical universe.

Vedanta has no difficulty in accepting the accuracy of scientific methods, and its authority over the *vyāvahārika* (empirical) truths of the physical universe. But regarding the *Pāramārthika* (absolute) truth, Vedanta is independent of empirical beliefs and follows the subjective methods of enquiry and deep introspection called *dhyāna* and *nididhyāsana*, leading finally to direct realization. As a result, Vedanta does not clash with the scientific method. Both deal with different planes of reality and have different criteria of truth. Science does not derive its authority from Vedanta, nor does Vedanta derive its authority from science. Both are independent disciplines, but they supplement each other in giving the total picture of truth.

This principle of harmony has two important practical applications: Inter-religious understanding, and the creation of a universal religion. Inter-religious understanding is vitally necessary today for communal harmony, which is a major socio-political problem in today's world. The concept of universal religion is based on three principles. The first is the principle of direct experience; the second principle says that universal religion can be created only by accepting the best elements of all the religions. Each religion has made a special contribution to world culture, and these contributions must become the universal property of all. The third principle underlying universal religion is that it should suit the different temperaments of peoples. That is why Swami Vivekananda wanted to propagate a religion that will be equally acceptable to all minds. It must be equally philosophic (*jñāna*), equally emotional (*bhakti*), equally mystic (*dhyāna*), and equally conducive to action (karma).

Vision 6: Unity in diversity

Vedanta tries to find out the ultimate unity of things in the midst of all diversity. It is expressed in this interrogative way: 'What is that by knowing which everything else is known?' Every science, all human knowledge, is based upon finding unity in the midst of diversity. Nearly every chapter in the Upaniṣads starts with dualistic teaching, *upāsanā*. God is first taught as someone who is the Creator of this universe, its preserver, and unto Him everything goes at last. He is the one to be worshipped, the Ruler, the Guide of nature, external and internal, yet appearing as if He were outside of nature and external.

One step further, and we find the same teacher teaching that this God is not outside of nature, but immanent in nature. And at last both ideas are discarded, and the conclusion is: whatever is real is He; there is no difference. *Tattvamasi śvetaketo*. There is no compromise, no fear of others' opinion. Bold truth has been taught in bold language. This boldness is one of the characteristics of Vedanta. It declares openly, 'This *ātman* cannot be reached by mere oratorical skill, not by the power of intellect, nor even by the study of the scriptures.'[12]

No religions in the world dare to say that Truth cannot be reached merely by the study of scriptures, because they are either scripture-based or personality-based. This boldness is one of the signal visions of Vedanta.

This principle of unity in diversity points to another cardinal tenet of Vedanta, namely, the basic solidarity of the universe. This solidarity or oneness of the universe is apparent at all levels of existence—material, mental, social, and spiritual. In the material level, science has discovered the whole universe as one mass, one ocean of matter, in which we all, the sun and the moon, and everything else are but the names of different whirlpools.

Mentally speaking, it is one universal ocean of thought in which we are similar little whirlpools. And as spirit it moves not, changes not. It is the one unchangeable, unbroken, homogeneous *Atman*. To put it in another way, the whole universe, in spite of all its diversity, is one in the Supreme Spirit which pervades everything. This immanence of the spirit proves the solidarity of the universe. From the moment we learn to make this principle of solidarity our own property, all sense of hatred and jealousy towards each other will vanish altogether.

Even caste problems can be released from its sinister effect of disparity in privileges. In practical life if privileges cannot be avoided at all, let the lower class people get more chances, more facilities than the higher ones, who have been enjoying till now so much of privileges. So, to keep the balance, let the circle be turned the other way round. Swami Vivekananda said 'Let the poor fellow enjoy himself a little, and then he will raise himself up, and renunciation will come to him of itself.'[13]

Vision 7: Principle of direct experience

In the spiritual history of the world, Swami Vivekananda for the first time made direct experience (*anubhūti*) the sole test and criterion of the validity of religious truths. Before him the earlier mystics restricted mysticism to minor movements and groups. Vivekananda made mysticism the main current of religion and showed that everyone can and should attain superconscious experience, and thereby become a prophet, a seer, in his own right. In other words, he said that transcendental truth can be realized by everybody. This proposition at once refutes the mistaken notion that Vedanta is esoteric, *rahasya-vidyā*, fit for only a limited few; and very importantly, it infuses great mental strength in an aspirant. The new idea then dawns upon one's mind that he need not have to depend helplessly on other people for welfare.

In the *Bṛhadāraṇyka Upaniṣad* the sage Yājñavalkya exhorts: *ātmā vā are draṣṭavyaḥ; śrotavyo, mantavyo, nididhyāsitavyaḥ*—this *Ātman* has to be realized by listening to the scriptural verdicts, pondering over them, and later meditating and relating them to one's own life. If man fills himself with the thought of his almightiness, his majesty and glory, then all his actions will be magnified, transformed, and deified by the very power of that thought.

And against the wrong notion that Vedanta is the personal property of a handful of Brahmin priests, Vedanta itself exhorts that this truth can be realized by each individual, and that each one of us can become seers. This will free man from the clutches of the priest class and prevent one from having recourse to sorcerers, magicians, or astrologers. Man need not have to believe whatever the priest says when he realizes for himself.

Vivekananda wanted to propagate a religion that will be equally acceptable to all minds. It must be equally philosophic (*jñāna*), equally emotional (*bhakti*), equally mystic (*dhyāna*), and equally conducive to action (karma). The Vedantic visions point to the fact that such a religion is already there in Vedanta. In this age of globalisation and consumerism also the Vedantic concepts will shower in torrents the elixir of life with a completely new outlook.

End Notes

1. 'M', *Gospel of Sri Ramakrishna*, Chennai, conversations on 28 October 1882, pp.148-49.
2. *Kenopaniṣad*, 1:3.
3. *Iśāvāsyopaniṣad*, 5.
4. *Complete Works, volume* 2, page 303.
5. *Mundaka Upanishad,* 3.1.6.
6. *Brahmavid iva vai somya bhāsi, ko nu tvānuśaśāseti— Chāndogya-Upaniṣad*, 4:9:2.
7. *Complete Works, volume* 8, page 523.
8. *Complete Works, volume* 9, page 215.
9. *Complete Works, volume* 2, page 225.
10. Cf. *Complete Works, volume* 4, page 207.
11. ND 5:158-59.
12. Cf. *Mundaka Upanishad,* 3.2.3.
13. *Complete Works, volume* 3, page 150.

Spontaneity and the Soul

Essential nature

THE EXPONENTS of Advaita Vedanta, in explaining the non-dual philosophy, often cite an analogy of a prince who is lost. Suppose a prince gets lost from the palace at a tender age and falls into evil company. Neither he nor his new associates know his real identity. At last, a courtier of his father's palace rescues him from the clutches of the bad people and brings him back to the palace with a grand ovation. What happens to the prince? He simply gets back his lost identity. In other words, he becomes what he already was.

The non-dual state can be defined as the homecoming of the soul. Similarly, spontaneity is a state of the soul that feels total identity with its higher dimension. Some people call this God; others call it super-soul; yet others consider it as the sum-total of the internal as well as external nature. But the fact remains that spontaneity is a state of the soul's atonement with everything that exists. It is the essence of the soul, and not merely an attribute or quality of it.

The soul or *ātman* is an abstract idea which cannot be

grasped by the senses or gross intellect. And the concept of spontaneity is also an abstract one. The two concepts are so intrinsically and inseparably connected that one cannot be thought of without the other. It is, as Sri Ramakrishna said, like milk and its whiteness. These essential natures cannot be separated from their respective sources even in thought.

When in the depth of meditation the Self is stripped of all its attributes, it recoils from its objectivity to a totally subjective experience in which the objective world connected to the soul vanishes, and emerges as the soul itself. The soul then lives fully in the present, while the past and the future cease to exist for it. The soul just likes to remain in harmony with its nature which is its own manifestation. All the cravings of the heart stop for that moment, at that state nothing remains to be craved.

The soul in its true nature is described as Being-Consciousness-Joy *(sat-cit-ānanda),* so also spontaneity is said to have these three dimensions.

Way to recognize

Spontaneity finds expression in the world in innumerable ways. According to the Vedantic view, the soul is immanent in everything—sentient and insentient, manifested and unmanifested—in the universe. It is not that all is a part of that soul; rather everything is the soul, and nothing other than the soul exists. Śaṅkarācārya expressed this idea of immanence within just half a verse: *brahma satyam jagan-mithyā jīvo brahmaiva nāparaḥ* (Brahman alone is truth, the world is false; the soul is nothing but Brahman.) Swami Vivekananda echoed this very idea in his beautiful doggerel to Mary Hale. (see previous chapter, *Complete Works,* volume 8, page 166)

There's a ceaseless communion between the soul and the manifested universe. It has got its own language. A baby in the cradle is an ideal example of this spontaneity. It goes on playing with itself, unmindful of the surroundings. Again, children below ten years of age are often seen to *play* alone, talk to some invisible being, when left to themselves. Sometimes they perceive the whole nature as living. Sri Ramakrishna gave a scintillating example from life:

> At Kāmārpukur I used to talk to Shibu, who was then a lad four or five years old. When the clouds rumbled and lightning flashed, Shibu would say to me, 'There, uncle! They're striking flints again!' one day I noticed him chasing grasshoppers by himself. The leaves rustled in the nearby trees. 'Hush! Hush!' he said to the leaves. 'I want to catch the grasshoppers.' He was a child and saw everything throbbing with consciousness. One cannot realize God without the faith that knows no guile, the simple faith of a child.

The *Chāndogya Upaniṣad* (4:4:1, 2…) narrates a story of a boy Satyakāma, who satisfied his preceptor, sage Gautama, by his courage to hold on to truth. The sage accepted him as a disciple on grounds of his truthfulness, and sent him to the woods with a herd of famished cows. He ordered the disciple to return only when the cows regain their health and become double in number. The disciple took up the job purely as a spiritual practice and kept his heart open with full awareness to receive spiritual wisdom. The story has it that the burning faith and eagerness of the disciple fetched him the rarest of wisdom. It all came through his communion with nature. Some animals and birds imparted to him the knowledge necessary for the supreme realization. This story may seem absurd on the face to the modern mind. But a little introspection will reveal that if we can live in tune with nature without the least vanity of our superiority or without animosity towards other beings; if we stand close by the river called life which is in a flux, changing and renewing every moment, and can listen carefully to the voice of the river without even a trace of bias towards anything passing by in that river of life; then it is guaranteed that we will get the same wisdom that came to Satyakāma.

Some of the poets, philosophers, artists and novelists also had such profound experiences of oneness with nature, even though for a short while. William Wordsworth expressed his trance in similar situation in his memorable poem *The Excursion*. Apart from that, Tennyson, Longfellow, Einstein, Newton, and many other illustrious people testify to the truth that it is possible to live in harmony with nature and gain a rare kind of wisdom.

In recent years, the renowned German novelist Hermann Hesse in his short novel, *Siddhartha,* has expressed in idyllic style the natural transformation of consciousness followed by the supreme realization that came to the hero—a sincere spiritual seeker and follower of the Buddha—in his life buffeted by ups and downs. At long last, with a heart bereft of all desires, he started listening to the communication conveyed by the river that became his constant companion. He started understanding the mute eloquence of the ever-dynamic river. The river has no attachment to anything or anybody. It keeps perennially moving toward the sea, its ultimate destination.

Vivekananda in his memorable poem *In Search of God*

(see *Complete Works,* volume 7, page 452) describes this beatific revelation:

The moon's soft light, the stars so bright,
The glorious orb of day,
He shines in them; His beauty—might—
Reflected lights are they.
The majestic morn, the melting eve, the boundless billowy sea,
In nature's beauty, songs of birds,
I see through them—it is He.

Such revelations came down to us from generation to generation. The basic teachings of the Vedic sages command us to realize this natural harmony—which they named *ṛtam*—and to live in tune with it. To live in harmony is life; to break this harmony, either intentionally or through callousness, is death. Vālmīki, the renowned sage, the author of the greatest tragic epic of human life—the *Rāmāyaṇa*—conceived this epic from the pitiable sight of wailing of a poor bird whose mate was killed by a hunter while they were engrossed in making love to each other and nature outside was pulsating with harmony. The cruel hunter broke the harmony while the sage mooted the immortal tragedy of Rāma and Sītā for posterity.

Spontaneity may come to man at any stage of life, at any moment. When it comes, the person knows for certain that he is living in truth. None of his thinking, feeling, and acting faculties remain compulsive any more, but become self-directed. On careful scrutiny, our daily actions—even our thoughts and emotions—are found to be directed by some external forces. They are called indirect actions. Spontaneity is a state of being in oneself uninfluenced by any such force. From the *Bhagavad Gītā,* chapter 3, verses 27-28, we get an echo of this clear knowledge of all actions. The Lord says:

> All actions take place in time by the interweaving of the forces of nature. But the man lost in selfish delusion thinks that he himself is the actor. The man who knows the relation between the forces of Nature and actions, sees how some forces of Nature work upon other forces of Nature, and becomes not their slave.

Spontaneity is thus a direct and immediate experience of an integral whole of which one's own self is an essential part. It is by far divorced from free expression of thoughts or feelings that come up from the unconscious level to the surface of the conscious mind, which are called 'instinctual drives.'

Dimensions of spontaneity

One whose personality simmers with spontaneity has nothing to worry about, be it the busiest or the loneliest place in the world.

Spontaneity can be expressed in two ways—active and passive. The passive component is expressed in a sort of meditative state. Sri Ramakrishna named it 'open-eyed meditation,' while the Zen masters term it as 'walking meditation,' 'sitting meditation,' and so on. In other words, the passive state of spontaneity is chiefly meant for the individual aspirant.

The active part of spontaneity can act as an eye-opener for those who look askance at its utility. It has two components—love and work. Most of us talk glibly on love without knowing its implication in depth. Love in the physical level often gets jumbled up with sensuality, sex, or attachment. Spontaneous love is not the dissolution of the self in another person; nor does it imply possessing another person.

In our interpersonal relationships, we are often heckled by our friends in the name of love. They take an upper hand on us, exploit our trust, and we feel betrayed. Still we eulogize such a relationship as love. However, the dynamic quality of love springs from the need of overcoming separateness and maintaining one's individuality simultaneously.

Śaṅkarācārya, in his masterpiece entitled *Vivekacūḍāmaṇi (Crest-Jewel of Discrimination)*, has beautifully depicted this free love in the master-disciple relationship. As the disciple, at the end of his vast, bookish learning, being plagued and scorched by worldly blows, takes shelter in the master out of a sense of helplessness and complete surrender, the master, an embodiment of compassion that he is, showers on the disciple the great assurance of fearlessness spontaneously.

The word *sahasā* has been used there to define the spontaneous spring of love that comes out effortlessly from the heart of the master. This is true love in contrast with our day-to-day love-hate relationship. Spontaneous love knows only to give without expecting anything in return. Nor does such giving exhaust oneself, since this love cascades from a never-ending fountainhead and it suffers from no waxing or waning.

The next component of active spontaneity is work. It is not the work done under compulsion, or to escape boredom. Nor can this work be compared to a saleable service or commodity that we find in the modern world. It is the work of creation. This type of creative work, though rarely found, is responsible for the upkeep of man's true personality. Creative, self-directed work opens the door of our 'inner chamber?'

and though in the beginning some of our shortcomings raise their ugly heads, we learn to accept ourselves and know for certain our true face. This acceptance makes our life more real. We then stop posing ourselves as someone else.

Creative, spontaneous activity is so rare only because in today's money-oriented world it does not necessarily fetch money. An artist's art is valued only if it fetches a good market. This marketing orientation of everything in the modern world makes the flow of spontaneity difficult. Creative work on the other hand gives one the meaning of life.

When Śankara refused to make a synthesis between work and knowledge, he meant by the term 'work' the unconscious, machine-like repetitive type of work which, besides creating bondage for man, weans him away from true knowledge.

Spontaneity in the eastern context

Nowhere else is this idea of spontaneity so expressly stated as in Zen Buddhism. Its followers, mainly the Japanese, made spontaneity the very foundation of their philosophy. Taoism in China advocates living in harmony with nature. Taoists believe that the essential features of nature are continuous flow and change. There are certain patterns in this change, which the enlightened person recognizes. He directs all his actions keeping harmony with this change.

Zen has converted this concept of spontaneity into a wonderful system of work philosophy, bringing religion in the day-to-day life of man. In Zen Buddhism, spontaneous activity finds an essential place in spiritual practice. There are two principal schools of Zen in Japan: the Rinzai or 'sudden' school, and the Soto or 'gradual' school. Both the schools attach importance to 'sitting meditation,' to be practised everyday for hours together.

Zen also asserts that enlightenment manifests itself in everyday affairs. This concept enabled the Japanese to bring all sorts of work like painting, calligraphy, garden design, serving tea, arranging flowers, martial arts, archery, judo, and fencing, within the purview of Zen.

All these acts can be done with spontaneity, simplicity, and presence of mind. For example, archery can be practised as a ritual by means of spontaneous and effortless movements. In this process, even the art of drawing the bow from the quiver is taught for years as a spiritual lesson. At the peak of perfection, the bow, arrow, bull's eye, and archer, all merge into one and the archer does not shoot intentionally; the process takes place automatically.

Zen Buddhism has earned worldwide popularity. Like the proponents of Hinduism, Zen masters also look upon the polarities of right and wrong as merely relative terms, to be treated indifferently. If one wants to live in harmony with nature with a view to achieving the natural state of spontaneity, one must learn to go beyond the pairs of opposites and not hang on to either of them.

Removing impediments

What impedes our growth in spontaneity is the constant conceptualisation that takes place in our minds. Since our childhood we are taught to develop certain pre-conceived notions. It is like feeding a computer with a fixed set of data. The computer cannot act or 'think' in any other way. Likewise, human minds also act after the fixed set of information only. That is why if anyone wants to live in spontaneity, the first thing he must do is to chuck aside all preconceived notions that have influenced his personality till now. Once this is done, living in the present no more remains difficult. He must be able to stop choosing for himself. We are too vociferous about the idea of duty, the sense of right and wrong. We hold fast to these petty ideas like the child who refuses to part with some toy holding it fast to its bosom. But so long as we continue to live with that mental bent, spontaneity remains a far cry to us.

According to *Aṣṭāvakra Saṁhitā* [18:3], the idea of duty is like the scorching midday sun that plagues the soul. These factors are like the waves and ripples that keep forming incessantly in a river. A river is an integral whole comprising the current, flow, tide, waves, ripples, and whirlpools. One who goes to swim in the river must be ready to encounter all these. Similarly, one who wants to cross the river of life must take in his stride many such conflicts of polarities, unprecedented problems and so on.

Application in life

Spontaneity is one of the hallmarks of sainthood. One may profess any religion like Christianity, Islam, Hinduism, Confucianism, Buddhism, Taoism or Zen. But the real test of spiritual realization is spontaneity. This word traces its origin in the Latin word sponta, meaning 'of one's free will.' It points to the fact that the will of a realized person becomes absolutely free and stripped of all bias.

Sri Ramakrishna's whole life is an ideal illustration of this concept. Right from his childhood he learnt to communicate with nature. His power of impartial observation and analysing facts was legendary. A swarm of milk-white cranes on the backdrop of a dark, pervasive cloud threw him into a trance at the thought of such beautiful contrast. Again, in acting the role of Śiva he identified himself completely with the deity. Truth, compassion, and love were spontaneous with him. To those who troubled him so much, he bore no malice; rather he took shelter in Divine Mother like a helpless child. Divine Mother, in his eyes, was responsible for the spontaneity or perfect rhythm of the universe, and She could also break the rhythm at will.

During his days at Dakshineswar all types of people from all walks of life flocked round him. He never posed himself as superior to them. Instead, when people unburdened their agony, he narrated episodes of his own life under similar situations and hinted at holding fast to the only reality that is God. Swami Vivekananda, who understood Sri Ramakrishna in the right perspective, took up this idea of spontaneity from him and translated it in his own life. Smiling at all the tribulations of his life, he said at the fag end of his life, 'I am glad I was born, glad I suffered so, glad I made big blunders, glad to enter peace.' (*Complete Works,* volume 6, page 432)

The most pertinent question in this context is: what change does spontaneity bring to one's life? Sure enough, spontaneity does not fetch wealth and riches from outside. But it does enrich a person from inside. One gets back one's lost wealth and becomes his original self. With the dawn of spontaneity man learns to accept himself with his capacities as well as limitations. With most people, unfortunately the reverse is the case. They claim that they know themselves very well, while in truth they know very little about themselves. Then, again, man does not want to accept his limitations. The general tendency is to patch up the serious shortcomings in the name of 'feeling good.' That is a wrong approach.

Accepting oneself makes one's life more real and simple. For spontaneity to flow in and through the personality, simplicity is a must.

Then we will find our life meaningful, not only when we are happy, but also during suffering. As life has a meaning, so death also has some meaning. If God is meaningful, the world also is meaningful, though in a vaster sense, since the world is pervaded by the Divine.

Swami Vivekananda wrote in a letter that the Hindus may get the credit of arriving at Advaitic harmony and oneness earlier than other races; yet practical Advaitism was never developed among the Hindus universally. That is why he proposed to bring Vedanta to bear upon the everyday life of man. When he spoke of abolishing all distinctions between the sacred and secular, he simply meant to practicalise the idea of spontaneity.

Then and then alone will we find no distinction between the sacred and secular. To labour will mean to pray; conquering will be synonymous with renouncing; to have and hold will become as stern a trust as to quit and to avoid.

All the differences between service of man and worship of God, between true righteousness and spirituality will vanish. The workshop, the study, the farmyard and the field will merge into the cell of the monk or the door of the temple—the places for the meeting of the soul with God.

Nivedita:
Blend of Lion and Lamb

Juxtaposing opposite natures

ONCE IN an interview with a representative of the then American daily *Detroit Free Press* the questioner asked Swami Vivekananda, 'Will it not be an impossibility to find in the great combative Western countries, where such tremendous energy is needed to develop the pressing practical necessities of the nineteenth century, this spirit which prevails in placid India?' To this he replied with a smile, 'May not one combine the energy of the lion with the gentleness of the lamb?'[1]

In later years, when Swami Vivekananda returned to India, once again he expressed the very same idea in his plans for the universal temple of Sri Ramakrishna. In his conversation with Prof Ranadaprasad Dasgupta, founder of Calcutta Jubilee Art Academy, he said, 'On the two sides of the door will be represented the figure of a lion and a lamb licking each other's body in love—expressing the idea that great power and gentleness have become united in love.'[2]

Did this idea of his ever materialize in human form? 'Yes,' comes the emphatic answer, 'in many of his torch-bearers.' But the name that leads all the rest is Nivedita, also known as Miss Margaret Elizabeth Noble! In fact, the nineteenth century India witnessed a number of her western benefactors who did a lot in spreading education among boys and girls of India. David Hare, Derozio, Lord Bethune, and many such persons did indeed contribute a lot in educating the Indian people.

But they all did it in a spirit of compassion for the helpless. Besides, their aim was to introduce English education to Indians. On the other hand, Sister Nivedita first moulded her whole personality into the Indian pattern—she became a whole-hearted Indian woman, and then looked through the eyes of her pupils in their own way. Instead of forcing into them a foreign culture, she insisted on their learning in the ancient Indian way, and that too in their mother tongue.

She first learnt in detail about the rich stock of Indian culture from her master Swami Vivekananda, and then realized how foolish it is to ignore that great culture which ran through the nerve currents of every Indian. It was a herculean task; yet she did it braving all the pains to learn not only the Bengali language but even the household customs of conservative Bengal. In effect, she identified herself with the Indian mind. Even when the great poet Rabindranath Tagore approached her to teach his youngest daughter English, she refused point-blank. That is why she stands before the Indian mind head and shoulders above all other western reformers and 'friends' of India.

Childhood environment and upbringing

How did she blend in her the strength of a lion and the mildness of a lamb? To know the secret we should look into her whole life-stream starting from her very birth, as also her upbringing that made her develop such a unique attitude towards life. By the will of Providence she was born in an Irish protestant family at a period when the age-old conflict between the Roman Catholics and the Protestants was reconciled at least temporarily by her noble-hearted grandfather John Noble. His able son Samuel was also a representation of idealism and independence, which he passed on to his eldest daughter Margaret (later Nivedita) as a legacy.

One evening Samuel declared to his mother that all commercial transaction was nothing but 'legalized theft.' (Remember Sri Ramakrishna's attitude towards businessmen, lawyers, and doctors.) So, leaving his infant daughter to the care of his mother, he went with his wife to England to join as a theological student in the Wesleyan church in Manchester. Margaret grew up under the personal care of her grandmother with a happy childhood which, however, did not last long.

Soon she was taken to her father's home at Oldham and subsequently to Great Torrington, and found herself as a guardian of her two siblings—sister May, who was three years old, and the new-born brother Richmond. Her father Samuel had set an example of perfect self-abnegation with his strict habit of 'living religion.' This left a marked impression in Margaret's mind and she realized that integrity alone could save her from the punishment of the Almighty.

Samuel died at just 34 years. As a last message to his wife, he whispered Margaret's name and said: 'When God calls her, let her go. She will do great things.' This was a clear sign that his daughter was divinely ordained to dedicate her life to God. And Swami Vivekananda was intuitively aware of this secret; so in later years he initiated her into the most fitting Sanskrit name 'Nivedita,' meaning, the dedicated.

When Margaret and her sister May were sent to Halifax College, they met their headmistress, Miss Larrett, who unleashed upon her students a wave of genuine religious fervour bolstered by self-sacrifice and repentance. The exercise of personal sacrifice became part of the general training. Thus, Margaret's training at home and school remained centred around self-sacrifice and purity of soul.

Miss Larrett was succeeded by Miss Collins who taught Margaret the beauty of art and music. Under her careful guidance, Margaret gradually came to realize that religion was a vaster science than all other sciences, and that one had to find within oneself, by personal experience, the answer to all spiritual issues. In spite of the strict regime of life—imposed by Miss Larrett earlier—she underwent in her school, Margaret's mind happened to escape now and then into the realm of dreams and fantasies commonly found in artists, musicians, and spiritual persons.

She would lead her dormitory companions into that world through suitable lively stories. Again, the philosophical wisdom of Miss Collins aroused in Margaret the age-old conundrum that once assailed many spiritual aspirants like Nachiket in the *Kathopanishad*: 'Can death really destroy life? What happens to the life element during death if nothing is ever destroyed in the successive transformations?' Miss Collins, sensing clearly the innate potentials of Margaret, allowed her freedom to think and do as she pleased. Margaret passed her examinations brilliantly and left school with the pronounced determination to earn her own living.

After passing from school at eighteen years, Margaret

embraced her new career as a teacher in the summer of 1885. There she gradually developed her own way of examining her students' reaction instead of imposing a prepared course of study. The headmistress of the school was astonished at her new science of teaching. Later, she wanted to conduct another new experiment to test her powers of renunciation and sacrifice. She chose to teach in an orphanage in Rugby, where twenty girls—charity pupils—were being brought up to be domestic servants. There she shared her pupils' manual labour and taught them to feel the joy of fulfilment through that labour while living after the ideal of their faith.

Yet it seemed she was never too satisfied in testing her own spirit of self-abnegation in newer fields. So, she joined another secondary school at Wrexham, a large mining centre, to gain experience in social welfare work. Through her association with the students and their families she went to the heart of the working man's existence and learnt a lot about the wretched conditions of the miners there. At the heart of the mining centre there stood a church where Margaret enrolled as a district worker, undertaking welfare research, visiting slum households, searching out pregnant women in factories, looking for waifs and strays.

She started giving assistance without discrimination to the poor, to people who never went to church, even to members of other congregations. As an inevitable consequence she was met with serious obstacles which seemed to paralyse her efforts and stir up strife. So, she gave up that work. But dauntless as she was, she gave vent to her pent up feelings and sent an open letter to the North Wales Guardian, exposing the Church's internal policy.

The tremendous upshot of this effort made her discover

that the power of her pen, properly wielded, could exert a greater influence than her social activities. So, she set herself to the task of applying this trait to the service of the oppressed at the mining centre. Such a daring spirit to forge through new ventures, however adverse, and to stick to them through thick and thin can only be attributed to a lion.

After this experience, Margaret's interest gradually grew up in a new method of education, and she felt that the best way to impart education is to concentrate on the pupil individually.

Time was ripe for Margaret to put into practice her own generalized conclusions about a child's personality. She was offered a teacher's job in a newly founded school in Wimbledon, which she accepted wholeheartedly. Her personality now underwent a great transformation, as she threw away all the restrictive influences she experienced from the world so far. The grave schoolteacher 'imparting knowledge' to the pupils gave way now to the 'real educator' guiding her pupils step by step towards a world of new discoveries. Her object was now to develop new personalities full of candour and confidence.

Her new method of education consisted in playing with the children between four and six years of age, thus allowing them freedom to express their inherent urges in accordance with each one's inner harmony. Free from all restrictions, they now set themselves to create various things according to their ingenuity. Margaret would suggest games in which the keener student could encourage the duller ones, and would tell stories that drew the attention of even the difficult students. She made the children discover their own geniuses by rightly appreciating their creations. But the children failed to know how they progressed with an invisible hand of their beloved teacher behind all their endeavours.

Through her free association with the children, Margaret discovered many more facts about them. She often spoke in meetings, demanding a complete liberty of expression for the child. She boldly declared, 'The child's worst enemies are overfond parents whose love is possessive and exclusive, or their first teachers who compel them to follow their own conception of life without troubling about the child's own individuality.'

Soon Margaret opened her own school, the Ruskin School at Wimbledon, teaching not only children but also adults who wished to study modern educational methods. Thus, all her efforts and successes invisibly led Margaret to the long-awaited task of her life set by the divine. Her honest and candid search for truth made her knock at many doors of individuals and groups of faith, but everywhere she discovered the undercurrents of intolerance, hatred, and sectarianism. She wanted to get at the spiritual Truth, which was of prime significance to her above all other goals.

The historic meeting

At long last, the Messiah could not but respond to her inner call and did come. 'What matters is intense yearning. Everything is bound to take shape in the ripeness of time,' Sri Ramakrishna used to say. Through some acquaintance, Margaret learnt of a Hindu Yogi who had been invited by Lady Isabel Margesson to speak at her residence. She went there just to appease her curiosity. There, amid a 15-strong audience, sat Swami Vivekananda with a regal bearing and other-worldly look.

The talk commenced; but it was not a mere talk. A feeling of complete emptiness gradually engulfed Margaret, annihilating her will power and critical sense, followed by a new force making her mind reach out to broader and vaster regions. The yogi's voice reverberated like a distant echo in the minds of all present: 'Man, the infinite dreamer, dreaming finite dreams!' All our struggle is for Freedom; we seek neither happiness nor misery but Freedom, Freedom alone.'[3]

He lifted the hearts of the hearers into eternity.

The lecture ended. Margaret's heart was filled with a profound peace. She felt that the truth she was seeking so long had come close to her. Yet she was not to give in without further test. So, she started asking questions along with others at the end of each of the parlour talks she attended. Vivekananda also gave satisfactory replies to all the queries untiringly. He was well aware of the capacity of his questioners, and so he slowly lifted their minds far beyond their limits of intellect into the spiritual realm. Margaret found herself struggling to feel her own way. He sensed this, and described to her in detail all the stages in spiritual life, from the faithful worshipper protected by the rites of his church or sect, to the worshipper projected into the freedom of the realized soul.

He taught Margaret the joy of renunciation, of love bereft of all possessiveness, of becoming a patient instrument of God's will. Margaret could only vaguely feel the idea of freedom; yet she did not give up her power of reason, for reason works only within the intellectual level which she was yet to transcend. And in the course of the question-answer session she discovered a religion that could smilingly bear the onslaught of scientific reasoning, while maintaining contact between spiritual and practical life, and which relied exclusively on the noblest and best traits in mankind.

After Vivekananda left for America in November 1895, Margaret got the opportunity of thinking in a free mind. She studied his teachings sufficiently to become convinced of its coherence. His words kept reverberating in her brain: 'The universe is like a cobweb and minds are the spiders; while no religion is true in the way commonly claimed, all were equally true in a very real way; the impersonal God, seen through the mists of sense becomes personal; the spirit behind an act is more powerful than the act itself.'[4]

Margaret started studying, one after the other, the *Gita*, *Upanishads*, Buddhist philosophy, beside her own. At times, merged in those intricate systems, she would lose heart; but Vivekananda's words would ring in her ears, 'Never feel yourself forsaken. Do you know how God dwells in man? He hides himself like a Hindu lady of noble birth behind a lattice curtain. He is always there, like that lady who sees everything, though no one suspects her presence.'

When Vivekananda returned to London in April 1896, he found Margaret completely transformed. She was prepared to meet him with a series of questions. He was satisfied to find Margaret in the same state as he was for six long years fighting with his master. In her personal interviews with him, Margaret spoke of her experience among the miners at Wrexham. He listened with interest, and interpreted that experience of hers in spiritual terms.

Encouraged at Vivekananda's words she also took him to her own school and spoke warmly of her aims and efforts. 'Every day I discover new elements. These children are free but several of them are slow to develop because I do not know how to neutralize the complexes which impede them. The child in itself is an entire science. Each has a right to complete self-expression. That is the essential condition of development which I offer them.'

Vivekananda wept with joy. 'Ah,' he said, 'my poor, poor children of India, who are abandoned to the blackest ignorance. Their lot is so lamentable that they imagine they are born to be oppressed by all those who have money. They have completely lost their individuality. Can you imagine their misery? Even if we could give them free education in every village, the poor children would be forced to work in the fields to earn their living rather than attend school! We have no money and we cannot educate them. The problem seems hopeless, but I am looking for a solution...If the poor cannot come to school, the school must go to them, to the plough, to the factory, everywhere....'

The resolve and the call

Margaret felt she could assist Vivekananda in a thousand ways and offered her own lifetime service for those neglected and suffering people in India. She at last declared herself a disciple of Swami Vivekananda by addressing him as 'Master.' He knew that her resolve was not a mere outburst of emotion. He recognized her as the woman she was to become. He saw her beyond her ego and limitations, rich with the reserves she herself did not know, acknowledged the leonine strength of her character and her candid faith in truth. So he wrote to her on 7 June 1896: 'The world is in need of those whose life is one burning love, selfless. ...you have the making in you of a world-mover. ...Bold words and bolder deeds are what we want.'[5]

Yet he wanted to caution her in every way from the dark and unknown path she was going to tread voluntarily. After his return to India, he wrote to her on 29 July 1897 with a little more emphasis, speaking aloud his thoughts about her while warning against the odds that might stand in her way: 'Let me tell you frankly that I am now convinced that you have a great future in the work for India. What was wanted was not a man, but a woman, a real lioness, to work for the Indians—women especially.... Yet the difficulties are many. You cannot form any idea of the misery, the superstition, and the slavery that are here. You will be in the midst of a mass of half-naked men and women with quaint ideas of caste and isolation, shunning the white skin through fear or hatred and hated by them intensely. On the other hand, you will be looked upon by the whites as a crank, and every one of your movements will be watched with suspicion.... On my part I promise you, I will stand by you unto death whether you work for India or not, whether you give up Vedanta or remain in it. "The tusks of the elephant come out, but never go back".'[6]

These words of assurance which followed the forewarning deepened Margaret's resolve. She had already prepared herself to struggle till death. So, feeling her genuineness and dauntless spirit, he again wrote to her on 1 October 1897 much more expressly of his readings about her: 'Many feel, but only a few can express. It is the power of expressing one's love and appreciation and sympathy for others that enables one person to succeed more in spreading an idea than others. What you call your Celtic outspokenness is just the thing necessary for work like ours, and I am quite satisfied now that you are the lioness born for the work, and I shall die quite content if you are spared.'[7]

Margaret was long waiting for a positive nod from her master. So, she set sail for India for the first time sometime during December 1897 and landed in Calcutta port on 28 January 1898 where Swami Vivekananda was waiting with one of his brother disciples and a large crowd to greet the new guest.

Training of the disciple

In the meantime, Mrs Sarah Ole Bull and Miss MacLeod, who had already been acquainted with Margaret, came to India to see for themselves the real spirit of India. They were accommodated in the Belur Math guest house. Swami Vivekananda would join the party, alone or with some of the novices at the Math, and unleash sublime ideas that rose in his mind. He would speak highly of the religious ardour of Indian people and called upon his disciples to spur the masses to action so as to make them realize their inherent latent abilities. 'Let each of them understand that he is divine; let them hear and know it; let us awaken them. The aim of all education should be this.' And his teaching, particularly to Margaret, was: 'Open your hearts wide to receive the treasure of the poor. For them you are like God entering their house.'

But Margaret had come to India with the definite purpose of opening a school for girls. Vivekananda didn't show interest. He wanted her not to become merely a charitable missionary worker but a full-fledged Hindu woman before becoming an educator of the Hindu women. She must acquire knowledge of all that a Hindu woman inherits at birth. So he told her the stories of Sita, Savitri, Gargi, Maitreyi, Mirabai, Ahalya, and others.

Giving up her uncontrolled impulses, she must take up as model the quiet and modest attitude of the Hindu woman. The lioness must first get special training to love the lamb. He wanted her to submit to all the restrictions and limitations imposed upon women in India until she understood their sense and values. Then he taught her the secret of entering into the solitude of the soul, the perfect silence. No one at that time realized that Vivekananda's purpose of training her into absolute mental obedience was to inspire her with total liberty of action.

One salient feature always came out: as soon as Vivekananda appeared before the people, a wave of love was released to flow over and through all around him. This idea was accentuated when she discovered him in a new form in the house of Nava Gopal Ghosh in connection with the consecration of the shrine there. He was in the centre of a group, dancing like a mad man, completely lost in joy, and intoxicated with love, to the accompaniment of devotional song and other musical instruments. The emotion came like frenzy upon all present and engulfed them. It was a totally unprecedented sight to her! As the procession drew up in front of the house, Swami Vivekananda prostrated himself in the dust, smearing his head with ashes, and then went to set up Sri Ramakrishna in the shrine.

One day Vivekananda was explaining to her the role of the guru who is above father and mother, the friend, the spiritual instructor, who knows the disciple's most intimate thoughts in seed form. Margaret hid her face in her hands and gave way to the tumults of the long-hidden questions within her. He understood her unspoken questions and yet kept quiet. On 11 March 1898, to make her acquainted with the elite of the Bengali society, he asked her to speak at the Star Theatre on *The Influence of Indian Thought in England.* She passed the test to Vivekananda's satisfaction.

Initiation into a new life

The birth anniversary of Sri Ramakrishna was celebrated in the last week of February 1898. The festival was arranged on a large scale with special worship in the temple, religious discourses, devotional songs, and processions. From morning till dusk poor people by thousands were fed sumptuously. The air was full of the sweet smell of incense sticks, perfumeries, and echoes of hallelujah in the name of Sri Ramakrishna.

Vivekananda initiated fifty novitiates belonging to the three castes in Hinduism—Kshatriya, Vaishya, and Shudra—into the life-long vow of celibacy by initiating them with the Gayatri Mantra. It was a daring attack on the orthodox scholars. Vivekananda went one step forward, and declared boldly that the Vedas have given clear injunction that such ordination could also be given to fit recipients, even if one were a foreigner. Earlier, on several occasions, he had raised the question, 'He is an Arya or a Rishi who brings a universal interpretation of the Vedic truths, no matter whether he is a *Mleccha* or a *Yavana.*'[8]

To emphasize his assertion he asked, 'Who was Nanak? Who was Chaitanya? Who was Kabir? Who was Dadu? Who were all these great preachers, one following the other, a galaxy of stars of the first magnitude? Did not Ramanuja feel for the lower classes? Did he not try all his life to admit even the pariah to his community? Did he not try to admit even Mohammedans to his own fold? Did not Nanak confer with Hindus and Mohammedans, and try to bring about a new state of things?'[9]

Thus, Vivekananda widened the scope of the meaning of the Vedas. He had already read the English commentaries of the Vedas and other sacred books of the East by Max Müller; he was well acquainted with the Vedantic thoughts of Paul Deussen, Maurice Bloomfield, Monier Williams, and many such foreigners who looked upon the wisdom of the Vedas as the beacon light on their path.

So, in order to give a concrete shape to his conviction, he decided to confer the vow of Brahmacharya to his Irish disciple Margaret. About a month after the birth anniversary of Sri Ramakrishna, he ordained her in the presence of two American ladies—Sarah C Bull and Josephine MacLeod—on 28 March 1898. She now became a full-fledged *brahmacharini*, so as to be in the same rank as her future Indian students who led austere lives.

She received the special name 'Nivedita.' Long ago, during Margaret's birth, her mother had dedicated the baby to God. This was a critical moment in her life when all she had been, and all she was, became crystallized into an act of total submission to Swami Vivekananda, her guru. Margaret was now conscious of what she was sacrificing—her life itself. She realized that henceforth her body, mind, and intellect, would no more belong to her anymore; that the preceptor would now mould her character in his own hands. Thus, before presenting her to the Holy Mother, Vivekananda sanctified her in body, mind, and spirit.

That day, after the spiritual fervour was over, Vivekananda rose to speak to Nivedita, revealing his long-cherished dream to her. Pointing to the opposite bank of the Ganges he said, 'Nivedita, that is where I should like to have a convent for women. Like a bird that needs two wings to fly, India must have both educated men and educated women.'

The next thing he did was to introduce her to the Holy Mother Sri Sarada Devi along with Mrs Bull and Miss MacLeod. He wanted to acquaint Nivedita with the intimate household of an orthodox Hindu widow, to feel that sparkling joy which radiated from the Holy Mother. At the same time, he was apprehensive on whether the Holy Mother would accept the foreign guests. Her acceptance would make a landmark to bridge the gulf between the East and the West. He sent the ladies upstairs to the Mother's room and himself stayed behind.

The Holy Mother, with her natural serenity, surprised the foreigners by ordering in low voice for some fruits, sweets, and a cup of milk. But some more surprise was waiting. The Mother started eating with her children from overseas by breaking all barriers of vapid orthodoxy. When Vivekananda came to know of this historic event, he was beyond himself in joy. Mother's acceptance meant to him the acceptance of the entire society! And Mother did not stop there!

Through a woman who knew English, she started conversing with her Christian daughters asking intimate questions such as: How the Lord is worshipped in their houses, what homage He is paid, are their parents still alive, and so on. And at long last she greeted Nivedita, 'My daughter, I am glad you've come.' Bathed in tears, Nivedita felt blessed.

This acceptance became the talk of the neighbourhood and Nivedita was accepted by the women as one of them. But a still greater surprise was waiting to amaze the three foreign ladies, whose next destination was the residence of Gopaler

Ma, an orthodox, devout Brahmin widow, who looked upon Sri Ramakrishna as her chosen deity Gopal. In course of time her eyes could see only Gopal in every soul. When the ladies went to meet her, she saw her beloved Gopal in each of them, and as she could not speak English, she expressed the warmth of her sympathy by holding the hands of her foreign friends and stroking them. She loved them all equally, but felt a stronger bond with Nivedita.

Knowing India in depth

The next task at hand was to acquaint Nivedita with India as a whole. The three foreign ladies and four monks joined Vivekananda in their journey via Naini Tal to Almora. Vivekananda looked at his motherland with the eyes of an artist, a poet, and a mystic. He explained to his foreign disciples how custom and religion are one and the same thing. He wanted them to see India through his eyes. He pointed out that every theme of life in India was like a prayer of the soul. To him the Hindu greeting the sun thrice a day, and the Muslim bowing five times to Allah are the epitome of Indian life and culture.

At Naini Tal they were allowed to visit the temple of Naina Devi by courtesy of Rajah Ajit Singh of Khetri. There, among the local crowd, were two young women draped with jewellery and richly dressed. They pleaded to see Swami Vivekananda. But the crowd protested, calling them prostitutes. Eventually the accompanying monks made way for the two at the behest of Vivekananda. They prostrated before him, and laid several pieces of gold at his feet as a contribution to his work. He blessed them, spoke a few words of tenderness, and sent them away without any vestige of reproach or condemnation.

Nivedita felt something welling up within her; she wished to put herself in the place of those women and receive the manna of compassion from Vivekananda.

After they reached Almora, Vivekananda again put Nivedita to a severe test. He wanted her to stand alone, face to face with herself without any external support, even from her guru; to find peace with the fervour of renunciation. He was convinced that the leonine spirit of Nivedita would surmount all obstacles to reach the summit of spirituality.

So he withdrew himself from her. Failing to understand this, the disciple got irritated. So far all her endeavours hovered around her master. She did everything for the love of her guru. But Vivekananda just disliked that. He wanted her to be more impersonal in her efforts. So, initially she reacted with obstinacy. A great war was going on within her. She felt abandoned. The more she fought with herself and tried to analyse, the more she was brought back to the subtle attachment to her guru. Vivekananda wanted to eradicate that to free her mind to work in her own field.

On the other hand she wanted to assume the role of Mary at the feet of Jesus. This was the main reason of the conflict. The tension between the two rose to such a degree that Mrs Bull had to come between them at last for a truce. Vivekananda listened without a reply. That evening he came back and, addressing the three ladies, said, 'You were right; there must be a change. I am going away into the forest alone, and when I come back I shall bring peace.' And he kept his words. After his return he blessed Nivedita with raised hands and said, 'Let us begin a new life.' After he had left, Nivedita felt that her sorrow had also left her. She felt a new life springing up within her. All the previous conflicts were resolved by themselves.

Through this act Vivekananda transformed Nivedita into one who loved India for itself and could enter into the life of its people without caring for disapproval, comparison, or even comment. Nivedita had looked upon India from outside till now, comparing her new experiences with what she had heard before.

But Vivekananda perceived that an entirely new problem had arisen in India, with the Western civilization superimposing upon India's ancient national heritage. They offered the Indians the prospect of a modern life completely dissociated from the foundations of their religion. And Nivedita was not aware of this. So she pitied the wretched folk of India and talked, like many other foreigners, about charity and funds to be raised. But Vivekananda said sharply to her: 'All I want you to see is that, with the majority of people, charity is nothing but the expression of an egoistic interest. You will have to set yourself to Hinduism. Your thoughts, deeds, conceptions, habits, your life, internal and external, will have to be like an orthodox Brahmacharini's. You have to forget your own past, and cause it to be forgotten. You have to lose even its memory!'

Thus, Vivekananda offered her to Kali, and there his duty towards her ended. He left a significant message to Nivedita: 'Call upon Mother! She will come because you belong to Her. But be ready to welcome Her when She takes hold of you.' Nivedita started worshipping that Kali who passes when the waves roar, the mountains shake; life and death are stirred up in Her creative movement. With one hand She snatches, with the other She blesses. She smiles at him who sees Shiva dancing in the sunlight of dawn. She is the point of balance in the continual interplay of powers! Gradually her verbal prayers gave way to the feeling of movement of Kali springing up within her.

Nivedita's whole being was uplifted towards Her, and she saw spirit and matter wedded together like the sun and the earth. Divine Mother then started speaking from within her: 'Shrink not from defeat; embrace despair. Uproot every interest that would conflict with mine. Look for no mercy for thyself, and I shall make thee bearer of the great vessel of mercy to others.'

The real work begins

Nivedita returned to Calcutta with renewed vigour to plunge into the practical experience of Hindu life. And now Vivekananda wanted to know of her plan of work. But when she gave him a picture of it as an experiment based on religious life of the Hindu women and the cult of Sri Ramakrishna, Vivekananda said: 'So you want to create a sect in order to rise above all sects. Yes, I understand.' Later he added, 'I don't criticize your plan. I regard you as much inspired as I am. So I shall help you do what you think best.'

Nivedita was then taken to Bagbazar to spend a fortnight with the Holy Mother and at the same time make preparations for the future life as a yogini. She observed and followed the household daily schedule of Mother, which was far more than rigorous austerity for her western body and mind, and at last Mother gave her permission with blessings to leave and start her own mission. 'Now your work is about to begin.'

The house where she was taken in stood almost next door to the Mother's. All the women in the Mother's household, including Gopaler Ma, even all the neighbours, bade her goodbye standing on their doorways. It was the house number 16, Bose Para Lane.

On 12 November 1898 (Kalipuja festival day) she opened her school. It was part of the plan for the women's convent Vivekananda hoped to build. Her first pupils were three puny and timid little Hindu girls. Its schedule of lessons was entirely irregular, since the children did not come at set hours. Even its plan was not definitely formed. The Holy Mother was its first guest of honour. Accompanied by several women, she arrived, and blessed the school. She was followed by Vivekananda and two other monks. He pointed out to Nivedita, 'Your work among the women is important. Stir them up! The manhood of Europe was kept up by the women who hated unmanliness. When will Bengali girls play their part and drown in merciless ridicule every display of feebleness on the part of men? You will learn everything from your pupils.'

And to achieve this end, he never stopped short of putting her on a rigorous regime. 'You must unite within yourself the practical spirit and culture of the perfect citizen, with love of poverty, purity, and complete abandonment of Self. Those are the conditions under which your faith will blossom. Never complain of not having enough time for prayer and meditation. You will have to discipline yourself through a stern *tapasya*. Reveal your inherent leonine power once again after you have completely renounced it. Remember, my mission is not Ramakrishna's, nor Vedanta's, but simply to bring manhood to these people.'

The three girls were so shy that whenever anyone so much as looked at them they hid their faces in their hands.

If they were spoken to, tears would fill their eyes. But they did not run away, and were glad to stay in 'Sister's house.' And Nivedita welcomed them as her teachers. It was Sri Ramakrishna's way of gaining the in-depth knowledge of Christianity, Islam, and other religions by living in every detail like them. Nivedita watched them living their own life unwatched by others.

They were irregular in their attendance. She observed that they were most familiar with acts of worship; they made some unknown image with clay and would offer flower petals to it; yet they played with it like a doll, lulling it to sleep; and when their game was over, they would smash it into tiny bits. She observed that the Hindu child had a concrete awareness of life. Their mothers had made them learn by heart countless episodes from the epics. They also knew how to conduct themselves with dignity and find their places in the family hierarchy.

Each of the children was given a particular task. They learnt unconsciously to relate the three R's with time and space in a playful spirit, instead of swallowing them like parrots. They discovered the relation between thoughts and words describing nature, and the value of numbers. Gradually the number of students swelled to thirty by March 1899. The Holy Mother took special interest in the school and would often visit on special days to distribute sweets to the children.

None of the children paid the monthly fee of one rupee; instead, Nivedita had to provide them with clothing, medical treatment, and everything.

In the meantime, Calcutta was affected once again with bubonic plague. Every day people died by hundreds. Vivekananda set aside all other cares and engaged Nivedita and two of his monastic disciples for practical aid with health measures to all, irrespective of caste prejudices. Sweepers were badly needed.

She had been patiently waiting for her turn to wage an implacable war. So, she forthwith set herself to this risky task along with the brother-monks. The list of desiderata seemed unending: nurse, vaccine, medicine, and so on. She went through the localities making a survey, preparing lists of needs; she opened a makeshift dispensary for treating patients; organized groups of volunteers to continue the cleaning campaign.

The whole work was done so enthusiastically by the people themselves that when the government health official came to inspect the area, he found that everything needed had been accomplished long before. The volunteers raised money from the public by groups, and distributed disinfectants to the houses. Nivedita had given them a new concept for civic life through the practice of self-sacrifice. She too joined hands with them to the extent of scavenging the lanes when initially the neighbouring ladies did not yield to her hygienic suggestions.

At long last, on 25 March 1899 at Belur Math old shrine, Vivekananda ordained her into a Naishthik Brahmacharini, a title which gave her the lifelong dignity of a nun. It was a landmark in her life. She felt purified from all sufferings, and represented love bereft of servitude. Her guru said to her, 'It is when half a dozen people learn to love like this that a new religion begins. Give me half a dozen disciples like that and I will conquer the world.'

Nivedita offered her life to the service of India. She became a true Hindu in every respect. Benefactors of India from foreign lands are no less in number today, but such a soul will be rare indeed who lives the life of the afflicted, with a regal spirit within. This is real empathy, and it is here that all her success lay—in harmonizing the dormant lion spirit with the mellowed nature of a lamb; in making worthy women and men for India, and above all, in identifying with the Indian soul.

End Notes

1. *The Complete Works of Swami Vivekananda*, Mayavati Memorial Edition (CW), volume 7, page 289.
2. *Complete Works,* volume 7, page 205.
3. *Complete Works,* volume 8, page 251.
4. Cf. *The Complete Works of Sister Nivedita*, Advaita Ashrama, Vol.1, pages 21-2.
5. *Complete Works,* volume 7, page 501.
6. *Complete Works,* volume 7, page 511.
7. Unpublished letter of Swami Vivekananda to Sister Nivedita.
8. *Mlecchā vai yavanās-teṣu eṣā vidyā pratiṣṭhitā/Ṛṣivat te'pi pūjyante...//*
9. *Complete Works,* volume 3, page 187.

Key to Transliteration and Pronunciation

Devanagari	Transliteration	Example Sound/Word
अ	a	rural
आ	ā	father
इ	i	fill
ई	ī	police
उ	u	full
ऊ	ū	rude
ऋ	ṛ	merrily
ॠ	ṝ	marine
ए	e	prey
ऐ	ai	aisle
ओ	o	go, stone
औ	au	Haus (German)
ॐ	aum	—
क्	k	kill
ख्	kh	lockhorn
ग्	g	gun, dog
घ्	gh	loghut
ङ्	ṅ	sing, king
च्	c	church
छ्	ch	churchhill
ज्	j	jump
झ्	jh	hedgehog
ञ्	ñ	singe
ज्ञ्	jñ	—
ट्	ṭ	tank
ठ्	ṭh	at home
ड्	ḍ	drum
ढ्	ḍh	ad hoc
ण्	ṇ	fund

त्	t	Istanbul
थ्	th	thorn
द्	d	this
ध्	dh	breathe here
न्	n	nut
प्	p	park
फ्	ph	uphill
ब्	b	rub
भ्	bh	abhor
म्	m	map
य्	y	yet
र्	r	red
ल्	l	lull
व्	v	view
श्	ś	shaft
ष्	ṣ	bush
स्	s	hiss
ह्	h	hit
ḥ	—	aspirate
ँ (अनुस्वार)	ṁ	m (nasal)